Music Theory

Third Edition
by Michael Miller

ALPHA

A member of Penguin Random House LLC

Publisher: Mike Sanders
Associate Publisher: Billy Fields
Acquisitions Editor: Lori Cates Hand
Development Editor: Phil Kitchel
Cover Designer: Lindsay Dobbs
Book Designer: William Thomas
Compositor: Ayanna Lacey
Proofreader: Lisa Starnes
Indexer: Tonya Heard

Third American Edition, 2016
Published in the United States by DK Publishing
6081 E. 82nd Street, Indianapolis, Indiana 46250

Copyright © 2016 Dorling Kindersley Limited
A Penguin Random House Company
16 17 18 19   10 9 8 7 6 5 4 3 2 1
003-292193-JULY2016

Published in the United States by Dorling Kindersley Limited.

IDIOT'S GUIDES and Design are trademarks of Penguin Random House LLC

ISBN: 9781465451675
Library of Congress Catalog Card Number: 2015956733

Note: This publication contains the opinions and ideas of its author(s). It is intended to provide helpful and informative material on the subject matter covered. It is sold with the understanding that the author(s) and publisher are not engaged in rendering professional services in the book. If the reader requires personal assistance or advice, a competent professional should be consulted. The author(s) and publisher specifically disclaim any responsibility for any liability, loss, or risk, personal or otherwise, which is incurred as a consequence, directly or indirectly, of the use and application of any of the contents of this book.

DK books are available at special discounts when purchased in bulk for sales promotions, premiums, fund-raising, or educational use. For details, contact: DK Publishing Special Markets, 345 Hudson Street, New York, New York 10014 or SpecialSales@dk.com.

Printed and bound in the United States of America

idiotsguides.com

Contents

Part 1: Tones 1

1   **Pitches and Clefs** 3

Understanding Musical Tones 4

Tones Have Value 6

   Tuning Into a Frequency 6

   Play by Numbers 7

   Do Re Mi 8

Tones Have Names 9

   Learning the ABCs 9

   Notes on a Piano Keyboard 10

   Notes on a Staff 11

   Above—and Below—the Staff 12

Different Clefs 13

   The Treble Clef 13

   The Bass Clef 14

   The Grand Staff 15

   Specialty Clefs 15

   The Percussion Clef 16

Exercises 17

2   **Intervals** 19

Be Sharp—or Be Flat 20

Steppin' Out … 21

A Matter of Degrees 22

   First Things First 22

   Major and Minor Intervals 23

   Perfect Intervals 24

   Augmented and Diminished Intervals 25

   Beyond the Octave 26

   Intervals and Half Steps 27

Mod-12 28

Exercises 29

3   **Scales** 31

Eight Notes Equal One Scale 32

Major Scales 33

Minor Scales...36

    Natural Minor..36

    Harmonic Minor...39

    Melodic Minor..41

In the Mode..44

    Ionian..45

    Dorian...45

    Phrygian..46

    Lydian...47

    Mixolydian..47

    Aeolian..48

    Locrian..49

Exercises...50

4   Major and Minor Keys **53**

Keys to Success..54

    Using Key Signatures...54

    Determining the Key Signature..54

    Major Keys..55

    Minor Keys..57

The Circle of Fifths..58

Accidents Will Happen...60

Changing Keys...61

Exercises...62

Part 2:   Rhythms **65**

5   Note Values and Basic Notation **67**

Taking the Measure of Things...68

Taking Note—of Notes...68

    Whole Notes...69

    Half Notes...69

    Quarter Notes..70

    Eighth Notes..71

    Sixteenth Notes...71

Taking Count..72

Taking a Rest..73

Taking a Note—and Dotting It..73

Taking Two Notes—and Tying Them Together.............................74

Taking the Beat and Dividing by Three..75

Exercises...76

6   Time Signatures **79**

Measuring the Beats 80

    Quarter-Note Time 80

    Eighth-Note Time 82

    Half Time 83

Changing the Time 84

Grouping the Beats 85

Exercises 86

7   Tempo, Dynamics, and Navigation **89**

Taking the Pulse 90

    Beats per Minute 90

    Italian Tempo Terms 91

Speeding Up—and Slowing Down 92

Hold That Note! 93

Getting Loud—and Getting Soft 94

    Dynamic Markings 94

    Changing Dynamics 95

    Play It Harder 95

Finding Your Way 96

    Repeating Sections 97

    Repeating Measures 99

    Repeating Notes 99

    Repeating Rests 100

Exercises 101

Part 3: Tunes **103**

8   Melodies **105**

Combining Tones and Rhythms 106

Common Melodic Techniques 106

    Dvořák's New World Symphony 107

    Bach's Minuet in G 108

    "Michael, Row the Boat Ashore" 108

    Pachelbel's Canon in D 109

The Building Blocks of Melodic Form 110

    The Motif 110

    The Short Melodic Phrase 110

    The Long Melodic Phrase 111

Composing Your First Melody 111

Exercises 114

9   Chords **115**

Forming a Chord 116

Different Types of Chords 117

Major Chords *117*

Minor Chords *118*

Diminished Chords *119*

Augmented Chords *120*

Chord Extensions 121

Sevenths *121*

Other Extensions *124*

Altered, Suspended, and Power Chords 126

Altered Chords *126*

Suspended Chords *127*

Power Chords *128*

Inverting the Order 129

Adding Chords to Your Music 130

Exercises 132

10   Chord Progressions **135**

Chords for Each Note in the Scale 136

Creating a Progression 139

It's All About Getting Home 139

One Good Chord Leads to Another 140

Ending a Phrase 142

Perfect Cadence *142*

Plagal Cadence *143*

Imperfect Cadence *143*

Interrupted Cadence *143*

Common Chord Progressions 144

I-IV *144*

I-V *144*

I-IV-V *145*

I-IV-V-IV *145*

I-V-vi-IV *146*

I-ii-IV-V *146*

I-ii-IV *146*

I-vi-ii-V *146*

I-vi-IV-V *147*

I-vi-ii-V7-ii *147*

IV-I-IV-V *147*

ii-V-I *148*

Circle of Fifths Progression...148

Chromatic Circle of Fifths...148

Singing the Blues...149

Chords and Melodies...149

Fitting Chords to a Melody...150

Chord Writing Tips...152

Writing a Melody to a Chord Progression...153

Exercises...154

11   Phrases and Forms...**157**

Parts of a Song...158

Introduction...158

Verse...158

Chorus...158

Bridge...159

Ending...159

Putting It All Together...159

Exercise...160

Part 4:   Accompanying...**161**

12   Transcribing What You Hear...**163**

Training Your Ear...164

Listening—Actively...165

Developing Super Hearing...166

Hearing Pitch...167

Hearing Intervals...168

Hearing Rhythms...171

Hearing Melodies...172

Hearing Keys...172

Hearing Chords and Chord Progressions...173

Writing It All Down...173

Exercises...174

13   Accompanying Melodies...**177**

What's the Score?...178

Working from a Lead Sheet...178

Working from a Chord Sheet...179

Working from a Melody...179

Working from Nothing...180

Working the Form 181

Playing the Part 181

    Block Chord Accompaniment *181*

    Rhythmic Accompaniment *182*

    Arpeggiated Accompaniment *184*

    Moving Bass *185*

One Good Strum Deserves Another 186

Exercises 186

14   Transposing to Other Keys **189**

Move Your Notes Around 190

Why You Need to Transpose 190

Four Ways to Transpose 191

    Step-Wise Transposition *191*

    Degree-Wise Transposition *193*

    Interval-Based Transposition *194*

    Software-Based Transposition *195*

Exercises 196

Part 5:   Embellishing **199**

15   Harmony and Counterpoint **201**

Two Ways to Enhance a Melody 202

Living in Harmony 203

    Voicing and Inversions *204*

    Making Harmony Parts More Melodic *206*

    Voice Leading *206*

Making a Point—with Counterpoint 208

    Keys to Successful Counterpoint *208*

    Creating Your First Counterpoint *209*

What to Avoid 212

Exercises 213

16   Chord Substitutions and Turnarounds **215**

Extending a Good Thing 216

Altering the Bass 217

Two Chords Are Better Than One 218

One Good Chord Can Replace Another 218

    Diatonic Substitution *218*

    Major Chord Substitutions *219*

    Minor Chord Substitutions *220*

Dominant Seventh Substitutions *220*

Functional Substitutions *221*

Turnarounds 222

Exercises 224

17   Special Notation **227**

Throwing a Curve 228

Ties *228*

Slurs *228*

Phrases *229*

The Long and the Short of It 229

Tenuto *229*

Staccato 230

When Is a Note More Than a Note? 230

Grace Notes 230

Turns *231*

Trills *231*

Glissandi *232*

Arpeggiated Chords *232*

Getting Into the Swing of Things 232

Getting the Word 233

Exercises 234

Part 6:   Composing and Arranging **237**

18   Musical Genres and Forms **239**

Classical Music 240

Classical Music Through the Years 240

Classical Forms *241*

Blues and Jazz 242

The Blues *243*

Jazz *244*

Popular Music 245

Exercises 246

19   Composing Your Own Music **247**

How to Become a Composer 248

Different Approaches to Composition *248*

Learning How to Write Your Own Music *249*

Composing with Chords...250

   Using Chord Leading..251

   Establishing a Harmonic Rhythm..251

   Fitting Melodies to Your Chords...252

Making Memorable Melodies...254

   Center on a Pitch..254

   Make Sure You End Up at Home...255

   Go Pentatonic..255

   Find the Hook..256

   Create Variations...256

   Make It Move...257

   Take Small Steps..258

   Stay in Range...258

   Set Up—and Resolve—Tension...259

   Follow the Words...260

Fitting Chords to a Melody..260

   Try the Obvious...260

   Use the Melodic Outline...261

   Work Backward...262

Exercises...263

20   Arranging for Voices and Instruments 265

Vocal Arranging...266

   Voice Characteristics...266

   Vocal Ranges...266

Instrumental Arranging..267

   Instrument Characteristics...267

   Transposition...270

   Good Keys and Bad Keys...273

Choosing Instruments for an Arrangement..274

Common Ensembles...275

   Choir..275

   Symphonic Orchestra..276

   Chamber Orchestra..277

   String Orchestra..278

   String Quartet...278

   Concert Band..278

   Marching Band..278

   Big Band (Jazz Band)...279

   Rock Band (Rhythm Section)...280

Exercises...281

21 **Lead Sheets and Scores**..**283**

Follow the Rules 284

Take the Lead..285

Make It Simple..286

Chord Sheets *286*

The Nashville Number System 287

Sing It Loud..289

Jazz It Up for Big Bands 290

Strike Up the (Concert) Band..292

Make the Big Score—for the Symphonic Orchestra 294

Use the Computer..296

Exercise 297

Coda 298

Appendixes

A **Glossary** 301

B **Music Theory Ear Training Course**..........................311

C **Answers to Chapter Exercises**...............................321

Index 335

Introduction

Back when I was in high school and college (a long time ago, and getting longer every day), many, if not most, of my fellow students regarded music theory as only slightly more fun than listening to paint dry. I didn't share that opinion, and still don't; I think music theory is interesting and fun and an essential part of any serious music education.

Still, if all you live for is to play your instrument (or to sing) 24 hours a day, taking time out from practicing to move a bunch of notes around on paper might not be tremendously appealing. In fact, I believe introductory-level music theory classes are the second most-skipped classes in college music schools, with only music history classes being less well received. (Some enterprising soul is bound to combine the two classes into a "Theory of Music History"—or "History of Music Theory"—course, thus creating new levels of student apathy.)

I'm not sure why so many budding musicians are so down on theory. Maybe it's because of the way it's presented. (Let's face it: Some instructors can be fairly boring when they present this material, and most music textbooks are stultifyingly dull.) Maybe it's because of the way music theory resembles sentence diagramming and other dreary grammar-related stuff. I don't know; maybe to some people, it just seems like a lot of work.

But the fact remains: every musician needs to know some music theory. That's a bold statement, and one that you might take issue with. After all, you've gotten this far in your music studies without knowing theory—why do you need to start studying theory now?

Music Theory Is Important

Most musicians, if they want to communicate with other musicians—to play in a band, or teach them their songs—have to know at least the basics about how music works. These basics—notes, chords, and so on—are what we call music theory.

Notes and chords are the building blocks of the language of music. Music theory defines the many different ways you can arrange those blocks into songs and compositions. Without the theory, all you have is noise; applying music theory, you can create great works of art.

Musicians apply music theory every time they sit down to play or sing—whether they know it or not. When you read a piece of music, you're using music theory. When you write down a series of notes, you're using music theory. When you play a chord, you're using music theory. When you sing a harmony line, you're using music theory.

Even musicians who don't have any formal training use music theory. When they put their hands on the piano, they might not know that they're playing a major ninth chord with the fourth in the bass, but they *do* know that those notes fit together well, even if they can't tell you why, or the strict chord construction.

Now, if they did have formal training, they could go beyond just playing the notes to sharing those notes with others. Instead of pointing at their fingers and saying "play this," they could actually write their notes and chords down on paper, in a format universally understood by musicians the world over. After all, it's a lot easier to tell someone to play a CM9/F chord than it is to say "put your first finger here, and your second finger here," and so on.

The knowledge of how different notes work together also helps you expand on the simple melodies you're currently playing. When you know theory, you know how to accompany a melody with chords and how to voice those chords so that they sound good to your ears. You also can learn how to turn that simple melody into a full-blown arrangement for groups of voices and instruments, and how to create your own melodies and compositions.

Without a knowledge of basic music theory, you won't be able to fully express your musical ideas; nor will you be able to share those ideas with others.

Music Theory Is Useful

Of course, it isn't just professional musicians who need to know theory. Even if you're just playing music or singing for your own personal enjoyment, a knowledge of theory will help you better appreciate it.

Here's an example: let's say you're helping out at your daughter's school and someone, knowing that you're a musician, asks you to work up an arrangement of "Mary Had a Little Lamb" for the upcoming school pageant. There are two girls and one boy in the class who sing pretty well, and another boy who knows how to play trumpet. You'll accompany them on guitar.

This doesn't sound like a tall order, but it does require a lot of theory to complete! First of all, you need to know how to read and write music—which includes the knowledge of clefs and keys and time signatures. Then you need to know about chords and chord progressions and how to create harmonies and counterpoint. You also need to know how to arrange music for different voices and instruments, and even how to transpose music from one key to another. (That's because the trumpet reads music in a different key from everybody else.)

You see the problem. If you don't know your theory, you won't be able to complete this rather simple assignment. It's as simple as that.

When you know the theory behind the music, playing and singing gets a lot more interesting. With a little grounding in theory, it's easier to understand why some melodies are more appealing than others, and why certain chord progressions work better with certain melodies. You'll see how harmony works, which will really help if you're singing background or accompanying someone on piano or guitar. You'll even be able to arrange music for your choir or band, or to create your own compositions.

And here's the neat part: music theory isn't hard. Once you learn the basic notes and scales, the rest falls together fairly easily. After all, a chord is just three notes played together. That's all—just three notes. And a song is nothing more than a few chords strung together in a series, along with a melody—which is just a series of notes all in a row. Figuring out what goes where (and which notes sound good together) is what theory is all about.

Music Theory Is for Nonmusicians

Music theory isn't just for musicians, either. A lot of listeners out there are curious about how music is created. Just what makes a particular song so special? Why does some music sound uplifting, and other music sound sad? And just what are your musician friends talking about when they say things like "cool changes" or "take this up a third"?

You don't have to be a music student to be interested in how music works—just as you don't have to have a literature degree to be interested in how words and sentences fit together. Basic music theory is for anyone who is interested in music; the more you know, the more you can appreciate the music that you listen to.

Music Theory and Me

There are many different ways to learn music theory. Your school might have music theory classes you can take. Your music teacher also might teach a little theory, or know a private teacher you can study with. Or you can learn theory the way I did: by yourself, from a book.

I taught myself music theory back when I was in eighth grade. My junior high school had the usual general music classes, as well as choir and band, but didn't have any theory classes. So, because I wanted to arrange some tunes for a band I was in, I had to teach myself the theory behind the arranging.

My theory education came from a lot of trial and error, and from two books: Dick Grove's *Arranging Concepts: A Guide to Writing Arrangements for Stage Band Ensembles* (1972) and David Baker's *Arranging and Composing for the Small Ensemble* (1970). Both of these books are still in print today (but in newer editions), and still as valuable as they were back then. I recommend you check them out.

Now, if you look at the titles of those books, you'll see that they really don't have anything to do with basic music theory. There's theory in the books, of course, but you really have to read between the lines (so to speak) to pull it out. I would have given my right arm back then for a book that focused on beginning-level theory, written at a level that I could comprehend.

Well, 30 years later, I wrote that book.

It's interesting. I was a fairly serious musician throughout my junior high and high school years, and went on to attend the prestigious Indiana University School of Music, in its even more prestigious jazz studies program. But something shifted along the way, and I ended up graduating IU with a business degree, and found myself some years later working in the book publishing industry. After serving my time in the corporate world, I became a full-time writer, writing books about all manner of topics, from computers to business management to home theater systems.

Then, in 2000, I was asked to write a music book—*The Complete Idiot's Guide to Playing Drums* (available at a bookstore near you). Things had finally come full circle, and I was writing about the music that I loved, and lived, so many years ago.

That book led to my writing other music books, chief of which is the one you hold in your hands—*Idiot's Guides: Music Theory*. The first edition of this book, published in 2002, became an overnight success—one of the best-selling music theory books of all time, with more than 250,000 copies sold worldwide. I'm still amazed at how well this book has been received, and am grateful to the hundreds of thousands of readers who helped to make it so successful. I'm glad to have had the opportunity to introduce a new audience to the joys of music—in, I hope, a manner that is easy to follow, reasonably comprehensive, and somewhat practical. And I'm pleased to present this updated third edition of the book, made even more useful by the inclusion of the *Music Theory Ear Training Course* online.

As to the book itself, *Idiot's Guides: Music Theory, Third Edition,* is designed to be a self-teaching tool for anyone wishing to learn music theory. The book starts with basic notes and rhythms; advances through scales, melodies, chords, and harmony; and ends with valuable information about accompanying, arranging, and conducting your music. In short, it presents pretty much everything you'll need to know about music theory—for musicians of any level.

Of course, I always recommend studying with a good teacher. Even if you're reading this book, you can learn even more by supplementing the material in these pages with the hands-on instruction you can get from a real human being. To me, that's really the best of both worlds: self-paced study accompanied by interaction with a good music theory instructor.

What You'll Find in This Book

However you decide to learn, I hope you find the information in this book useful. I've arranged the material in such a way that even if you know nothing about music or music theory, you can start on page one and progress through the book, moving from the basics to more advanced concepts. If you do know some theory, you can skip those chapters that you already know and go right to the new material you want to learn. And, once you've learned what you need to know, you can still use this book as a reference, to look up those scales or chords that you never can seem to remember.

Idiot's Guides: Music Theory, Third Edition, is composed of 21 chapters, each of which presents a different aspect of music theory. The chapters are organized into six general parts, as follows:

Part 1, Tones, gets you started with reading music. You'll learn about the notes on a piano, the intervals between different notes, and how those notes combine into different scales. You'll also learn about clefs and keys—both major and minor.

Part 2, Rhythms, shows you how to arrange your notes sequentially in space. You'll learn how to count and how to notate your music, using whole notes, half notes, quarter notes, and more. You'll also learn about different time signatures, and about tempo, dynamics, accents, and other musical effects.

Part 3, Tunes, helps you combine tones and rhythms to create your own melodies. You'll learn how melodies and chords are constructed; you'll also learn about chord progressions and different song forms.

Part 4, Accompanying, shows you how to make more out of your basic melodies. You'll learn how to write down the songs you hear on the radio, how to accompany simple melodies on piano or guitar, and how to add harmony and counterpoint to your songs.

Part 5, Embellishing, goes beyond basic theory to present advanced music notation and show you how to transpose music to other keys. You'll also learn how to spice up your music by substituting more sophisticated chords in your arrangements.

Part 6, Composing and Arranging, presents real-world advice for creating your own music—and taking it public. You'll learn how to compose music in various genres and forms, create lead sheets and scores, use music notation software to create sophisticated arrangements, and arrange for groups of instruments and voices.

In addition, you get three appendixes, including a glossary of musical terms, a guide to ear training files available online, and the answers to this book's exercises (found at the end of each chapter).

Speaking of online, at the book's website, idiotsguides.com/musictheory, you'll find a slew of audio files, a chord reference, charts of instrument ranges, and a bonus chapter on performing your music.

Music Theory Ear Training Course Online

 The web page that accompanies this book (idiotsguides.com/musictheory) is your gateway to the *Music Theory Ear Training Course.* This is a self-paced guide, in the form of streaming audio files, to improving your musical hearing. Work through the online examples and exercises to learn how to recognize scales, intervals, chords, and rhythms. It's a great way to learn how to understand and transcribe the music you hear. (You can check your answers in Appendix B.)

Although you don't need to listen to the online audio files to learn from the book, I've tried to tie the ear training lessons in with the content presented throughout the book. For example, when you read Chapter 2, you can listen to Lesson Two online (track #11), which lets you hear what all those intervals actually sound like. Look for the Ear Training icon at the beginning of a chapter to discover which track online corresponds to the information being presented.

What You Need to Use This Book

Any practicing or aspiring musician can learn basic music theory from *Idiot's Guides: Music Theory, Third Edition*. You don't need any initial knowledge to get started; you can use this book even if you don't know how to read music or play an instrument.

However, it will help if you have access to some sort of keyboard instrument. That can be a piano or organ, or some sort of inexpensive synthesizer or consumer-grade music keyboard. You can even use a keyboard app on your smartphone or tablet. It doesn't have to be a great keyboard or a big one; you'll use it mainly to perform some of the examples and exercises in the book. (You can use this book without having a keyboard, but then you'll have to envision some of the examples in your head.)

Most of the examples and exercises can be performed on any instrument—piano, guitar, trumpet, or whatever. If you don't play an instrument, you can sing most of the exercises. If you can't play or sing, I suggest you go the cheap keyboard route, so that you have some way of hearing the theory presented.

It will also help if you have some blank music paper at your disposal. And, of course, a computer, tablet, or smartphone with an internet connection, so you can listen to the *Music Theory Ear Training Course* online.

How to Get the Most Out of This Book

To get the most out of this book, you should know how it is designed. I've tried to put things together in such a way to make learning music theory both rewarding and fun.

Each chapter presents a basic concept of music theory, and progresses through that concept using a combination of text and musical examples. In some chapters you'll find pages of reference material—scale listings, chord charts, and the like—that you can turn back to whenever necessary.

At the end of each chapter are exercises based on the theory presented in that chapter. Work through these exercises to test your newfound knowledge—and find out what areas you need to work on a little more! (The answers to these exercises are in Appendix C.)

Throughout the entire book, you'll see a number of sidebars that present additional advice and information. These elements enhance your knowledge or point out important pitfalls to avoid. Here are the types of sidebars you'll see scattered throughout:

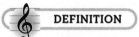
DEFINITION

These sidebars contain definitions of terms pertaining to aspects of music theory.

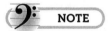
NOTE

These sidebars contain additional information about the topic at hand.

TIP

These sidebars contain advice about how best to use the theory presented in the text.

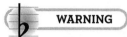
WARNING

These contain cautions about what to avoid when you're reading and writing music.

Let Me Know What You Think

If you want to learn more about me and my other books, check out my personal website at millerwriter.com. Search or click through to find the page for this book to find any corrections or clarifications we've posted.

You can also use the contact form on my website to contact me with questions or comments. I always love to hear from my readers—especially when the readers are fellow musicians! I can't promise that I'll answer every message, but I will promise that I'll read each one!

Dedication

This book is dedicated to Beth Ogren, who has been a good friend for more years than I remember. She's been waiting a long time for me to write a book about a topic she's interested in—so here it is, Beth.

Acknowledgments

I had assistance from dozens of individuals in the creation of this book and would like to thank the following for their help:

For the first edition of this book, I thank Marie Butler-Knight, Renee Wilmeth, Kathy Bidwell, and Joan Paterson, for helping to turn my original manuscript into a printed book. For the second edition, I thank Jennifer Moore, Janette Lynn, and Cari Luna for their additional work. And for this new third edition, I thank Lori Cates Hand, Phil Kitchel, Billy Fields, and Mike Sanders for making the book better than ever.

In addition, special thanks to my junior high school music teacher and lifelong friend, Phyllis Fulford, for suggesting some important changes to the book's outline, and for encouraging my talents way back when.

Thanks, as well, to another old friend, Orson Mason, who helped me arrange contact with Harry Miedema, and who also deserves many thanks for turning me on to a lot of great jazz at the Jazz Kitchen in Indianapolis—and equally tasty jambalaya at Yats next door!

Thanks also to Harry Miedema for agreeing to write the original foreword for this book.

Special thanks go to Allen Winold, professor emeritus in the Department of Music Theory at Indiana University, for graciously taking time out of his busy schedule (and his vacation!) to review the manuscript of the first edition of this book. Allen jumped into this project with a very welcome enthusiasm, and his comments and suggestions helped to make this a better book than it otherwise would have been.

Even more thanks go to Dr. Frank Felice, composer, educator, and all-around good guy, for providing a thorough review of this book's audio ear training course and for writing a new foreword for the second edition. He helped ensure the accuracy of the ear training files and accompanying text, and offered many valuable comments on content and approach—and helped to make the second edition of this book even better than the first.

I'd be remiss if I didn't thank my lovely wife, Sherry, and the rest of my family. They put up with all my nonsense, some (but not all) of which is undoubtedly related to the writing of this and other books.

Finally, I'd like to thank all the readers of this book's first and second editions, for their kind comments and useful suggestions. It's you folks who made this book such a resounding success, and I'm extremely grateful for your support.

Special Thanks to the Technical Reviewer

Idiot's Guides: Music Theory, Third Edition, was reviewed by an expert who double-checked the accuracy of what's presented here to help us ensure learning the ins and outs of music theory is as easy as it gets. Special thanks are extended to Jay Fuchs, PhD.

Dr. Jay Fuchs is the head of the Music Theory Department at McNally Smith College of Music, located in St. Paul, Minnesota. He holds a PhD in music theory and composition from the University of Minnesota and is a respected music educator, authoring the popular musicianship series Doctor Jay's Music Lessons. He also is a popular singer and pianist.

Tones

Discover the building blocks of all music: the pitches you play or sing. You'll learn about the notes of a scale, the different types of clefs and staves, the intervals between notes, major and minor scales, and all sorts of different keys and key signatures. (That's a lot for just four chapters!)

Pitches and Clefs

 Lesson 1, Track 2

As you can tell from the title, this is a book about music theory. But what exactly is music theory? And, even more basic than that, what is *music?*

There are lots of different definitions of the word "music," some more poetic than practical. For example, William Shakespeare called music the "food of love," George Bernard Shaw called music the "brandy of the damned," and Gottfried Wilhelm Leibnitz called music "sounding mathematics."

Interesting definitions all, but not really what we're looking for here. Let's try another definition:

> Music is the art, the craft, and the science of organizing sound and silence in the framework of time.

Now that's a little more helpful, but it's still fairly broad. This definition could describe a tremendous range of activities— a mother singing a lullaby to her child, an orchestra playing a Mozart symphony, a rock group performing their latest hit, a group of Native Americans playing ceremonial drum beats, Louis Armstrong playing trumpet in a jazz quartet, a group of sailors chanting "yo heave ho," or a nightingale warbling a

In This Chapter

- Understanding musical tones
- Assigning names to specific pitches
- Putting notes on a staff
- Using the treble, bass, and other clefs

serenade. You probably didn't buy this book to learn about all these things, although all of them can be called "music."

So we'll use a slightly different definition of music in this book. This definition is a lot more specific:

> Music is a succession of tones arranged in a specific rhythm.

Better? This definition doesn't cover *everything* that's ever been called "music," but it probably covers those types of music that you're familiar with—primarily, twentieth- and twenty-first-century popular music, from ragtime to reggae to rock, and everything in between.

Now to the word "theory." In scientific circles, this word is used as the formulation of a hypothesis, such as Einstein's theory of relativity. Although academic music theorists sometimes do formulate hypotheses in this scientific fashion, that's not what this book is about.

In our context, we'll use the word "theory" to mean a study of the rudiments of music—the basic things that performers and listeners need to know to produce and enjoy this marvelous art. This goes back to the root meaning of the word, which means "a way of looking." If we broaden this definition to include not just looking, but also listening and performing, then we're set.

Now that we've defined our terms, it's time to learn the theory behind the music. Let's go back to our definition of music, which says that music is a succession of tones, arranged in a specific rhythm. To study music, then, we have to learn about notes, and about arranging them.

We'll get to the "arranging in a specific rhythm" bit starting with Chapter 5. That lets us focus our attention, for the time being, on tones.

Understanding Musical Tones

So what's a tone? The definition is simple: a tone is a sound that is played or sung at a specific *pitch*.

When you hum (go ahead …), you're humming a tone. When you whistle, you're whistling a tone. When you go "aaaahhhh," you're sounding a tone. If you put two or more hums, whistles, or "aaaahhhhs" together, you have music.

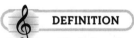 **DEFINITION**

Pitch describes the specific frequency or tuning of a tone.

You can hum lots of different tones, high or low. The higher tones are referred to as *higher pitched;* lower tones are called *lower pitched.*

Here's an exercise: hum a tone. Now hum a tone higher than the first tone.

What you've just hummed are two separate tones, at two separate pitches. The second tone was higher pitched than the first tone.

Different voices and different instruments produce different ranges of tones. For example, women tend to have higher voices than men; the tones most women sing are higher pitched than the tones most men sing. (There are exceptions to this rule, of course; listen to some of the doo-wop singers of the 1950s and you'll hear some fairly high male voices!)

In the world of musical instruments, physically larger instruments tend to produce lower-pitched tones, whereas smaller instruments tend to produce higher-pitched tones. This is because bigger instruments move more air than smaller ones do, and more air means a lower pitch. This is why the small cylinder of a flute produces higher notes than the big brass tubing of a tuba, and why the thin strings on a guitar are higher pitched than the thick strings.

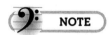 **NOTE**

Some instruments produce tones that aren't at specific pitches. These instruments—such as drums and cymbals—are called *unpitched* or *nonpitched* instruments. The tones they produce can be high or low, but typically don't correspond to specific note pitches.

Some instruments produce a broader range of tones than other instruments. In particular, the piano has a very broad range. From the lowest tone (the key on the far left of the keyboard) to the highest (the key on the far right), the piano reproduces more tones than just about any other instrument—and certainly a lot more than the human voice!

Time for another exercise: hum the lowest tone you can hum; then gradually raise the pitch until you're humming the highest tone you can hum. You just hummed a whole lot of different tones. How, then, do you describe a specific tone so that someone else can hum the same tone?

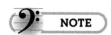 **NOTE**

You'll find lots of musical terms in this book, but you need to know that musicians tend to use a lot of these terms interchangeably. A conductor who says, "That *note* was wrong," might mean that the *pitch* was wrong, or that the *note value* (rhythm) was wrong. That's because the word "note" can be used in place of either more specific definition. So don't get hung up on the differences between "tones" and "pitches" and "notes." While there are specific definitions for each word, it's acceptable to be a little loose on the usage. I might even substitute one word for another in this book. You'll understand what I mean from the context.

Tones Have Value

When it comes to describing a tone, it helps to know that every tone you can sing or play has a specific value. You can measure that value scientifically, and use that value to describe the tone—or, more precisely, its pitch. If that's too complicated, you also can assign an arbitrary name to each tone. (Go ahead: hum a note called "Bob.")

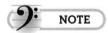 **NOTE**

One good way to determine a specific pitch is with a *tuning fork,* which is a fork-shaped piece of metal that resonates at a specific frequency when struck. Most tuning forks resonate at 440Hz, which is the pitch A. Some people have what is called *perfect pitch,* in that they can hear absolute pitches in their heads. However, most people need the guidance of a tuning fork, pitch pipe, piano, or other musical instrument to fix a specific pitch.

Tuning Into a Frequency

If you plug a microphone into an oscilloscope, and then hum a tone into the microphone, the oscilloscope will measure the *frequency* of the tone. This is actually a measurement of how fast the molecules of air are vibrating; the faster the vibrations, the higher the pitch.

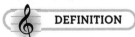 **DEFINITION**

Frequency is a measurement of how fast air molecules are vibrating.

These vibrations are measured in *cycles per second,* and there are a lot of them. (Cycles per second are often called *hertz,* abbreviated Hz.) If you hum the pitch we call middle C (the white key in the exact center of a full 88-key piano keyboard, or the first fret on the second string of a guitar), the oscilloscope will measure 261.6Hz—that is, the air is cycling back and forth 261.6 times per second.

So one way to identify specific pitches is by their frequency. Unfortunately, writing out even a simple melody in terms of frequency gets a tad unwieldy. For example, here's the first half of "Mary Had a Little Lamb" ("Mary had a little lamb, little lamb, little lamb") notated by frequency:

```
659Hz, 587Hz, 523Hz, 587Hz, 659Hz, 659Hz, 659Hz,
587Hz, 587Hz, 587Hz,
659Hz, 783Hz, 783Hz
```

Not easy to read, is it? That's why we don't use the frequency method to write music.

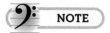

NOTE

The "standard" pitch today that most musicians tune to is the A above middle C, which equals 440Hz; all the other notes are pitched in relation to this note. In earlier times and cultures, this note had other values—as low as 376Hz in early eighteenth-century France, and as high as 560Hz in early seventeenth-century Germany (referred to as *North German church pitch*).

Play by Numbers

An easier way to designate tones is to number each individual pitch. But before we start numbering, it helps to know a little bit about how different pitches relate to each other.

When you hum a pitch, you can "slide" that pitch from lower to higher and back again, which might make you think there are an infinite number of pitches available. (You can certainly see this when you look at frequencies; you have one tone at 256Hz, another at 257Hz, another at 258Hz, and so on.)

Although that might be true in theory, in practice some pitches are too close together to clearly distinguish them. For example, if you hum a 256Hz tone and a 257Hz tone, they sound almost identical in pitch because there isn't a big enough *interval* between the tones.

We need to place a reasonable interval between tones, enough for our ears to notice, and then assign values to those main pitches that result. What you end up with is a series of pitches called a *scale*. (You'll learn more about scales in Chapter 2.) Each scale starts on a specific tone, and ends on a higher-pitched version of that same tone.

In the Western world, we divide our scales into seven main notes—eight if you count the top note, which is the starting note repeated higher at the end of the scale. Because there are seven notes, it's easy to number them—one through seven. Using this numbering system, here's what the first half of "Mary Had a Little Lamb" looks like:

```
3 2 1 2 3 3 3
2 2 2
3 5 5
```

If you're reading ahead and want to see how the numbering system applies to traditional music notation, here's what the C Major scale looks like, by the numbers:

Numbering the notes in the C Major scale.

Now, not to be confusing here, but there are actually notes *between* some of these main notes—enough of them that we really have *12 pitches* before they start repeating. These in-between pitches are equally spaced in what we call *half steps,* where the major pitches (A, B, C, etc.) have either one or two half steps between them, depending on the note. (I know, it's getting confusing already ….)

For the time being, we're going to focus on the seven main notes of a scale since that's easiest to understand. We'll leave the half steps for Chapter 2. Feel free to read ahead if you're interested.

Do Re Mi

Another way to remember each tone is by assigning a simple syllable to each tone. Remember the song from *The Sound of Music* that goes "Do, a deer, a female deer"? That's what we're talking about here.

In this particular method, called *Solfeggio* or *Solfège* (pronounced *sol-FEZH*), each of the seven notes of a scale has its own name. The following table shows the words to use.

 TIP

Solfeggio is a method of naming musical tones using a set of syllables—do, re, mi, and so on. These syllables come from the initial syllables of the first six words to "The Hymn to St. John the Baptist"; the seventh syllable (Ti) is derived from the name St. John, in Latin.

The Solfeggio Method

Tone	Solfeggio Name	Pronunciation
1	Do	Doh
2	Re	Ray
3	Mi	Mee
4	Fa	Fah
5	So (Sol)	So
6	La	Lah
7	Ti	Tee
8	Do	Doh

Here's what the first half of "Mary Had a Little Lamb" looks like using the Solfeggio method:

```
Mi Re Do Re Mi Mi Mi
Re Re Re
Mi So So
```

If you're reading ahead and want to know how the Solfeggio names apply to traditional music notation, here's what the C Major scale looks like:

1	2	3	4	5	6	7	8
Do	Re	Mi	Fa	So	La	Ti	Do

The Do Re Mis of the C Major scale.

Tones Have Names

It's important to know that both the numbering and the Solfeggio methods are relative ways of naming musical tones. That is, the first note in a scale is always number one, and is always called Do. The second tone is always number two, and is always called Re. It doesn't matter what actual tone you start with, these names always apply.

The problem with using relative naming is that it doesn't tell you what precise pitch to start with. You might start your Do Re Mi on a low pitch, and your neighbor might start hers on a higher pitch, and your duet will end up sounding like two water buffaloes in heat.

And that's not good. (Unless you're a water buffalo, of course.)

No, what we need is a way to designate specific pitches—without resorting to the cumbersome frequency method.

Learning the ABCs

The accepted way of naming specific musical pitches uses the first seven letters of the alphabet—A, B, C, D, E, F, and G. Although the numbering method is relative (the number 1 can be assigned to any pitch), the letter method is absolute. This means that A always refers to a specific frequency. When you tell someone to sing or play an A, they'll always sing or play the same pitch.

The only problem with this method is that you can sing or play more than one A.

Try this exercise: sing A B C D E F G A (think "Do Re Mi Fa So La Ti Do"). The first A and the second A should be the same tone, with the second A an *octave* higher than the first A. (You'll learn about octaves a little later in this chapter—suffice to say it's a way of presenting a lower or higher version of the same note.)

You can play an A with a low pitch, and an A with a higher pitch—and other As both below and above those. Now, all the As will have the same tone; they're just higher or lower versions of the basic pitch.

How, then, do you tell which A to play or sing?

Notes on a Piano Keyboard

A good way to visualize the seven basic notes (A through G) is to look at a piano keyboard. Each white key on the keyboard corresponds to one of these seven main notes, as shown in the following figure. (And ignore the black keys, for the time being.)

The white keys on a piano keyboard.

As you can see, the black and white keys on a piano form a certain pattern. If you start in the right place, you'll see that the black keys are arranged in groups of threes and twos. The first white key to the left of a group of *three* black notes is always assigned to the tone of F. The first white key to the left of a group of *two* black notes is always assigned to C. Once you know where F and C are, you can figure out the location of the other tones.

To figure out which A (or F or C) to play, know that the C located in the very middle of a full-size piano keyboard—directly underneath the manufacturer's logo or pull-down door handle—is called *middle C*. (It's the C in the middle of the keyboard—easy to remember.) All other notes can be described relative to middle C—as in "the F above middle C" or "the D below middle C."

    TIP

Some musicians identify the specific pitch by placing a number after the note name. Using this method (which is sometimes called *scientific pitch notation*), the lowest C on a grand piano is notated C1. The next C up from that is C2, then C3, C4, and so on—and the same for all the other notes. (In this notation, middle C is C4.)

Notes on a Staff

Now that you know the seven basic notes and where they lie on a piano keyboard, how do you go about communicating those notes to others? You could just spell out a song; if you used this method, the first half of "Mary Had a Little Lamb" would look like this:

```
E D C D E E E
D D D
E G G
```

Now, that's more specific than using numbers or Solfeggio, but it's still somewhat difficult to read. A better way to notate pitches is to do so *visually*, using a graphic that in some ways resembles a basic piano keyboard. This graphic is called a *staff*.

The basic music staff is composed of lines and spaces, like this:

A blank staff.

As you can see, the staff has precisely five lines and four spaces. Each line or space represents a specific pitch. The pitches are determined by the clef at the beginning of the staff; the staff we're looking at here uses what's called the treble clef. (There are several different types of clefs, which we'll discuss later in this chapter.)

The notes of a staff (treble clef).

This treble clef staff pictures the notes in the exact middle of a piano keyboard—just above middle C. (The bottom line of the staff represents the E above middle C.) The following figure shows how the notes of the staff relate to specific piano keys.

The notes on a staff and where they appear on a piano keyboard.

Back to "Mary Had a Little Lamb," here's what the first part of that song looks like on a music staff:

The notes of "Mary Had a Little Lamb" on a music staff.

Above—and Below—the Staff

The basic staff describes nine basic notes—five on the lines, four in the spaces. But what about all those notes either above or below these nine notes—like that last note in "Mary Had a Little Lamb"?

Notes higher than the F at the top of the staff are written in the lines and spaces *above* the staff. For example, the first space above the staff is the first note after F: G. The first line above the staff is the first note after G: A. You can keep adding spaces and lines above the staff to describe higher and higher notes, as shown in the following figure.

Notes above the staff.

Just as you can add lines and spaces above the staff, you can also add lines and spaces *below* the staff to describe lower notes. For example, the first space below the staff is the first note before E: D.

The first line below the staff is the first note before D: C. The following figure shows the first few notes below the standard staff. By the way, the first line below the staff is middle C.

Notes below the staff.

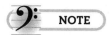

The lines you add above or below a staff are called *ledger lines*.

Different Clefs

Up till now, we've been looking at a staff that represents the notes just above middle C on the piano keyboard. The notes of this staff are determined by the type of *clef* that appears at the beginning of the staff—and there are several different types of clefs.

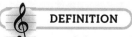

A **clef** is a graphical symbol placed at the beginning of a staff or piece of music that establishes the pitch of a specific line or space on the staff; thus it determines the pitch of all the other notes on the staff.

The Treble Clef

The clef we've been working with so far is called the *treble clef;* it looks like this:

The treble clef.

As you've already learned, in real-world terms the treble clef is positioned just above middle C. The bottom line of the treble clef staff is an E; the top line is an F.

The treble clef, like all clefs, fixes the position of a single pitch, from which you can figure out where all the rest of the notes go. In the case of the treble clef, the pitch it fixes is G, which is the second line on the staff. (If you look closely at the treble clef itself, you see that the big round part of the clef circles around the second line of the staff.) For this reason, the treble clef is sometimes called the G clef—and the clef itself looks a little like a capital G.

If you ever have trouble remembering which note goes with which line or space on a staff, here's an easy way to remember them. The lines of the treble clef staff are assigned, bottom to top, to the notes E, G, B, D, and F. You can remember the lines by recalling the first letters in the phrase "Every Good Boy Does Fine." The spaces of the treble clef staff are assigned, bottom to top, to the notes F, A, C, and E. You can remember the spaces by remembering the word "FACE."

Most higher-pitched instruments and voices use the treble clef. This includes trumpets, flutes, clarinets, and guitars, as well as singers singing the soprano, alto, and tenor parts.

The Bass Clef

When you need to write music below the treble clef, you can use a different clef, called the *bass clef*. The bass clef is positioned just below middle C, and is sometimes called the F clef. (That's because the two dots on the clef surround the fourth line, which is F.)

NOTE

The word "bass," as in "bass clef," is pronounced *base*—like the bottom of things, not like the fish.

Here's what the bass clef looks like, with the notes of a bass clef staff:

The bass clef.

Most lower-pitched instruments and voices use the bass clef. This includes trombones, tubas, bass guitars, and singers singing the bass part.

An easy way to remember the lines of the bass clef is with the phrase "Good Boys Do Fine Always." (The first letter of each word describes each line of the staff, from bottom to top.) To remember the spaces of the bass clef, remember the first letters in the phrase "All Cows Eat Grass."

The Grand Staff

If you play or write for piano, there's another staff you need to know. This staff, called the *grand staff,* links together a treble clef staff and a bass clef staff. (That's because you play the piano with two hands; each staff roughly corresponds to each hand.)

The grand staff looks like this:

The grand staff.

When you use a grand staff, it's important to note that the two staffs neatly flow into each other. The A at the top of the bass clef extends above that staff to a B and a C. The C is then linked to the treble clef, goes on up to a D, and then the E on the bottom line of the treble clef.

The neat thing is that the C—which just happens to be middle C—is halfway between each staff. So when you write a middle C on a grand staff, it might extend down from the treble clef staff or extend up from the bass clef staff, depending on where the surrounding notes are placed.

Specialty Clefs

There are a handful of specialty clefs you must learn, although you probably won't use them much. These clefs are designed for instruments whose ranges don't fit comfortably within the traditional treble or bass clefs.

One of the most common specialty clefs is the *alto clef,* shown here:

F	G	A	B	C	D	E	F	G

The alto clef.

The alto clef is used primarily by the viola, which is a slightly bigger version of a violin. The pointer on this clef points at middle C, which is the third line, in the exact middle of the staff.

The *tenor clef* looks a lot like the alto clef, except the pointer points at a different line. (It still points to middle C, but middle C is positioned at a different point on the staff.) The tenor clef looks like this, and is sometimes used by bassoons, bass violins, and tenor trombones.

| D | E | F | G | A | B | C | D | E |

The tenor clef.

Although there are several other specialty clefs (including the baritone, subbass, and French violin clefs), you probably won't run into them too often; they're not widely used. However, you might run into what is called an *octave clef,* which looks like a normal treble or bass clef with the number 8 either above or below the clef. When you see this type of clef, you're supposed to transpose the normal treble clef notes either up (if the 8 is above the clef) or down (if the 8 is below the clef) an octave.

Octave clefs.

The Percussion Clef

There's one more clef you should know, and it's really the easiest of them all. This clef is used when you're writing for drums and other percussion instruments—those that don't play a fixed pitch. It's called either the *percussion clef* or the *indefinite pitch clef,* and it can be written one of two ways:

The percussion clef—version one and version two.

The neat thing about this clef is that the lines and spaces don't correspond to any specific pitches. Instead, you assign different instruments to different parts of the staff.

For example, if you're writing for drum set, you might assign the bass drum to the bottom space, the snare drum to the third space, and two tom-toms to the second and fourth spaces; you can put the ride cymbal on the top line of the staff.

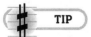
TIP

There really aren't any rules for how to assign instruments to a percussion clef, so you're pretty much on your own. It's probably a good idea to consult a few drummers or look at a few percussion parts to get a better idea of how to use the percussion clef.

Exercises

Exercise 1-1

Write the name of each note below the note.

F   B   A   E   F   D   C   G   G   C

Exercise 1-2

Write the name of each note below the note.

C   A   A   G   D   G   C   B   E   E

Exercise 1-3

Write each note on the staff.

A   C   G   F   B   G   D   E   D   B

Exercise 1-4

Write each note on the staff.

E   F   D   G   C   A   B   G   A   C

Exercise 1-5

Draw the indicated clefs on the staff.

Bass   Treble   Alto   Tenor   Treble (octave above)

Exercise 1-6

Write the following notes above the staff.

G   B   A   D   C   B   D   C   E   F

Exercise 1-7

Write the following notes below the staff.

C   D   B   A   G   F   E   C   D   B

Exercise 1-8

Identify the following notes on the piano keyboard.

C   F   G   B   D   E   F   A   G   B

The Least You Need to Know

- Music is a succession of tones arranged in a specific pattern; a tone is a sound that is played or sung at a specific pitch.

- There are many different ways to describe a specific pitch. You can describe a pitch by its vibration frequency, by where it lies numerically compared to other pitches, or by using the Do Re Mi (Solfeggio) method.

- Established music notation assigns letters to the seven basic pitches, A through G. The letters repeat as you generate higher pitches.

- Pitches are assigned to specific keys on a piano keyboard, and to specific lines and spaces on a musical staff.

- The clef placed at the start of a staff determines which notes appear where on the staff. The most used clef is the treble clef; the bass clef is used for lower-pitched instruments and voices.

Intervals

Lesson 2, Track 11

In the previous chapter you learned all about musical pitches: how they're named and how they're presented on a staff. In this chapter we'll go beyond that by looking at how pitches can be raised and lowered, and how you can describe the differences between pitches in terms of *intervals*.

To make things as simple as possible, we'll discuss these pitches and intervals in terms of the C Major scale—that is, the notes between one C on the piano keyboard and the next C above that. The basic concepts can be applied to any scale, as you'll see; it's just that sticking to a single scale makes it all a little easier to grasp. (And, at least on the piano, the C Major scale is the easiest scale to work with—it's all white keys!)

In This Chapter

- Changing pitches with sharps and flats
- Understanding half steps and whole steps
- Counting the intervals between notes
- Using major, minor, perfect, diminished, and augmented intervals

Be Sharp—or Be Flat

As you learned in Chapter 1, the lines and spaces on a music staff correspond exactly to the white keys on a piano. But what about those black keys? Where are they on the staff?

When we say there are 7 main pitches in a Western musical scale (A through G), that's a bit of an oversimplification: there actually are 12 possible notes in an octave, with some of them falling between the 7 main pitches.

Just count the keys between middle C and next C on the piano—including the black keys, but without counting the second C. If you counted correctly, you counted 12 keys, which represent 12 pitches; each pitch/key is the same *interval* away from the previous pitch/key.

These black keys are called *sharps* and *flats.* Sharps and flats are halfway between the pitches represented by the white keys on a piano; a sharp is above a specific key, and a flat is below a specific key.

Put another way, a sharp raises the natural note; a flat lowers the note.

Take the black key above the middle C key, for example. You can refer to this key as *C-sharp,* because it raises the pitch of C. It also can be called *D-flat,* because it lowers the next white key up, D. It may be a little confusing, but it's true—C-sharp is the same note as D-flat. And whenever you have two notes that describe the same pitch—like C-sharp and D-flat—the notes are *enharmonic.*

Here are the dual names you can use for a piano's black keys:

The black keys on a piano keyboard.

On a music staff, sharps and flats are designated by special characters placed before the affected note. These characters, called *accidentals,* look like this:

♯   ♭   ♮

A sharp, a flat, and a natural sign.

That third character is called a *natural*. When you see a natural sign on a piece of music, it means to return the specific note to its natural state, without any sharps or flats.

It's important to know that you can add sharps and flats to any note—even those keys on a piano that don't have black notes between them. So, for example, if you add a flat to the C note, you lower it to the next note on the keyboard—which happens to be B natural. (This means B natural is the same pitch as C-flat.)

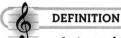 **DEFINITION**

An **interval** is the space between two pitches. The smallest interval in Western music is a half step; intervals are typically measured in the number of half steps between the two notes. Two notes that sound the same but can be spelled differently are called **enharmonic** notes. Any modification to a natural note is called an **accidental.** Sharps and flats are accidentals; the natural sign (used to return a sharped or flatted note to its natural state) is also an accidental.

Steppin' Out ...

The smallest interval in Western music is the *half step*. On the piano keyboard, half steps appear between the white keys B and C and between E and F. In all other cases they appear between a white key and a black key—for example, D to D-sharp, or F-sharp to G.

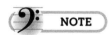 **NOTE**

In some musical circles, a half step is called a semitone, and a whole step is called a tone. On a guitar, a half step is the distance of a single fret. A whole step is the distance of two frets.

Two half steps equal one *whole step*. The interval between F and G is a whole step; the interval between B and C-sharp is also a whole step.

Now that you know about steps, it's a little easier to understand how sharps and flats work. When you sharpen a note, you move the pitch up a half step. When you flatten a note, you move the pitch down a half step.

Take the note C, for example. When you add a flat to C, you take it down a half step. Because the first key (white or black) to the left of C is the white key B, this means C-flat equals B. When you add a sharp to C, you take it up a half step. The first key to the right of C is the black key we call C-sharp. (This black key is also the first key to the left of D, which means C-sharp is the same as D-flat.)

You can use the step method to describe the intervals between two notes—although once you get more than a few steps away, the counting becomes a tad difficult. When you're trying to figure out which note is seven half steps above middle C (it's G, in case you're counting), it's time to use another method to describe your intervals.

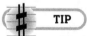

TIP

The half step is the smallest interval in Western music, but music from other parts of the world often contains intervals smaller than a half step. Some Indian music, for example, divides an octave into 22 steps, each about half as large as a Western half step.

A Matter of Degrees

A more accepted way of describing intervals is to go back to the seven main notes of a scale and revisit the relative numbering method. You can use the numbers of the scale to denote the basic intervals between notes, and thus apply this numbering to any scale.

First Things First

As you learned in the previous chapter, you can use numbers to describe the seven main notes in any scale. The first note is numbered one, the second note is numbered two, and so on. This method of numbering actually describes the seven *degrees* of a musical scale.

There also are fancy musical names you can use in place of the numbers, which you might run into in some more formal situations. The following table presents these formal degree names.

Degrees of the Scale

Degree	Name
First (*Root*)	Tonic
Second	Supertonic
Third	Mediant
Fourth	Subdominant
Fifth	Dominant
Sixth	Submediant
Seventh	Leading Note
Eighth (Octave)	Tonic

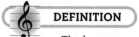

> **DEFINITION**
>
> The lowest note of an interval, chord, or scale, is called the **root**.

To be honest, you probably won't use all of these fancy degree names; musicians will know what you're talking about if you just say first, second, third, and so forth. If you only memorize a few of these formal names, focus on *tonic* and *dominant*–the first and the fifth degrees are most important in real-world situations. (All this will become more important when you learn about chord progressions in Chapter 10.)

There are a few more terms you need to know before we proceed. When two notes of the exact same pitch are played by two different instruments or voices, they're played in *unison*. Two identical notes with the same name, played eight degrees apart, form an *octave*. (The word "octave" comes from the Latin word "*octo*," for "eight"—because an octave is eight notes above the beginning note.)

For example, if you go from middle C to the next C up the keyboard, that's an octave; F to F is another octave, and so on.

These musical degrees come in handy when you're describing intervals between notes. Instead of counting half steps and whole steps, you can simply describe an interval by using these relative numbers.

For example, let's say you want to describe the interval between C and D. If you count C as number one (the first degree), D is number two, and the interval between them is called a *second*. The interval between C and E (the first and third degrees) is a *third*; the interval between C and F (the first and fourth degrees) is a *fourth*, and so on.

Pretty easy, once you get used to it!

The following figure shows the basic intervals, starting with a unison and ending with an octave, with C as the root.

Unison   Second   Third   Fourth   Fifth   Sixth   Seventh   Octave

The basic intervals, starting on C.

Major and Minor Intervals

When you describe intervals by degree, you still have to deal with those pitches that fall above or below the basic notes—the sharps and flats, or the black keys on a keyboard.

When measuring by degrees, you see that the second, third, sixth, and seventh notes can be easily flattened. When you flatten one of these notes, you create what is called a *minor* interval. The natural state of these intervals (in a major scale) is called a *major* interval.

Here's what these four intervals look like, with C as the root, in both major and minor forms.

Major 2nd   Minor 2nd   Major 3rd   Minor 3rd   Major 6th   Minor 6th   Major 7th   Minor 7th

Major and minor intervals, starting on C.

 NOTE

Remember, in this chapter we're dealing with intervals within a major scale. Minor scales (described in Chapter 3) have different "natural" intervals between degrees of the scale.

Perfect Intervals

Certain intervals don't have separate major or minor states (although they can still be flattened or sharpened). These intervals—fourths, fifths, and octaves—exist in one form only, called a *perfect* interval. You can't lower these intervals to make them minor or raise them to make them major; there's no such thing as a minor fifth or a major octave. The intervals, because of their acoustical properties, are perfect as-is.

Here are the three perfect intervals, with C as the root.

Perfect   4th   Perfect   5th   Octave

Three perfect intervals, starting on C.

Over the years, I've found that perfect intervals tend to confuse some beginning music students. (And some more advanced ones, too!) The fact that they don't have major and minor forms puts them in stark contrast to the other intervals.

Now, it's perfectly (sorry …) okay to just accept that fourths and fifths and octaves are different from other intervals and let it go at that. But it's the *why* behind these unique intervals that vexes many students.

The big question I get asked is, "Why is a perfect interval so perfect?" It all has to do with frequencies, and with ratios between frequencies. In a nutshell, perfect intervals sound so closely related because their frequencies are closely related.

For example, a perfect octave has a ratio of 2:1 between the two frequencies—the octave is twice the frequency of the starting pitch (which is called the *fundamental*). If the fundamental is 440Hz, the octave above is twice that frequency, or 880Hz. Similarly, a perfect fifth has a ratio of 3:2; you take the starting pitch and multiply it by $\frac{3}{2}$ to get the perfect fifth above (660Hz for a 440Hz fundamental). A perfect fourth has a ratio of 4:3; multiply the fundamental by $\frac{4}{3}$ to get the perfect fourth (586Hz for a 440Hz fundamental).

Other intervals have more complex ratios, which makes them less perfect. For example, a major third has a ratio of 5:4, not quite as simple—or as perfect—as a 2:1, 3:2, or 4:3 ratio. And the minor third ratio of 6:5 is even less perfect.

Put into a series, each increasingly complex interval ratio forms what is called a *harmonic series,* and the intervals (in order) are called *harmonics.* The simpler harmonics of the perfect intervals sound more pleasing to our ears because they're less complex—there's less stuff going on, sonically.

To make a long story short, the reason we call octaves, fifths, and fourths "perfect" is because they're simpler and more consonant—that is, they sound better and more natural than do the less perfect intervals. The nomenclature is somewhat arbitrary, admittedly, but that's just the way things are. My advice is not to lose too much sleep over all this and just learn which intervals are which. They're not going to change.

Augmented and Diminished Intervals

Okay, now you know that perfect intervals can't be major or minor. That doesn't mean that they can't be altered, however. You can raise and lower fourths and fifths—however, the result is not called major or minor. When you raise a perfect interval a half step, it's called an *augmented* interval. When you lower a perfect interval a half step, it's called a *diminished* interval. So don't call the new intervals major or minor—call them augmented or diminished.

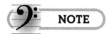 **NOTE**

An augmented fourth and a diminished fifth are enharmonically the same note.

For example, if you use C as the root, F is a perfect fourth away from the root. If you sharpen the F, the resulting note (F-sharp) is an augmented fourth above the root.

Along the same lines, G is a perfect fifth above C. When you flatten the G, the resulting note (G-flat) is a diminished fifth above the root.

Here are the key augmented and diminished intervals, with C as the root.

Diminished 4th   Augmented 4th   Diminished 5th   Augmented 5th

Augmented and diminished intervals, starting on C.

Now, just to confuse things, other types of intervals can also be called diminished and augmented—and these intervals have nothing to do with the perfect intervals.

To start, you can also create a diminished interval by lowering a minor interval by another half step. For example, F to D-flat is a minor sixth; if you flatten the D-flat (yes, there's such a thing as a double flat), the resulting interval is called a diminished sixth.

You can also create an augmented interval by raising a major interval by another half step. For example, F to A is a major third; if you sharpen the A (to A-sharp), the resulting interval is an augmented third.

Fortunately, you don't have to deal with either type of diminished or augmented interval that often. But you still need to know what they are, just in case!

Beyond the Octave

You don't have to stop counting intervals when you get to the octave. Above the octave are even more intervals—ninths, tenths, elevenths, and so on.

Intervals that span more than an octave are called *compound intervals* because they combine an octave with a smaller interval to create the larger interval. For example, a ninth is nothing more than an octave and a second; an eleventh is an octave and a fourth … and so on.

The following table describes the first six intervals above the octave.

Compound Intervals

Interval	Combines
Ninth	Octave plus second
Tenth	Octave plus third
Eleventh	Octave plus fourth
Twelfth	Octave plus fifth
Thirteenth	Octave plus sixth
Fourteenth	Octave plus seventh

Compound intervals can have all the qualities of smaller intervals, which means a compound interval can be (depending on the interval) major, minor, perfect, augmented, or diminished.

Intervals and Half Steps

It might be easier for you to think of all these intervals in terms of half steps. To that end, the following table shows how many half steps are between these major and minor intervals.

Half Steps Between Intervals

Interval	Number of Half Steps
Perfect unison	0
Minor second	1
Major second	2
Minor third	3
Major third	4
Perfect fourth	5
Augmented fourth	6
Diminished fifth	6
Perfect fifth	7
Minor sixth	8
Major sixth	9
Minor seventh	10
Major seventh	11
Octave	12
Minor ninth	13
Major ninth	14
Minor tenth	15
Major tenth	16
Perfect eleventh	17
Augmented eleventh	18
Diminished twelfth	18

continues

Half Steps Between Intervals   (continued)

Interval	Number of Half Steps
Perfect twelfth	19
Minor thirteenth	20
Major thirteenth	21
Minor fourteenth	22
Major fourteenth	23

And take special note of those intervals that are enharmonically identical—such as the augmented fourth and the diminished fifth. What you call that particular interval depends on which direction you're heading, and which notation is the easiest to read in a given piece of music.

Mod-12

What you've learned so far is traditional Western music notation—but it's not the only way to notate musical pitches. Some educators today use what is called the *Mod-12* system to teach notes and intervals. In this system, the intervals between the 12 half steps in an octave are numbered, from 0 to 11. (If you count the 0, that adds up to 12 intervals.)

For example, the interval we call unison has zero half steps between notes, and is called "interval 0." The interval we call a minor third has three half steps, and is called "interval 3."

The nice thing about using this system is that you don't have to worry about enharmonics. A diminished fifth and an augmented fourth both have six half steps, and are both called "interval 6."

You can also use the Mod-12 system to describe individual notes—based on their interval from tonic. Tonic, of course, is note 0. The minor second degree is note 1, and the major second degree is note 2. If you wanted to describe the tonic, the major third degree, and the perfect fifth degree, you'd use the numbers 0, 4, and 7.

Some people like to use the Mod-12 system to teach intervals, but I prefer the old-fashioned method presented here earlier in this chapter, for the sole reason that this is what you'll run into in the real world. When you're playing in a concert band or a jazz trio, you won't hear other musicians say "play 4, 7, 11." You *will* hear them say "play the major third, fifth, and major seventh."

Still, if Mod-12 works for you, use it. It's a perfectly acceptable way to learn the 12 tones we use in Western music—and it makes it a lot easier to deal with enharmonic notes.

Exercises

Exercise 2-1

Add sharps before each of these notes.

Exercise 2-2

Add flats before each of these notes.

Exercise 2-3

Enter a new note an octave above each of the following notes.

Exercise 2-4

Enter a new note a specified number of half steps from the previous note. (Remember to start each new note after the previous note you entered!)

Down three half steps (minor 3rd)	Up one half step (minor 2nd)	Up one whole step (major 2nd)	Up two whole steps (major 3rd)	Down seven half steps (perfect 5th)	Down two whole steps (major 3rd)	Up one whole step (major 2nd)	Up seven half steps (perfect 5th)	Down one whole step (major 2nd)

Exercise 2-5

Name each of the following intervals.

Major   third   _____   _____   _____   _____

Exercise 2-6

Using the first note as the root, enter a second note to create the specified interval.

Perfect   fifth   Major   third   Perfect   fourth   Minor   third   Major   second

Exercise 2-7

Using sharps, flats, and naturals, change the following major intervals to minor.

Exercise 2-8

Using sharps, flats, and naturals, change the following minor intervals to major.

The Least You Need to Know

- The smallest interval between any two notes is called a half step. Two half steps equal one whole step.

- A sharp raises the value of a note by a half step. A flat lowers the value of a note by a half step.

- The intervals between any two notes are described in terms of degree. For example, the interval between the first and third notes is called a third.

- In a major scale, seconds, thirds, sixths, and sevenths are called major intervals. You can create a minor interval by flattening these notes.

- In a major scale, fourths, fifths, and octaves are called perfect intervals. When you flatten a perfect interval, you create a diminished interval; when you sharpen a perfect interval, you create an augmented interval.

Scales

 Lesson 3, Track 24

In the first two chapters we discussed the seven key notes (A through G), and how they relate to each other. We also tossed around the word "scale" to describe all seven of those notes together.

In this chapter we further examine the concept of the musical scale, which (no surprise) is seven notes all in a row, in alphabetical order. (If you count the first note, repeated an octave higher at the top of the scale, it's eight notes.)

What might be surprising is that there are so many different types of scales. You can have a major scale, a minor scale (three different types of minor scales, actually), or any number of different modes within a scale. It sounds confusing, but it's really fairly simple once you understand how scales are constructed, using different intervals between the various notes. (What's a mode, you ask? You'll have to read this entire chapter to find out!)

Scales are important because you use them to create melodies, which you'll learn about in Chapter 8. In fact, you can create a nice-sounding melody just by picking notes from a

In This Chapter

- Putting eight notes together to form a scale
- Creating major and minor scales
- Discovering the different modes within a major scale

[handwritten annotations:]
Major: WWWHWWH
G# Major: Ab Major
G#M: G#A#B#C#D#E#FxG#

single major scale. For example, use the C Major scale (the white notes on a piano) and pick and choose notes that sound good when played together. Make sure you start and end your melody on the C note itself, and you've just written a simple song.

Eight Notes Equal One Scale

A scale is, quite simply, eight successive pitches within a one-octave range. All scales start on one note and end on that same note one octave higher.

For example, every C scale starts on C and ends on C; an F scale starts on F and ends on F; and they all have six more notes in between.

The eight notes of a scale; C Major, in this instance.

The first note of a scale is called the *tonic,* or *first degree,* of the scale. Not surprisingly, the second note is called the *second degree,* the third note is called the *third degree,* and so on—until you get to the eighth note, which is the tonic again.

The major exception to the eight-note scale rule is the scale that includes *all* the notes within an octave, including all the sharps and flats. This type of scale is called a *chromatic scale,* and (when you start with C) looks something like this:

The C chromatic scale. The top staff shows the scale using sharps; the bottom staff shows the scale using flats.

Now, any given scale has specific relationships between the different degrees of the scale. That's how you can describe different types of scales: a major scale has different intervals between specific notes from those you'll find in a similar minor scale. These different intervals give each type of scale its unique sound.

TIP

When you're playing a piece of music, you typically stay within the notes of the designated scale. Any notes you play outside the scale are called *chromatic* notes; notes within the scale are said to be *diatonic*. For example, in the C Major scale, the note C is diatonic; the note C-sharp would be chromatic. Even though chromatic notes might sound "different" than the normal scale notes, they can add color to a piece of music. (That's where the term comes from, by the way; chroma means "color.")

The most common scale is called the *major scale*. Major scales are happy scales; they have pleasant and expected intervals at every turn. (Just sing "Do Re Mi Fa So La Ti Do" and you'll hear this pleasant quality.)

The mirror image of the major scale is the *minor scale*. Minor scales are sad scales; the intervals between the notes sound a little depressing.

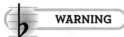

WARNING

Most musicians don't capitalize the word "minor," or any of its abbreviations. Major chord notation is (almost) always capitalized, and minor chord notation is (almost) always lowercase.

Both major and minor scales can start on any note—from A-flat to G-sharp. No matter which note you start with, each scale has its own specific combination of intervals between notes.

The following sections go into more detail about both major and minor scales.

Major Scales

What makes a major scale major are the specific intervals between the notes of the scale. Every major scale uses the same intervals, as shown in the following table.

The Intervals of the Major Scale

Note	Half Steps to Next Note
Tonic	2
Second	2
Third	1
Fourth	2
Fifth	2

continues

The Intervals of the Major Scale   (continued)

Note	Half Steps to Next Note
Sixth	2
Seventh	1

Put another way, the intervals in a major scale go like this: whole, whole, half, whole, whole, whole, half.

If you start your major scale on C (the C Major scale), you end up playing all white keys on the piano. C Major is the only major scale that uses only the white keys; all the other scales have black keys in them.

To make things easier for you, the following table shows all the notes in the 15 major scales.

The 15 Major Scales

Scale	Notes
C Major	
C-sharp Major	
D-flat Major	
D Major	
E-flat Major	
E Major	

Scale	Notes
F Major	
F-sharp Major	
G-flat Major	
G Major	
A-flat Major	
A Major	
B-flat Major	
B Major	
C-flat Major	

Note that several of these scales are enharmonic. (Remember that word from Chapter 1? It means two notes that are identical, but spelled differently.) So C-sharp Major and D-flat Major are just different ways of describing the same notes, as are F-sharp Major and G-flat Major, and B Major and C-flat Major.

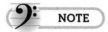

NOTE

The seventh note of any scale is sometimes called the *leading note* because it leads up to the tonic of the scale.

Minor Scales

Minor scales sound a little less "up" than major scales. This is partly because the third note of the minor scale is a minor interval, whereas the third note of the major scale is a major interval. That little half step between a minor third and a major third makes all the difference in the world!

Not to confuse you, but whereas there was a single type of major scale, there actually are three types of minor scales: natural, harmonic, and melodic. We'll look at each scale separately.

Natural Minor

The easiest minor scale to construct is the *natural minor scale.* You can think of the natural minor in terms of its corresponding major scale. When you start and end a major scale on the sixth note, instead of the tonic, you get a natural minor scale.

Here's an example: play a C Major scale (C D E F G A B C). Now move up five notes to the sixth note—or just move down two notes. (It's the same thing—up five or down two—both put you on the A.) Now play an eight-note scale, but using the notes in C Major. What you get—A B C D E F G A—is the A minor (natural) scale.

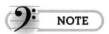

NOTE

If you start your natural minor scale on A (the A minor scale), you will play all white keys on the piano. The A natural minor scale is the only minor scale that uses only the white keys; all the other scales have black keys in them.

As you can see, each natural minor scale shares the same tones as a specific major scale. The following table shows you which minor scales match up with which major scales.

Relative Major and Minor Scales

Major Scale	Related Natural Minor Scale
C Major	A minor
C-sharp Major	A-sharp minor

Major Scale	Related Natural Minor Scale
D-flat Major	B-flat minor
D Major	B minor
E-flat Major	C minor
E Major	D-flat (C-sharp) minor
F Major	D minor
F-sharp Major	D-sharp minor
G-flat Major	E-flat minor
G Major	E minor
A-flat Major	F minor
A Major	F-sharp (G-flat) minor
B-flat Major	G minor
B Major	G-sharp minor
C-flat Major	A-flat minor

Every natural minor scale uses the same intervals, as shown in the following table.

The Intervals of the Natural Minor Scale

Note	Half Steps to Next Note
Tonic	2
Second	1
Third	2
Fourth	2
Fifth	1
Sixth	2
Seventh	2

Put another way, the intervals in a natural minor scale go like this: <u>whole, half, whole, whole, half, whole, whole</u>.

To make things easier for you, the following table shows all the notes in the 15 natural minor scales.

The 15 Natural Minor Scales

Scale	Notes
C minor	
C-sharp minor	
D minor	
D-sharp minor	
E-flat minor	
E minor	
F minor	
F-sharp minor	
G minor	
G-sharp minor	

Scale	Notes
A-flat minor	
A minor	
A-sharp minor	
B-flat minor	
B minor	

Harmonic Minor

The *harmonic minor scale* is similar to the natural minor scale, except the seventh note is raised a half step. Some musicians prefer this type of minor scale because the seventh note better leads up to the tonic of the scale. (It's a half step up to the tonic, as opposed to the whole step in the natural minor scale.)

The following table details the intervals between the notes in the harmonic minor scale.

The Intervals of the Harmonic Minor Scale

Note	Half Steps to Next Note
Tonic	2
Second	1
Third	2
Fourth	2
Fifth	1

continues

The Intervals of the Harmonic Minor Scale   (continued)

Note	Half Steps to Next Note
Sixth	3
Seventh	1

Put another way, the intervals in a harmonic minor scale go like this: whole, half, whole, whole, half, whole and a half, half.

To make things easier for you, the following table shows all the notes in the 15 harmonic minor scales.

The 15 Harmonic Minor Scales

Scale	Notes
C minor	
C-sharp minor	
D minor	
D-sharp minor	
E-flat minor	
E minor	
F minor	

Scale	Notes
F-sharp minor	
G minor	
G-sharp minor	
A-flat minor	
A minor	
A-sharp minor	
B-flat minor	
B minor	

Note: the "x" you see before several of the notes in the previous table is a *double sharp*. It means you raise the base note two half steps.

Melodic Minor

The only problem with the harmonic minor scale is that the interval between the sixth and seventh notes is three half steps—and you seldom have an interval in a scale wider than two half steps. (It's just too awkward to sing.) So the *melodic minor scale* raises both the sixth and seventh notes of the natural minor scale by a half step each, resulting in the following intervals.

The Intervals of the Melodic Minor Scale

Note	Half Steps to Next Note
Tonic	2
Second	1
Third	2
Fourth	2
Fifth	2
Sixth	2
Seventh	1

Put another way, the intervals in the melodic minor scale go like this: whole, half, whole, whole, whole, whole, half.

To make things easier for you, the following table shows all the notes in the 15 melodic minor scales.

The 15 Melodic Minor Scales

Scale	Notes
C minor	
C-sharp minor	
D minor	
D-sharp minor	
E-flat minor	

Scale	Notes
E minor	
F minor	
F-sharp minor	
G minor	
G-sharp minor	
A-flat minor	
A minor	
A-sharp minor	
B-flat minor	
B minor	

As if three minor scales weren't enough to deal with, some music theorists use this melodic minor scale only when you're going "up" the scale. (They call this the *ascending melodic minor scale.*) Going back "down" (the *descending melodic minor scale*), they use the notes in the natural minor scale. So the sixth and the seventh degrees are raised on the way up, but not on the way down. Theorists are split on this issue, however; some use the melodic minor scale both ascending and descending, and others use the two different scales. It's okay to use a single scale, as presented here, as long as you're aware of the alternate way of doing things.

In the Mode

If a scale is a combination of eight successive notes (in alphabetical order, of course), do any eight notes make a scale? Not necessarily. Once you get past the major and minor scales, all the other eight-note combinations aren't technically called scales; they're called *modes*.

There are seven essential modes, each of which you can think of as starting on a different degree of the major scale. You stay within the relative major scale; you just start on different notes. For example, the Dorian mode starts on the second degree of the major scale. In relation to the C Major scale, the Dorian mode starts on D, and continues upward (D, E, F, G, A, B, C, D). The same holds true for the Phrygian mode, which starts on the third degree of the related major scale—in C Major: E, F, G, A, B, C, D, E.

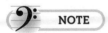

NOTE

It's convenient to think of modes in relation to a specific major scale, but modes are arrangements of intervals in and of themselves. In practice, any mode can start on any note.

Modes are important when you're constructing melodies. When you create a melody based on a specific mode, you get to create a different sound or feel while staying within the notes of a traditional major scale. You just start and stop in different places. (Melodies based around specific modes are called *modal melodies*.)

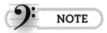

NOTE

Chronologically, modes were around long before scales. The major and minor scales we use today came after the introduction of the various modes, and were, in fact, based on the Ionian and Aeolian modes, respectively. Modes date all the way back to the ancient Greeks, and the findings of Pythagoras and Aristotle. The number and use of modes were expanded in the era of the medieval church, where they were called *church modes* and used in the form of plainsong called *Gregorian chant*.

Ionian

If you're a musician, you play the Ionian mode all the time without really knowing it because the Ionian mode starts on the tonic of the related major scale—and contains the same notes as the major scale. The following table details the half steps between the notes of the Ionian mode.

The Intervals of the Ionian

Note	Half Steps to Next Note
Tonic	2
Second	2
Third	1
Fourth	2
Fifth	2
Sixth	2
Seventh	1

The C Ionian mode consists of the following notes:

The C Ionian mode—just like the C Major scale.

Dorian

The Dorian mode can be thought of as starting on the second note of a major scale. It sounds a little like a natural minor scale, but with a raised sixth. (To get an idea what Dorian mode sounds like, listen to Simon and Garfunkel's "Scarborough Fair"; it's composed entirely in Dorian mode.) The intervals between notes in the Dorian mode are as follows.

The Intervals of Dorian Mode

Note	Half Steps to Next Note
Tonic	2
Second	1
Third	2
Fourth	2
Fifth	2
Sixth	1
Seventh	2

D Dorian is relative to the key of C, and consists of the following notes:

D Dorian mode, relative to the key of C.

Phrygian

The Phrygian mode can be thought of as starting on the third note of the related major scale. Like the Dorian mode, it sounds like a natural minor scale—but with a lowered second degree. The intervals between notes in the Phrygian mode are as follows.

The Intervals of the Phrygian Mode

Note	Half Steps to Next Note
Tonic	1
Second	2
Third	2
Fourth	2
Fifth	1
Sixth	2
Seventh	2

E Phrygian is relative to the key of C, and consists of the following notes:

E Phrygian mode, relative to the key of C.

Lydian

The Lydian mode can be thought of as starting on the fourth note of a major scale. It's an almost-major scale, but with a raised fourth. The intervals between notes in the Lydian mode are as follows.

The Intervals of the Lydian Mode

Note	Half Steps to Next Note
Tonic	2
Second	2
Third	2
Fourth	1
Fifth	2
Sixth	2
Seventh	1

F Lydian mode is relative to the key of C, and consists of the following notes:

F Lydian mode, relative to the key of C.

Mixolydian

The Mixolydian mode can be thought of as starting on the fifth note of the related major scale. Like the Lydian mode, it's sort of major sounding, but in this case with a lowered seventh. The intervals between notes in the Mixolydian mode are as shown in the following table.

The Intervals of the Mixolydian

Note	Half Steps to Next Note
Tonic	2
Second	2
Third	1
Fourth	2
Fifth	2
Sixth	1
Seventh	2

G Mixolydian mode is relative to the key of C and consists of the following notes:

G Mixolydian mode in the key of C.

Aeolian

The Aeolian mode contains the exact same notes as the natural minor scale. It can be thought of as starting on the sixth note of the related major scale. The intervals between notes in the Aeolian mode are as follows.

The Intervals of the Aeolian Mode

Note	Half Steps to Next Note
Tonic	2
Second	1
Third	2
Fourth	2
Fifth	1
Sixth	2
Seventh	2

You use the Aeolian mode a lot when you play blues and jazz tunes. A Aeolian is relative to the key of C, and consists of the following notes:

A Aeolian mode, relative to the key of C.

Locrian

The Locrian mode can be thought of as starting on the seventh note of the related major scale. It's probably the weirdest sounding of all the modes, because all the leading notes are in all the wrong places. Back in olden times, Locrian was a mode that existed in theory only; it wasn't used in actual music. Today, however, the Locrian mode is used in some jazz music, and in some new music compositions. The intervals between notes in the Locrian mode are as follows.

The Intervals of the Locrian Mode

Note	Half Steps to Next Note
Tonic	1
Second	2
Third	2
Fourth	1
Fifth	2
Sixth	2
Seventh	2

B Locrian is relative to the key of C, and consists of the following notes:

B Locrian mode, relative to the key of C.

Exercises

Exercise 3-1

Name the following major scales.

Exercise 3-2

Name the following minor scales.

Exercise 3-3

Enter the notes for the following major scales.

A   Major   Bb   Major   G   Major

D   Major   F   Major   Eb   Major

Exercise 3-4

Enter the notes for the following minor scales.

A   minor   G   minor   C   minor

B   minor   F#   minor   E   minor

Exercise 3-5

Name the natural minor scales related to the following major scales, and enter the notes for those scales.

F   D   Bb

Exercise 3-6

Enter the notes for the following modes, within the C Major scale.

Lydian   Aeolian   Dorian

The Least You Need to Know

- A scale consists of eight notes whose letter names are in successive alphabetical order.
- Scales can be either major or minor. (And there are three different types of minor scales!)
- All major scales have the same intervals between different notes, no matter what note they start on.
- A mode, like a scale, consists of eight notes in a row—but aren't limited to just major and minor. Modes are derived from the ancient Greeks and (later) the medieval church, and can be thought of as starting on different degrees of the related major scale.

Major and Minor Keys

In This Chapter

- Understanding major and minor keys
- Determining key by using key signatures
- Using the circle of fifths
- Applying accidentals and changing keys

If you're writing music within the C Major scale, you have it easy. All the notes fall in the lines and spaces of the treble and bass clefs; no sharps or flats are necessary. (And, if you're playing the piano, you don't have to use those tricky black keys!)

However, if you're writing music using another scale, you have to use accidentals to raise and lower notes beyond the white keys on the piano keyboard. For example, if you're using the F Major scale, you have a pesky B-flat to deal with.

Now, you could put a flat sign in front of every B-flat in your music. However, you'll end up writing a lot of flats—which is a major pain in the butt.

Fortunately, there's an easy way to designate consistent flats and sharps throughout an entire piece of music, without noting each and every instance. This approach requires the knowledge of musical *keys*—which just happen to correspond to the musical scales we discussed in the previous chapter.

Keys to Success

When a piece of music is based on a particular musical scale, we say that music is in the "key" of that scale. For example, a song based around the C Major scale is in the key of C Major. A song based around the B-flat Major scale is in the key of B-flat Major.

When you assign a key to a piece of music (or to a section within a larger piece), it's assumed that most of the notes in that music will stay within the corresponding scale. So if a piece is written in A Major, most of the notes in the melody and chords should be within the A Major scale. (There are exceptions to this, of course; they're called *accidentals;* they're discussed later in this chapter.)

Using Key Signatures

One of the convenient things about assigning a particular key to a piece of music is that it enables you to designate the appropriate sharps and flats up front, without having to repeat them every time they occur in the music.

Here's how it works. You designate a key by inserting a *key signature* at the very start of the music, next to the first clef on the first staff. This key signature indicates the sharps and flats used in that particular key. Then, when you play through the entire piece, you automatically sharpen and flatten the appropriate notes.

For example, let's say you write a song around the F Major scale. The F Major scale, if you recall, has one flatted note: B-flat. So next to the first clef on the first staff, you put a flat sign on the B line. Now, when you play that song, every time you see a B, you actually play B-flat.

The key signature for the key of F. (Note the flat sign on the B line, indicating the automatic B-flat.)

The same would apply if you were playing in the key of G, which has one sharp: F-sharp. You put a sharp sign on the top F line on the first staff; then every time you see an F, you play an F-sharp.

Determining the Key Signature

How can you quickly determine which key signature you're looking at? It depends on whether the key signature contains sharps or flats.

If the key signature includes flats, the key (no pun intended) is to look at the next-to-last flat—the one next to the farthest one on the right. This note determines the key signature.

For example, if a key signature has two flats, you look at the next-to-last flat and determine that the key is B-flat, which it is. If the key signature has three flats, you look at the next-to-last flat, and determine that the key is E-flat. It's pretty easy.

But what do you do if there's only one flat? There's no next-to-last flat! For the key signature with a single flat, the key is F. You'll have to memorize that one, as you will the key with no flats or sharps—which is the key of C.

If the key signature includes sharps, the method is different. With sharps, know that the last sharp in the key signature represents the seventh degree of that particular scale, so the tonic of the scale is the next note up. In other words, look at the last sharp, and the next note up is the key.

Take, for example, the key signature with one sharp. That sharp is on the note F-sharp, so the next note up tells you that the key is G. If the key signature has two sharps, the last one is on the note C-sharp, and the next note up is D—which is your key. And so on for all the other sharp key signatures.

Major Keys

Just as there are 15 major scales (including three enharmonics), there are 15 major keys; each with its own key signature. The following table shows what each key of these key signatures looks like, along with its corresponding scale.

The 15 Major Keys

Key	Key Signature and Scale
C Major	
C-sharp Major	
D-flat Major	
D Major	

continues

The 15 Major Keys   (continued)

Key	Key Signature and Scale
E-flat Major	
E Major	
F Major	
F-sharp Major	
G-flat Major	
G Major	
A-flat Major	
A Major	
B-flat Major	
B Major	
C-flat Major	

Minor Keys

The key signatures used to indicate major keys also can represent natural minor keys. As you remember from Chapter 3, a natural minor scale is based on the same notes as a major scale, but starts on the sixth note of the scale. This same method applies to keys, so that (for example) the key of A minor uses the same notes—and the same key signature—as C major.

The following table shows the 15 minor keys, with their corresponding key signatures and scales.

The 15 Minor Keys

Scale	Notes	Same as This Major Key
A minor		C Major
A-sharp minor		C-sharp Major
B-flat minor		D-flat Major
B minor		D Major
C minor		E-flat Major
C-sharp minor		E Major
D minor		F Major
D-sharp minor		F-sharp Major

continues

The 15 Minor Keys   (continued)

Scale	Notes	Same as This Major Key
E-flat minor		G-flat Major
E minor		G Major
F minor		A-flat Major
F-sharp minor		A Major
G minor		B-flat Major
G-sharp minor		B Major
A-flat minor		C-flat Major

The Circle of Fifths

There's a quick way to remember how many sharps or flats to include with each key signature; it's called the *circle of fifths,* and it works like this.

Starting with the key of C, for every perfect fifth you move up, you add a sharp. So the key of G (a perfect fifth up from C) has one sharp. The key of D (a perfect fifth up from G) has two sharps, and so on.

The circle of fifths works in the other direction for flats. For every perfect fifth you move down from C, you add a flat. So the key of F (a perfect fifth down from C) has one flat. The key of B-flat (a perfect fifth down from F) has two flats, and so on.

The following drawing shows how all the major keys relate in the circle of fifths. When you move clockwise around the circle, you're moving up through the fifths (and the sharp keys); when you move counterclockwise, you're moving down through the fifths (and the flat keys).

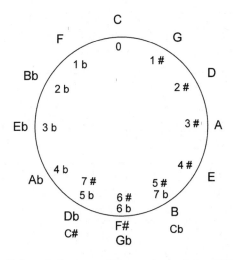

All the major keys are a fifth apart in the circle of fifths.

The next figure shows the circle of fifths for the 15 minor keys. It works just the same as the major-key circle; move clockwise for the sharp keys, and counterclockwise for the flat keys.

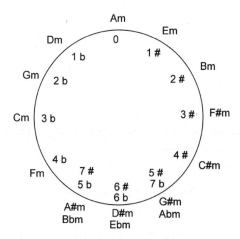

The circle of fifths works for minor keys, too.

Accidents Will Happen

When you assign a key signature to a piece of music, it's assumed that all the following notes will correspond to that particular key. How, then, do you indicate notes that fall outside that key?

First, note that you can play outside a key. For example, it's okay to play the occasional B natural when you're in the key of F, which normally has a B-flat. No one will arrest you for it—in fact, certain types of music regularly employ nonscale notes.

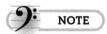

NOTE

Jazz and blues music often add flatted thirds and sevenths within the designated major key, which gives these styles their unique sound.

When you decide to write a note that isn't within the current key, you have to manually indicate the change in the music—by using sharp, flat, or natural signs. When musicians see the inserted sharp, flat, or natural, they know to play the note as written, rather than as indicated by the music's key signature.

These "outside the key" notes are called *accidentals* or *chromatic notes;* they're quite common.

For example, let's say a piece of music is in the key of F, which has only one flat (B-flat). You want your melody to include an E-flat, which isn't in the key. So when you get to that note, you insert a flat sign before the E to indicate an E-flat. It's as simple as that.

Use accidentals to indicate notes outside the current key signature.

WARNING

An accidental applies only from that point in the measure to the end of the measure. It doesn't affect those notes in the measure before the accidental appears.

The same approach applies if you want to include a B natural in the same piece, instead of the expected B-flat. Simply insert a natural sign before the B.

When you change a note with an accidental, that accidental applies until the end of the current measure. At the start of the next measure, it's assumed that all notes revert to what they should be in the current key. So if you flat an E in measure one of an F Major melody, the first E you write in measure two will be assumed to be natural, not flatted.

The one exception occurs when you tie a note from the end of one measure to the beginning of the next. The accidental carries over—thanks to the tie—to that first note in the second measure, as you can see in the following example. (Ties are explained in Chapter 5.) Note that the accidental doesn't apply to any subsequent notes in the second measure; it applies only to the tied note.

Accidentals apply to all notes tied over a measure.

If you think other musicians might be confused about whether a note has reverted back to normal, it's okay to use a *courtesy* sharp, flat, or natural sign. (This is a sign placed within parentheses.) This reminds the reader that the note has reverted back to its normal state in that key. You don't have to use courtesy signs, but when the music is complicated, it can be helpful.

A courtesy accidental reminds musicians that a changed note has reverted back to normal.

Changing Keys

Some long pieces of music don't always use the same key throughout the entire piece. In fact, some short pop songs change keys midway through. It's allowed.

When you change keys in the middle of a song, it's called *modulating* to another key. You can modulate to any key, although the most common modulations are up a half step (from E Major to F Major, for example), or up a fourth or fifth (from E Major to either A Major or B Major, for example).

 TIP

The half-step modulation is most common in twentieth-century popular music, and can add a "lift" to the end of a pop song. The fourth or fifth modulation is more common in classical music of the seventeenth through the nineteenth centuries.

When you want to change keys, you indicate this by inserting a new key signature in the first measure of the new key. It's as simple as that, as you can see in the following figure. (Note that some composers and arrangers also insert a double bar whenever there's a key change.)

To change keys, insert a new key signature.

  TIP

If you want, you can alert musicians to a key change by placing the appropriate sharps and flats at the very end of the last staff of the old key—as well as with a new key signature in the following measure. This approach is entirely optional; it's perfectly acceptable to signal the key change with a single key signature in the first measure of the new key.

The only complicated key change is when you're changing to the key of C—which has no sharps or flats. You indicate this by using natural signs to cancel out the previous sharps or flats, like this:

How to change to the key of C.

Exercises

Exercise 4-1

Label the following major key signatures.

Exercise 4-2

Label the following minor key signatures.

Exercise 4-3

Create the indicated major key signatures.

F Major   D Major   Eb Major   G Major   Bb Major

Exercise 4-4

Create the indicated minor key signatures.

C minor   D minor   E minor   C# minor   F minor

Exercise 4-5

Using the initial key signature as a guide, label each note in the following example.

Exercise 4-6

Determine what key signature you could use to write this melody without accidentals, and enter that key signature at the beginning of the staff.

Exercise 4-7

Determine what key signature you could use to write this melody without accidentals, and enter that key signature at the beginning of the staff.

Exercise 4-8

Following the circle of fifths, add the appropriate number of flats to each successive major key signature, and then label each key signature.

C   F   __   __   __   __

The Least You Need to Know

- You use key signatures to indicate what scale your music is based on.
- The sharps and flats in a key signature are automatically applied throughout the entire song.
- To indicate notes outside the current key, use accidentals—sharps, flats, and natural signs.
- To change the key in the middle of a piece of music, insert a new key signature.

Rhythms

You don't have to be a drummer to feel the beat. This part shows you how to notate any type of rhythm, from simple whole notes to sixteenth note syncopations. You also learn all about time signatures, tempo, and dynamics as well as how to navigate your way through a piece of music.

Note Values and Basic Notation

Lesson 4, Track 27

Part 1 of this book covered how to work with pitch—but that's only half of the music theory that you need to know. In this chapter, we'll deal with the other half of the equation, which is how you work with time—which, in music, is called rhythm.

Rhythm is what drives the music forward and gives it its beat. To learn rhythm, you have to learn about note values. This type of music notation isn't that hard, really. All you need is learn is a little basic math and how to count to four.

Before we start, however, let's lay down some ground rules for this chapter. Although a lot of songs are written with four beats to a measure—one, two, three, four—that isn't a universal. Some very popular songs only have three beats to a measure. (Think "My Favorite Things," from *The Sound of Music*.) And other tunes, especially in the jazz and classical genres, have *more* than four beats per measure.

In This Chapter

- Grouping beats into measures
- Understanding whole, half, quarter, eighth, and sixteenth notes and rests
- Using dotted notes and ties
- Dividing beats into triplets

To make it easier to learn the basics, in this chapter we're only going to address four-beat measures—what we call *4/4 time*. All the other types of beats—three, five, seven, whatever—will be covered in Chapter 6.

And *that's* why I said you only have to know how to count to four!

Taking the Measure of Things

Rhythm is about counting. Listen to your favorite pop song, and feel the beat. (Go ahead, tap your foot—it's okay!) You'll likely feel the beats fall into groups of four—one, two, three, four; one, two, three, four …. It's easy to hear because it's very natural.

Let's use a specific example: "Mary Had a Little Lamb." The notes of the song fall into groups of four; just replace the words "Ma-ry had a" with "one two three four" and you see how it works.

In this and other songs based around groups of four, each group of four beats is called a *measure*, a container that holds a specific number of beats. In standard 4/4 time, a measure holds the equivalent of four quarter notes. The beginning and end of a measure are signified by bar lines, like this:

A group of measures on a staff; each measure is separated by left and right bar lines.

The first beat in a measure is counted as one. The second beat is counted as two. The third beat is counted as three, and the last beat is counted as four. There is no five; if you count out five, you've counted too far! Whenever you hit four, the next beat is always one.

Every time four beats go by—one, two, three, four—another measure is completed. If you put enough measures together—one, two, three, four; one, two, three, four—you have a song.

Taking Note—of Notes

Every time you sing or play a tone, you're also singing or playing a note value. There are different types of note values, with each note value signifying a specific length of time—as measured by parts of a measure.

To better explain, we have to get into a little math. (Don't worry—there won't be any story problems!) You see, each note value lasts a specific duration, and each duration reflects a ratio to duration. As you can see from the following figure, each shorter note is precisely half the duration of the previous note. So if you can divide and multiply by two, this should be easy.

The most common rhythmic notes; each smaller note is exactly half the previous note.

Whole Notes

The most basic note is called the *whole note*. It's called a whole note because, in 4/4 time (we'll get to this soon—I promise!), it lasts a whole measure. Because 4/4 time has four beats in a measure, a whole note lasts four beats. A whole note looks like a big empty oval, nice and whole.

Whole notes, at different places on the staff.

When you put a whole note in a measure of 4/4 time, that's the only note that goes in that measure; no other notes will fit. When you play a whole note, you sing or play your instrument once at the very beginning of the measure (on beat one), and then you hold that tone through the entire measure. In other words, one whole note should last a whole measure.

Half Notes

The whole note is the largest note; let's go down one size and look at the next smallest note. Remember that I said each shorter note is exactly half the previous note? Let's apply a little math and divide a whole note by two to see what we get.

The next smallest note is called a *half note*. (It's half of a whole note—pretty simple, eh?) Because a whole note lasts a whole measure (in 4/4, anyway), a half note lasts a half measure, or two beats—half the duration of a whole note. Put another way, you can put two half notes in a measure, because two half notes equal one whole note.

A half note looks like a whole note with a line next to it. The line is called a *stem;* it can point up or down, depending on the pitch of the note. If the stem points down, it sits to the left of the *notehead*. If the stem points up, it sits to the right of the notehead.

Two half notes—one with the stem pointing up; the other with the stem pointing down.

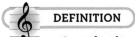

A **notehead** is the big, oval part of a note. The stem is always attached to the notehead.

When you play a half note, make sure the tone lasts a full two beats. If you let up after the first beat, you're playing only half a half note—which is what we'll discuss next.

If the notehead (the part of the note that isn't the stem) is on or above the third (middle) line of the staff, then the stem should point down from the notehead. If the notehead is below the third line of the staff, then the stem should point up from the notehead. The only exception to this guideline is when you have a run of connected notes—notes where all the stems are connected, like a run of eighth or sixteenth notes. It's okay to run two or more of these connected notes together with their stems in the same direction, even if they move past that third line of the staff, to make the music easier to read.

Quarter Notes

Let's keep going. If a half note is half a whole note, what is half a half note? Well, do your math, and when you divide ½ by 2, you get ¼. This means half a half note is a *quarter note.*

If a half note lasts two beats, then a quarter note—which is half that duration—lasts one beat. Put another way, you can fit four quarter notes in a measure; one to a beat. When you tap your foot to the beat of most popular songs, your foot is tapping quarter notes. One, two, three, four—each of those counts is a quarter note.

A quarter note looks like a half note with the notehead filled in, as shown here:

Two different quarter notes, pointing in both directions.

Eighth Notes

Just like those miniature superheroes Ant Man and the Atom (depending on whether you're Marvel or DC), notes just keep getting smaller. Again, we're operating on a 2-to-1 ratio, so let's take a quarter note and divide it in half. Doing the math, $\frac{1}{4} \div 2 = \frac{1}{8}$—so the next-smallest note is the *eighth note.*

Just as there are four quarter notes in a measure of 4/4 time ($4 \times \frac{1}{4} = 1$), each measure holds eight eighth notes ($8 \times \frac{1}{8} = 1$). Put another way, there are two eighth notes for every quarter note ($2 \times \frac{1}{8} = \frac{1}{4}$)—or two eighth notes for every beat.

An eighth note looks like a quarter note with a *flag* on it. If you have two or more eighth notes in a row, the flags can be replaced with horizontal beams at the end of the normal vertical stems. (The flags don't have to be joined together; sometimes it's just easier to read that way.)

A variety of eighth notes.

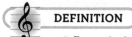

DEFINITION

A **flag** is the little doohickey dangling off the stem of eighth notes, sixteenth notes, and all smaller notes. (It actually looks like a flag flying on a mast.) The flag is always at the end of the stem, so if the stem is pointing up, the flag is above the notehead; if the stem is pointing down, the flag is below the notehead.

Sixteenth Notes

Okay, you know where this is going. Half an eighth note is (do the math!) a *sixteenth note* ($\frac{1}{8} \div 2 = \frac{1}{16}$). There are 16 sixteenth notes in a measure ($16 \times \frac{1}{16} = 1$), or 4 sixteenth notes per one quarter-note beat ($4 \times \frac{1}{16} = \frac{1}{4}$).

A sixteenth note looks like a quarter note with two flags on it. As with the eighth note, if 2 or more sixteenth notes are next to each other, the flags may (or may not) be joined together.

A variety of sixteenth notes.

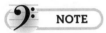

NOTE

Although we'll end this discussion with sixteenth notes, there are lots of notes even smaller than that. Each successive note is half the value of the previous note and is indicated by an additional flag on the stem. For example, the thirty-second note is the next-smallest note after the sixteenth note; it has three flags on its stem. After that is the sixty-fourth note, with four flags. In actuality, you won't run into too many notes smaller than the sixteenth note.

Taking Count

It's fairly easy to write down a series of notes—but how do you communicate notes and values to other musicians verbally? Do you go all mathematical and say things such as "the fourteenth sixteenth note" or "the eighth note after the two sixteenth notes on beat four"—or is there an easier way to describe your rhythms?

Just as you describe absolute pitches by using letters (A through G), you describe absolute rhythms by using numbers—and you need only to be able to count to four.

It starts fairly simple, in that each beat in a measure is counted as either one, two, three, or four. So if you're counting off four quarter notes, you count them as one, two, three, four. If you want to talk about the fourth quarter note in a measure, you call it "four," as in, "In the last measure, make sure you play a B-flat on four."

If the beat is always one, two, three, or four, what about the eighth notes that lay between the beats? It's simple: count them as "and" as in "one-and, two-and, three-and, four-and," all very even. You'd talk about an eighth note like this: "Make sure you play a C-sharp on the and after three."

This is pretty easy—but what about sixteenth notes? This gets a little tricky, but it'll seem natural once you get into it. Use the nonsense syllables "e" and "ah" to represent the sixteenth notes between eighth notes. So if you're counting a group of straight sixteenth notes, you'd count "one-e-and-a, two-e-and-a, three-e-and-a, four-e-and-a," all nice and even. Still not sure about this?

Examine the following figure, which shows how to count various groupings of notes.

One Two Three Four   One and Two and Three and Four and   One e and a Two e and a Three e and a Four e and a

How to count various types of notes.

Taking a Rest

If a note represents the duration of a pitch, what do you call it when you're not playing or singing? In music, when you're not playing, you're resting—so any note you don't play is called a *rest*.

When you see four quarter notes, you play or sing four tones—one per beat. When you see four quarter note rests, you don't play four tones; you rest over four beats.

Each type of note—whole note, half note, and so on—has a corresponding rest of the same duration. So you have a whole rest that lasts a whole measure, a half rest that lasts a half measure, and so on. Rests are used to indicate the spaces in between the notes and are just as important as the notes you play.

The following table shows all the notes you've just learned and their corresponding rests.

Notes and Rests

Duration	Note	Rest
Whole	o	—
Half	♩	—
Quarter	♩	𝄽
Eighth	♪	𝄾
Sixteenth	♬	𝄿

Taking a Note—and Dotting It

Sooner or later you'll run into something a little different: a note or a rest with a dot after it. When you run into one of these *dotted notes*, that note should have a longer duration than the normal version of that note—one and a half times longer, to be precise.

Here's where your math skills come back into play. Let's take a dotted quarter note as an example. A regular quarter note is worth a single beat. If you multiply $1 \times 1\frac{1}{2}$, you get $1\frac{1}{2}$ beats—so a dotted quarter note is worth $1\frac{1}{2}$ beats. You also could go about it by saying a quarter note equals four sixteenth notes, and $4 \times 1\frac{1}{2} = 6$, and 6 sixteenth notes equal $1\frac{1}{2}$ quarter notes. However you do the math, it comes out the same.

TIP

Another way to think about a dotted note is that it has a duration equal to three of the next-smaller note value. For example, a dotted half note equals 3 quarter notes, a dotted quarter note equals 3 eighth notes, and a dotted eighth note equals 3 sixteenth notes.

So when you see a dotted note, hold that note 50 percent longer than you would do normally, as shown in the following table.

Dotted Note Values

This Dotted Note ...	Equals This
𝅗𝅥.	𝅗𝅥 + ♩
♩.	♩ + ♪
♪.	♪ + ♬

You can also have dotted rests, which work the same as dotted notes. When you see a dot after a rest, that rest should last one and a half times the value of the main rest.

Taking Two Notes—and Tying Them Together

Another way to make a note longer is to tie it to another note. A *tie* is a little rounded connector placed between two notes; it essentially tells you to add the second note to the first note.

A tie makes one note out of two.

When you see two or more notes tied together, you play them as if they're a single note; for example, two quarter notes tied together equal one half note.

What do you do if the tied notes are on different pitches? Well, this may look like a tie, but it isn't really a tie—it's a *slur*. A slur is a way of indicating that two (or more) notes are to be played in a smoothly connected fashion, rather than as distinctly separate notes.

This isn't really a tie; it's a slur.

Taking the Beat and Dividing by Three

There's another little oddity in rhythmic notation—and this one is very important. Everything we've done up to now has divided notes and beats by two. What happens, then, if you divide by something other than two?

The most common division other than two is dividing by three; this is called a *triplet.* When you see the number three over a group of three notes (or three rests—or any combination of three equal notes and rests), you know that those three notes have to fit into a space that would normally hold just two notes.

The three notes of a triplet fit in the space of two regular notes.

Triplets have more of a rolling feel than straight notes and are counted as "trip-ah-let." You can have triplets of any note value, although quarter-note triplets (where three of them are spaced over two beats), eighth-note triplets (three on a single quarter-note beat), and sixteenth-note triplets (three in the space of a single eighth note) are the most common.

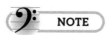 **NOTE**

Triplets are the most common uneven rhythmic division, but not the only one. You can divide a beat any way you like, which can lead to groups of five or seven or any prime number. (If you divide a beat by a nonprime number, you're actually dividing by two or more groups of a prime number. For example, if you divide a beat into six, you're really dividing into two groups of three—or two triplets.)

Exercises

Exercise 5-1

Name the following notes and rests.

Exercise 5-2

Write the count ("one-e-and-ah") below each of the notes in the following measures.

Exercise 5-3

Fill in the balance of these measures with eighth notes.

Exercise 5-4

Write the corresponding rests for the following notes.

Exercise 5-5

Fill in the balance of these measures with eighth-note triplets.

Exercise 5-6

Tie each group of two notes (but not the rests!) together.

Exercise 5-7

Enter four whole notes, followed by four half notes, followed by four quarter notes, followed by four eighth notes, followed by four sixteenth notes.

Exercise 5-8

Draw stems and flags on these notes to make them eighth notes; make sure to point the stems in the correct direction.

The Least You Need to Know

- Note values are named according to their duration. Whole notes last a whole measure (in 4/4 time), half notes last a half measure, and so on.
- Each smaller note lasts half as long as the previous note. A quarter note, for example, is half as long as a half note.
- Each note value has a corresponding rest of the same duration—which indicates not to play or sing.
- A dot after a note or rest extends the value of that note by 50 percent.
- When you fit three notes into a space that normally holds only two, those notes are called triplets.

Time Signatures

In the previous chapter, you learned about measures, those containers that hold the beats of a piece of music. The start and end points of a measure are marked by vertical bar lines, and multiple measures combine to create a complete song.

To simplify things, in Chapter 5 we limited our discussion to measures with four beats apiece, with each of those beats equaling a quarter note. That covers a lot of different songs, especially in popular music. Whatever type of music you listen to—rock-and-roll, soul, jazz, country, hip hop, or even reggae—most of the songs you hear are likely to adhere to this four-beat form.

However, not all music has four beats per measure, and not every beat is equal to a quarter note. To understand all the different numbers and types of beats per measure, you need only apply a little math—in the form of fractions.

In This Chapter

* Understanding how time signatures determine meter
* Learning both usual and odd time signatures
* Changing time signatures
* Subdividing odd time signatures

4 →How many per measure

4 ↙ Base note (quarter)

Measuring the Beats

Written music uses something called a *time signature* to signify how many beats are in a measure and what kind of note is used for the basic beat. A time signature looks kind of like a fraction, with one number sitting on top of another number. The top number indicates how many beats are in a measure; the bottom number indicates the note value of the basic beat.

Time signatures show how beats are organized in a particular piece of music. This organization is called *meter*, and time signatures are sometimes called *meter signatures*.

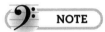

NOTE

Classical musicians tend to refer to the organization of beats as "meter," while jazz and pop musicians tend to refer to it as "time," as in "4/4 meter" or "4/4 time."

Let's take the four-quarter-notes-to-a-measure form we used in the previous chapter. Because we have four beats in a measure, the top number in the time signature is a four. Because the basic beat is a quarter note, the bottom number is a four (as in the 4 in ¼). So the standard form we've been using is called "four four" time (because of the 4 on top of the 4), and looks like this:

The time signature for 4/4 meter.

Other time signatures follow this same form. For example, if our measures have three beats instead of four, and still use a quarter note for the beat, we have a 3/4 time signature. If you have three beats per measure but the basic beat is an eighth note instead of a quarter note, that time signature is "three eight," or 3/8.

Read on to learn more about the different types of time signatures you're likely to encounter in the world of music.

Quarter-Note Time

The most common types of time signatures use a quarter note for the base beat. However, you're not limited to just four beats (quarter notes) per measure; quarter-note time signatures can have as few as one beat per measure, or as many as … well, as many as you like!

Although 4/4 is the most common quarter-note time signature, you'll almost definitely run into its close cousin, 3/4. In 3/4 time, you have three quarter notes per measure; the measures are counted "one, two, three; one, two, three." If you've ever heard a waltz, you've heard 3/4 time.

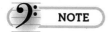

NOTE

In most rock and pop music, the second and fourth beats of a measure are accented, typically by the drummer, like this: one, TWO, three, FOUR; one, TWO, three, FOUR. (When you clap your hands to a song, you're probably clapping on two and four.) This heavy "backbeat" is what gives rock and roll its rolling rhythm; it is so common that it's noticeable when it is absent.

Another common quarter-note time signature is 2/4 time. This time signature is common in marches and other fast music, and is very easy to play. After all, two measures of 2/4 add up to one measure of 4/4!

Less common are quarter-note time signatures with more than four beats per measure. For example, 5/4 time feels a little awkward, especially if you're used to feeling the "backbeat" in a 4/4 pop song. But jazz musicians play a lot of 5/4—just listen to the Dave Brubeck Quartet's famous recording of "Take Five" if you want to hear a good example of playing in five.

The following table shows some of the more common quarter-note time signatures.

Quarter-Note Time Signatures

Time Signature	Beats per Measure
$\frac{4}{4}$	♩ 1
$\frac{2}{4}$	♩ ♩ 1 2
$\frac{3}{4}$	♩ ♩ ♩ 1 2 3
$\frac{4}{4}$	♩ ♩ ♩ ♩ 1 2 3 4
$\frac{5}{4}$	♩ ♩ ♩ ♩ ♩ 1 2 3 4 5
$\frac{6}{4}$	♩ ♩ ♩ ♩ ♩ ♩ 1 2 3 4 5 6
$\frac{7}{4}$	♩ ♩ ♩ ♩ ♩ ♩ ♩ 1 2 3 4 5 6 7
$\frac{8}{4}$	♩ ♩ ♩ ♩ ♩ ♩ ♩ ♩ 1 2 3 4 5 6 7 8
$\frac{9}{4}$	♩ ♩ ♩ ♩ ♩ ♩ ♩ ♩ ♩ 1 2 3 4 5 6 7 8 9

By the way, 4/4 time is sometimes called *common time*, and indicated by a large "C" for the time signature, like this:

4/4 time is common time—indicated by a big "C."

Eighth-Note Time

Not all music uses a quarter note for the beat. A lot of music—especially classical music—is based on an eighth-note beat.

When you have an eighth-note time signature, such as 3/8 or 6/8, every time you tap your foot you're tapping an eighth note, not a quarter note. So for a measure of 3/8, you'd tap three eighth notes; for a measure of 6/8, you'd tap six eighth notes.

When the eighth note is the beat, half a beat (the "and" after the beat, if you're counting) will be a sixteenth note. Also, if you see a quarter note in an eighth-note time signature, that note takes up two beats.

It's all about math, basically. When you play in an eighth-note time signature, all your normal note values take up half as much space as they do in a quarter-note time signature. It's simple division.

The most common eighth-note time signatures are those divisible by three: 3/8, 6/8, 9/8, and so on. When you're playing one of these time signatures and you're playing really fast, you might end up tapping your foot just once every three beats, like this: ONE, two, three, FOUR, five, six; ONE, two, three, FOUR, five, six. (In fact, many conductors will conduct 6/8 time with just two downbeats per measure—the one and the four.) These time signatures sound a lot like 3/4, the waltz time signature. The following table details the most common eighth-note time signatures.

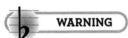

WARNING

Don't assume that an eighth-note time signature is automatically twice as fast as a quarter-note time signature. Although this might be true (and almost always is true when time signatures change in the middle of a song), the speed of the beat (what musicians call tempo) is independent of the time signature. Thus, a song in 3/8 time actually could be played slower than a song in 3/4. (Learn more about tempo in Chapter 7.)

Eighth-Note Time Signatures

Time Signature	Beats per Measure
$\frac{1}{8}$	♪ 1
$\frac{2}{8}$	♪ ♪ 1 2
$\frac{3}{8}$	♪ ♪ ♪ 1 2 3
$\frac{4}{8}$	♪ ♪ ♪ ♪ 1 2 3 4
$\frac{5}{8}$	♪ ♪ ♪ ♪ ♪ 1 2 3 4 5
$\frac{6}{8}$	♪ ♪ ♪ ♪ ♪ ♪ 1 2 3 4 5 6
$\frac{7}{8}$	♪ ♪ ♪ ♪ ♪ ♪ ♪ 1 2 3 4 5 6 7
$\frac{8}{8}$	♪ ♪ ♪ ♪ ♪ ♪ ♪ ♪ 1 2 3 4 5 6 7 8
$\frac{9}{8}$	♪ ♪ ♪ ♪ ♪ ♪ ♪ ♪ ♪ 1 2 3 4 5 6 7 8 9

Half Time

If you move the other direction from the basic quarter-note time signature, you get into time signatures based on a half-note beat. In a half-note time signature, each half note gets one beat; quarter notes get half a beat, and eighth notes get a quarter of a beat. Whole notes, on the other hand, get just two beats. (It's not really that confusing; it's just more math to deal with.)

Half-note beats—2/2, 3/2, and the like—are typically used in classical music for slower, more sweeping passages.

The following table presents the most common half-note beats.

Half-Note Time Signatures

Time Signature	Beats per Measure
$\frac{2}{2}$	♩ ♩ 1 2
$\frac{3}{2}$	♩ ♩ ♩ 1 2 3
$\frac{4}{2}$	♩ ♩ ♩ ♩ 1 2 3 4

Just as 4/4 is sometimes called common time, 2/2 is sometimes called *cut time*. You can indicate 2/2 by either the normal time signature, or by a large C with a line through it, like this:

2/2 time is cut-time—thus you cut a "C" in half.

Changing the Time

You always indicate the time signature at the very beginning of a piece of music. However, you don't have to keep the same time signature through the entire song; you can change time anywhere you want in a piece of music, even for just a measure or two!

If the meter changes in the middle of a song, you insert a new time signature at the point of change. This new time signature remains in effect through the rest of the song, or until another new time signature is introduced.

    TIP

In most music notation, the time signature is shown only on the first line of music (or when there's a time change)—unlike the key signature, which is typically shown at the start of each line.

Here's what a time change looks like in the middle of a piece of music:

Changing time signatures in the middle of a song.

Grouping the Beats

If you see a piece of music in 9/8 and despair about counting that high (nine's a lot higher than four), there's a way around the problem. You can do as many musicians do: chop up each measure into smaller groupings.

When you're playing in odd time signatures—especially those with more than four beats per measure—it's common to subdivide the beats within a measure into an easier-to-grasp pattern. Using smaller groupings not only makes each measure easier to count; it also makes the music flow better. When you subdivide measures in this fashion, you create sub-rhythms behind the basic beat, which makes the music easier to listen to.

For example, if you're playing in 6/8 time, you could count all the beats evenly (one, two, three, four, five, six)—or you could subdivide the beat. The most common subdivision of 6/8 divides the measure into two equal parts, each containing three beats, like this:

Subdividing a 6/8 measure into two groups of three.

So you count the measure "one, two, three; one, two, three" or "one, two, three; two, two, three." Easier, isn't it?

Of course, you could also divide 6/8 into three groups of two, or one group of four and one group of two, or one group of one and one group of five, but the two groups of three is the most common way to play this particular time signature.

For another example, let's look at 5/4 time. In 5/4, measures are typically sub-divided into one group of three and one group of two, like this:

Subdividing 5/4 time into one group of three and one group of two.

You count each measure "one, two, three; one, two."

Of course, you could also reverse the groupings, and end up with two beats in the first group and three beats in the second—"one, two; one, two, three." It depends on the feel and the flow of the music.

The more beats you have in a measure, the more possible groupings you can come up with. To demonstrate, the following example shows three possible groupings of 7/4 time: 4+3, 3+4, and 2+3+2.

Three different ways to group 7/4 time.

Just for fun, count all the way up to 11, and see how many groupings you can come up with for a measure of 11/4!

Exercises

Exercise 6-1

Write the following time signatures on the staff.

3/4   7/8   2/2   5/4   9/8

Exercise 6-2

Enter the appropriate number of quarter notes per measure for each time signature.

Exercise 6-3

Enter the appropriate number of eighth notes for each time signature.

Exercise 6-4

Enter the equivalent eighth-note time signature for each quarter-note time signature.

$\frac{4}{4}$ = $\frac{2}{4}$ = $\frac{8}{4}$ = $\frac{3}{4}$ = $\frac{5}{4}$ =

Exercise 6-5

Enter the equivalent quarter-note time signature for each half-note time signature.

$\frac{2}{2}$ = $\frac{1}{2}$ = $\frac{3}{2}$ = $\frac{5}{2}$ = $\frac{4}{2}$ =

Exercise 6-6

Enter bar lines to divide the following piece of music into four measures of 3/4 time.

Exercise 6-7

Enter bar lines to divide the following piece of music into four measures of 7/8 time.

Exercise 6-8

Group the beats in the following measures three different ways each.

The Least You Need to Know

- You have to place a time signature at the beginning of a piece of music—or anywhere you change the basic meter or time.
- The top number in a time signature indicates the number of beats per measure.
- The bottom number in a time signature indicates what note is used for the basic beat.
- Odd time signatures are sometimes broken up into smaller groupings, to make each measure easier to count.

Tempo, Dynamics, and Navigation

You might not have noticed, but the first six chapters of this book taught you how to read and write music. That's right—all those bits about staves, clefs, notes, and rests comprise what we call the standard music notation, which is the common language of all musicians.

Think of it this way: the staff, clef, and key signature determine where a note is in terms of pitch. The time signature and note value determine where a note is in terms of time, or rhythm. By placing a note in this two-dimensional space, you tell a musician everything he or she needs to know to play that note—and all the notes that follow.

The only things you haven't yet learned about music notation are how to signify the speed (tempo) and loudness (dynamics) of a piece of music. We look at both topics in this chapter, along with some simple navigational aids to help you get from one point to another within a song.

In This Chapter

- Determining how fast to play
- Changing tempo
- Determining how loud to play
- Changing dynamics and accenting notes
- Repeating parts of a song

Taking the Pulse

In Chapter 6 you learned how to figure out how many beats there are in a measure. The question remains, however, how fast those beats should be played.

The speed of a piece of music—how fast the beat goes by—is called the *tempo*. A faster tempo means a faster beat; a slower tempo makes for a slower song.

You can indicate tempo in one of two ways: by indicating the precise number of beats per minute or by using traditional Italian terms. We'll discuss both methods next.

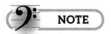

NOTE

As you'll soon see, many notation markings (especially for classical music) are in Italian. This speaks to the importance of Italian culture in the evolution of Western music, but it also means it wouldn't be a bad thing to know a little Italian—and I don't mean a short guy named Mario!

Beats per Minute

The most accurate way to indicate tempo is by specifying a certain number of *beats per minute*, or *bpm*. This gives you a very precise speed for your song, especially when you use a *metronome* or a *click track* on a computer or in a recording studio. You set your metronome or click to a specific bpm number, and it tick-tocks back and forth at the proper speed. When you play along to the metronome or click track, you're playing at exactly the right tempo.

Setting the tempo—120 quarter-note beats per minute.

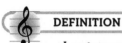

DEFINITION

A **metronome** is a device (invented by a contemporary of Beethoven named Maelzel; in classical music, the abbreviation MM, for Maelzel's Metronome, is used to represent beats per minute) that precisely ticks off beat after beat at a specified tempo. Metronomes can be either pendulum-type affairs or computerized devices that emit an electronic beat. When you're playing professionally (especially in recording studios), you might run into a **click track,** a type of electronic metronome. The click track is typically played on a synthesized instrument, like an electronic woodblock or cowbell. (To hear what a click track sounds like, listen to the rhythm and melody exercises provided online; I use a click to "count off" each of the exercises.)

Italian Tempo Terms

The second way to indicate tempo, typically found in orchestral music, is through the use of traditional Italian musical terms. These terms correspond to general tempo ranges, as indicated in the following table, which is arranged from the very slowest to the very fastest tempo.

Italian Tempo Terms

Tempo	Means ...
Slow Tempos (40–75 bpm)	
grave	Very slow; solemn
largo	Slow and dignified
larghetto	A little faster than largo
lento	Slow
adagio	Moderately slow
adagietto	A little faster than adagio
Moderate Tempos (70–115 bpm)	
andante	A "walking" tempo
andantino	A little faster than andante
moderato	Moderate pace
allegretto	Not quite as fast as allegro
Fast Tempos (110–220 bpm)	
allegro	Fast, cheerful
vivace	Lively
presto	Very fast
prestissimo	Very, very fast

 TIP

Sometimes you'll see these tempo terms accompanied by the word "molto," which means "very." So if you see *molto vivace*, you know that the music should be played "very lively."

These tempo markings are very approximate, and even the order is not always 100 percent observed. The important thing the Italian terms try to get across is the "spirit" of the music. For example, the word "allegro" in Italian really means "cheerful." When these markings are used, the precise tempo is always left to the discretion of the orchestra's conductor.

So when you see a piece of music marked "Allegro," such as Bach's *Brandenburg Concerto No. 6,* you know that it should be played fairly fast. If you see a piece marked "Largo," like the second movement of Dvořák's *New World Symphony,* you know that the tempo should be fairly slow. This method isn't terribly precise, but it will get you in the ballpark.

Specifying tempo using traditional Italian terms. (Play this one fast!)

Speeding Up—and Slowing Down

Some pieces of music retain the same tempo throughout the entire song (think most popular music here). Other pieces of music speed up and slow down at times, often for dramatic effect.

If a tempo change is immediate—that is, you go directly from one tempo to another, with no gradual transition—you indicate the change by inserting a new tempo marking of your choice. For example, if you've been playing at 120 bpm and want to switch to a faster tempo—160 bpm, let's say—all you have to do is insert a new 160 bpm tempo mark. If you're using Italian tempo markings, just insert the new marking where you want the tempo to change.

If you'd rather gradually speed up or slow down the tempo, it's time to learn a new set of Italian markings. There are several you can use, but the most common are *ritardando* (to gradually slow down the tempo) and *accelerando* (to gradually speed up the tempo). The following table presents the tempo-changing markings you're likely to encounter.

Indicating Tempo Changes

Indicator	Means ...
ritardando (rit., retard.)	Gradually slow down
rallentando (rall.)	Gradually slow down
ritenuto (riten.)	Hold back the tempo
accelerando (accel.)	Gradually speed up
doppio movimento	Twice as fast
a tempo	Return to the previous tempo
tempo primo	Return to the tempo at the beginning of the piece

Decreasing the tempo using a ritardando marking.

Hold That Note!

Sometimes you don't just want to slow down, you actually want to stop. When you want to ignore the beat and hold a specific note, you use what's called a *fermata,* which looks like a little bird's eye placed on top of a note (or a rest) and indicates a pause in the music. This means you hold that note (or rest) indefinitely or until the conductor cuts you off; then you start up with the next note after the fermata, at normal tempo.

When you see a fermata, hold the note.

Getting Loud—and Getting Soft

You now know how to indicate how fast or how slow a song should be played. How do you indicate how loud or how soft you should play it?

Dynamic Markings

A song's *dynamics* indicate how loud or soft you should play. In the world of music notation, there is a set range of volume levels, from very soft to very loud, that you use to indicate the dynamic level of a piece of music. These dynamic markings are shown in the following table.

Dynamic Markings

Marking	Dynamic	Means ...
ppp	pianississimo	Very, very soft
pp	pianissimo	Very soft
p	piano	Soft
mp	mezzo piano	Medium soft
mf	mezzo forte	Medium loud
f	forte	Loud
ff	fortissimo	Very loud
fff	fortississimo	Very, very loud

The dynamic marking, just like the tempo marking, typically appears at the beginning of the song. If you don't see a dynamic marking, that means the song should be played at a medium volume.

Use dynamic markings to indicate how loud a song should be played.

Changing Dynamics

Dynamics can—and do—change throughout the course of a piece of music.

To abruptly change the volume level at a specific point, insert a new dynamic marking. It's okay to indicate dramatic changes in volume; you can go from pp in one measure to ff in the next, if you want.

To gradually change the volume of a song, you have to use what we call *crescendo* and *decrescendo* marks. The crescendo mark (which looks like a giant hairpin, closed at the left and widening to the right) indicates that you gradually increase the volume from your current level to the new level indicated at the end of the crescendo. The decrescendo mark (which looks like a hairpin, open at the left and closed at the right) indicates that you gradually decrease the volume from your current level to the new level indicated at the end of the decrescendo.

Crescendos and decrescendos indicate gradual increases or decreases in volume.

Crescendos and decrescendos can be relatively short (just a beat or two) or extend over multiple measures. Obviously, the longer the crescendo or decrescendo, the more gradual is the change in volume.

 TIP

The way you can remember whether the marking means to get louder or softer is that the wider the "mouth" of the hairpin, the louder the music. When the mouth is at the left and then narrows, that means you start loud and get softer. When the mouth is at the right, that means you start soft and get louder.

Play It Harder

If you want a specific note to be played louder than the other notes around it, you'll want to place an *accent mark* (>) over that note. When a note is accented, you simply play it louder than a normal note.

To indicate that a note is to be played very loud (or hit very hard, if you're writing a percussion part), you place a *marcato* (^) over the note. This means you play or hit that extra hard—with a good solid punch!

Two accent marks and a marcato.

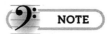 **NOTE**

Technically, the marcato is not an accent. The formal definition means to play the note "well marked," or distinct from the surrounding notes. In practice, however, this typically translates into a loud, long accent.

You can use three other markings to indicate a sudden accent. These markings, like all Italian notation, are placed under the note in question, as detailed in the following table.

Italian Accent Markings

Marking	Means ...
fz	Sudden accent (forzando)
sf	Forced (sforzando)
sfz	Even more forced (sforzando)

Finding Your Way

Reading a long piece of music is a little like reading a roadmap. You'll see various indications in a *score* that provide direction, to repeat a section or to jump to another section within the song.

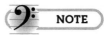 **NOTE**

A long piece of music (especially in the orchestral environment) is often called a score. More precisely, the score is the piece of music the conductor uses, which contains all the parts for all the instruments and voices. The music for each individual instrument is not technically a score, although sometimes people refer to it as such.

When you're playing a long piece of music, various parts of the song might be indicated by numbers or by letters. For example, you might see the letter A at the beginning of the first verse, and the letter B at the beginning of the second verse, and the letter C at the start of the chorus. This way other musicians can tell you to start at a specific point in the song by saying, "Start at letter B."

Alternatively, the measures of a song might be numbered. If this is the case, you can say "Start at measure 16"; everyone will know what you mean.

In any case, you need some way to determine just where you are in a piece of music; otherwise you'll always have to start at the beginning—even if all you need to practice is the very end!

Learn more about the various sections of a song in Chapter 11.

Repeating Sections

You can use various shorthand methods when writing or arranging a piece of music. Especially useful are various ways to indicate repeating sections, which saves you the trouble of writing out the exact same music two (or more) times.

When you have a section of music that should be repeated, you border that section by a pair of *repeat marks*. One repeat mark indicates the start of the section to be repeated; the other one indicates the end of that section. Unless noted otherwise, you repeat a section only once (that is, you play it twice), and then you move on to the next section.

Use repeat marks to indicate a range of measures to play twice.

Sometimes you'll need to repeat a section but play a slightly different ending the second time through. When you see this in the score—called a *first ending* and a *second ending*—you play the first ending the first time through, and then when you repeat the section you skip the first ending and play the second ending.

Use first and second endings to end a repeated section two different ways.

You also can repeat a section of a song by returning to a section designated with a sign (called a *segno*, which is Italian for "sign"). For example, when you see the notation "D.S. al Fine," you jump back to the segno and play through to the end of the song.

Another navigation technique uses a separate section of music called the *coda*. When you insert a coda sign in your music, that indicates that you should jump to the section marked coda. A common navigation technique is notated "D.C. al Coda" or "D.C. al Fine," where you jump to the beginning of the song and then follow through to the coda or the end (fine). The following table details these and other common Italian navigation markings.

 DEFINITION

"**D.S.**" is short for *dal segno*, which means "from the sign." "**D.C.**" is short for *dal capo*, which means "from the head" or "from the start." (*Capo* is Italian for "head"–literally, the top of the chart.)

Italian Navigation Markings

Marking	Means ...
D.C. al Fine	Go back to the beginning and play through to the end.
D.C. al Coda	Go back to the beginning and play to the coda sign; then skip to the coda section.
D.S. al Fine	Go back to the segno sign and play through to the end.
D.S. al Coda	Go back to the segno sign and play to the coda sign; then skip to the coda section.

Use the segno (left) and coda (right) signs to navigate a piece of music.

Repeating Measures

If you have only a single measure to repeat, you can use a *measure repeat* sign. Just insert this sign between the bar lines *after* the measure you want to repeat; musicians will know to repeat the previous measure.

Use the measure repeat sign to repeat the contents of the previous measure.

You can use the measure repeat sign in multiple measures. For example, if you have three measures worth of repeat signs, you play the original measure four times (the original time plus three repeats).

Repeating Notes

If you're really lazy, you'll like the fact that you don't always have to write each individual note in a piece of music. If you're repeating notes of the same rhythmic value and pitch, you can use *note repeat* notation to spare yourself the trouble of writing down all those eighth or sixteenth notes in a row.

TIP

You can also use note repeats on dotted notes. When you put a single slash on a dotted note, you play three of the shorter notes. When you put a double slash on a dotted note, you play six of the shorter notes.

Note repeats (sometimes called *reiterated notes*) are indicated by drawing slash marks through the main note. One slash mark is shorthand that indicates you add one flag or beam to the original note. So, for example, a slash on a whole or half or quarter note indicates you play eighth notes. A slash on an eighth note indicates you play sixteenth notes. And a slash on a sixteenth note means you play thirty-second notes.

This shorthand also indicates that you play as many of the shorter notes as necessary to fill the metric space of the original note. For example, if you draw a single slash through a quarter note, you play two eighth notes. (Two eighth notes equal one quarter note.) Two slashes through a quarter note means you play four sixteenth notes.

The following table indicates some common note repeat values.

Note Repeat Markings

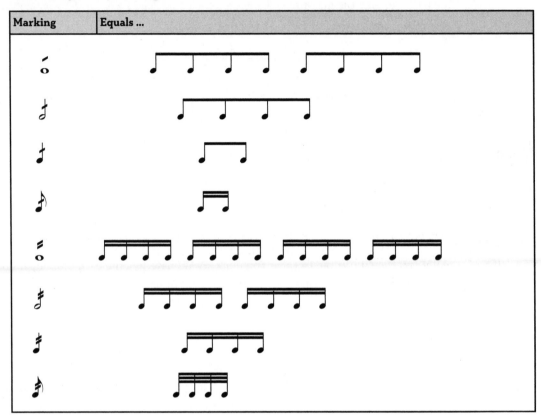

Marking	Equals ...

Repeating Rests

There's one last bit of repeat notation you need to know, and it concerns resting, not playing. In much orchestral music, each individual instrument spends a lot of time not playing. Although the composer could indicate all this inactivity by writing lots of individual measures full of whole rests, it is more common (and a lot easier) to indicate the total number of measures the instrument will rest.

This is done by using a multiple-measure rest sign in a single measure, with a number written above the rest. The number indicates how many measures of rest there are. For example, a multiple-measure rest with the number 6 written above indicates that that instrument is supposed to rest for six measures.

Use a multiple-measure rest sign to indicate multiple measures of rest—in this example, six measures.

Exercises

Exercise 7-1

Play or sing the following piece of music, paying strict attention to the tempo markings.

Exercise 7-2

Play or sing the following piece of music, paying strict attention to the dynamic markings.

Exercise 7-3

Play or sing the following piece of music, paying strict attention to the repeat signs and navigation markings.

The Least You Need to Know

- The tempo of a piece of music can be indicated by traditional Italian markings or by a specific "beats per minute" instruction.

- You indicate changes in tempo by using Italian markings such as ritardando (slow down) and accelerando (speed up).

- The volume level of a piece of music is typically indicated by the use of traditional Italian dynamic markings.

- You indicate changes in dynamics by using crescendo (get louder) and decrescendo (get softer) markings.

- When you want a single note played louder than normal, use an accent mark.

- You navigate an entire piece of music using repeat signs and various Italian markings. (For example, D.C. al Coda means to go back to the beginning, play to the coda sign; then jump to the coda section.)

Tunes

In this part, you discover how to put tones and rhythms together to create a melody and then learn how to add chords to your tunes. You also read about chord progressions and song forms—everything you need to know to create your own songs and pieces of music.

Melodies

Lesson 5, Track 36

In the first part of this book (Chapters 1 through 4), you learned all about notes and pitches. In the second part (Chapters 5 through 7), you learned all about note values and rhythms. By themselves, pitches and rhythms don't amount to much. But when you combine them, they create something wonderful—a melody.

Melody is defined as a logical progression of tones and rhythms—a tune set to a beat. But pay close attention to that word "logical." A melody isn't a random conglomeration of notes; the notes have to relate to and follow from each other. In other words, a melody has to make sense, or else it's just a bunch of noise.

All that said, this textbook definition of melody, however precise, doesn't go far enough for my tastes. To me, a melody is the most memorable part of a piece of music. It's the song you sing, the notes you hum, the musical line that stays in your mind long after the record is over or the band has stopped playing. The best melodies pack an emotional punch; they make us jump with joy or weep with sadness. When done right, melodies can tell a story without words, or reinforce the meaning of a song's lyrics.

In This Chapter

- Creating a melody from tones and rhythms
- Analyzing existing melodies
- Learning the building blocks of melodic form
- Composing your first melody

Combining Tones and Rhythms

If you think back to Chapter 1, you'll remember how we discussed various ways to describe the tones in the song "Mary Had a Little Lamb." We finally settled on the traditional labeling of tones using the letters A through G. Each tone in the song is assigned a letter corresponding to its precise pitch; anyone reading the letters knows which tone to sing or play.

Assigning tones, of course, is only half the story. When you sing "Mary Had a Little Lamb," you give each tone a specific rhythmic value; each tone takes up a specific place in time. The rhythm of the song is described by using different note values, the half notes and quarter notes that we call music notation.

By combining the pitch values with the rhythmic values, we can now notate the entire melody of "Mary Had a Little Lamb." The notes on the staff tell us what pitches to sing; the note values tell us how long to sing each pitch.

The result looks like this:

The complete melody for "Mary Had a Little Lamb."

All melodies are described using similar notation. You set the key signature and the time signature up front, and then fill in the notes of the melody from there. Naturally, you have to arrange the notes within measures, with each measure holding the appropriate number of beats. When you're done writing down the notes, you've written your melody.

Common Melodic Techniques

Every song—every piece of music—has a melody. Some longer pieces (such as much orchestral music pieces) have multiple melodies. Some melodies consist of multiple parts, with different parts repeated in different parts of the song. No matter how the music is constructed, the melody is the heart of the song—the part you should be able to sing or hum or whistle all by itself, with no other instruments needed.

To get a feel for how melodies are constructed, let's take a look at some melodies from well-known pieces of music. You'll see that, although they all have their distinct sound and feel, these melodies also have a lot of factors in common.

Dvořák's *New World Symphony*

We'll start with a tune from Antonín Dvořák's *Symphony #9 in E minor ("From the New World")*, more commonly known as the *New World Symphony*. This is a popular piece of orchestral music, and consists of several different sections; the melody we'll look at is just one of many used throughout the work, and it goes like this:

One of the main melodies in Dvořák's New World Symphony.

Let's first get a feel for the mechanics of the melody. As you can see, the time signature for this melody is 4/4, so there are four quarter-note beats in each measure. The key signature is D♭, with five flats. When you listen to it, the melody has a happy sound, which means it's in a major key—D♭ Major, to be precise. The piece of the melody we're looking at is four measures long.

If you look at (or listen to) this melody carefully, you'll see that it breaks into two, two-measure phrases. The first two measures end on a note (E♭) that doesn't feel like an ending note (it's the second note in the scale); this sets up a kind of tension that you want to hear resolved. The second two measures resolve the tension by effectively repeating the first two measures, but ending on a more satisfying tone—D♭, the tonic of the scale.

This is a common technique, setting up some sort of tension in the first part of the melody that is then resolved in the second part. This helps to make a melody interesting; if you think about it, it's also a very logical, symmetrical, almost mathematical construction. (If you look at it like a mathematical formula, the first half of the melody "equals" the second half.)

Another technique used in this melody is the repetition of specific rhythms. Look at the rhythmic pattern used throughout: dotted eighth note, sixteenth note, and quarter note. This "dum de duh" pattern is played twice in the first measure, and twice again in the third measure, establishing a kind of rhythmic signature for the entire piece. This rhythmic repetition helps to establish a familiarity for the listener; you hear the rhythm once, then you hear it again, and it feels familiar; almost comfortable. In fact, a listener expects to hear some repetition; if every measure of a melody is completely different from all the preceding measures, the melody will be difficult to remember.

Bach's *Minuet in G*

Our next example is Johann Sebastian Bach's *Minuet in G*—although you might be familiar with it as the melody of the pop song "A Lover's Concerto," performed by the Toys back in the mid-1960s.

The melody for Bach's Minuet in G—*also appropriated for the pop song "A Lover's Concerto."*

This melody differs from Dvořák's melody in a number of ways. First, it's in 3/4 time, not 4/4. Second, it's in the key of G, and is based on the G Major scale.

Beyond those differences, you can hear a lot of similar techniques in use. Note the rhythmic repetition between measures 1 and 2 and measures 3 and 4, and the continued repetition of the first measure in measures 5 through 7. Also note the very slight tension created in measure 4 (the end of the first half of the melody—it sounds like there's more coming), which is then resolved in the second half of the melody.

There's something else interesting about this particular melody. The first half of the melody has an insistent upward motion; the second half uses a downward motion to deposit you pretty much where you started. Even though not all the notes go up (or down), the general flow of the melody moves in those directions, and thus propels the melody forward.

You need to have some sort of motion in a melody, or you'll put the listener to sleep. That motion can be in the tune, or in the rhythm, but it needs to be there, to help the melody get from point A to point B.

"Michael, Row the Boat Ashore"

Next up is the traditional folk song "Michael, Row the Boat Ashore." The words to this tune, simple as they are, can actually help us see the melodic form. When you read the words, you can clearly see that the song consists of two near-identical halves—rhythmically, anyway. The first time Michael rows his boat ashore (hallelujah!), the melody has a slight upward motion, and ends with a slight bit of tension on the fifth note of the scale (A). The second time Michael goes boating, the melody sways downward slightly, and resolves itself by ending on the tonic of the key.

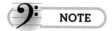

NOTE

The two quarter notes before measure one are called *pickup notes;* that little half measure is called a *pickup measure.* You use pickup notes and measures when the melody actually starts up before the first beat of the first measure.

Symmetry, repetition, tension, and release—these techniques are used over and over to create memorable melodies.

The melody for the folk song "Michael, Row the Boat Ashore."

Pachelbel's *Canon in D*

Our final melody is a bit different from the ones we've examined so far. It's different because rhythmically, it's very simple—nothing but half notes.

You've probably heard this melody before—it's Johann Pachelbel's *Canon in D* (sometimes just called "Pachelbel's *Canon*"—like he only wrote this one!), and it's been used in a number of different movies and television shows. It's a compelling melody, despite its rhythmic simplicity.

The very simple melody for Pachelbel's Canon in D.

This melody also is different in that it doesn't use a lot of symmetry or repetition. (Except for the repeated half notes, of course!) It's actually the stepwise intervals between the notes that propel this melody forward; each pitch leaning forward to the next, one after another, almost in a giant spinning circle of tones. And then the last note, C#, is the leading tone of the scale (D Major); you jump back to F# (the third of the scale) and start all over again.

The point of examining this particular melody is that you don't need fancy rhythms to create a memorable melody. Pure tones, played slowly and simply, can be quite lyrical—if you pick the right ones!

The Building Blocks of Melodic Form

Now that we've examined some simple melodies, let's look at how melodies are constructed. You'll need to know this if you want to compose your own melodies.

The Motif

For a melody to be truly memorable, there needs to be a piece of the melody that really reaches out and grabs the listener's attention. In pop music, this is called the *hook*, because it's the part of the song that hooks the listener. In more traditional music, this piece of the song is known as the *motif* or *motive*. Whatever you call it, it should be memorable enough that you want to repeat it not only within a longer melodic phrase, but throughout the entire composition. (And the listener wants to hear it again and again!)

A motif is typically fairly short—a few notes (think of the five whistling notes in Sergio Leone's theme from the movie *The Good, the Bad and the Ugly*) or, at longest, one or two measures. You can reuse a motif throughout a composition by varying it in one way or another—repeating the same tones with a different rhythm, playing the tones up or down a specified interval, playing different tones to the same rhythm, and so on.

A simple four-note motif.

The Short Melodic Phrase

The motif is often part of a more complete melodic phrase. This phrase is typically two or four measures long and contains a complete musical thought or statement. For want of a better term, we'll call this the *short melodic phrase* or the *short melody*.

A short melodic phrase typically defines itself by coming to some sort of easily identifiable endpoint, either in terms of chord structure or rhythmic complexity. In essence, the endpoint of a melodic phrase is where the music breathes. And these short melodies often function within an even longer musical phrase to set up and resolve tension.

The motif used within a two-measure short melodic phrase.

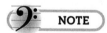
NOTE

Of all the short melodies within a longer composition (and there should be more than one), one of them should be memorable enough to become the *theme* of the composition. The melodic theme defines the composition, and is typically repeated several times throughout a piece.

The Long Melodic Phrase

Short melodic phrases combine into longer melodic phrases. You typically put two or four short melodic phrases together into a single *long melodic phrase*. The end of a long melodic phrase is a major breathing (or resting) point; after all those short melodies, your composition needs to take a significant break.

Four short melodic phrases combined into a single longer melodic phrase.

Composing Your First Melody

Now that you know some of the techniques you can use to create a melody, let's put those techniques to work.

As you learned with Pachelbel's *Canon*, a melody doesn't have to include complex rhythms. The right notes on the right pitches are all you need to start any new tune.

One of the primary rules of composing is to base your melody on a specific scale. And, as you'll learn in Chapter 9, there are three notes in a scale which, when played together, create what we call a *major triad*. These three notes represent a good place to start for our first melody.

For simplicity's sake, let's start in the key of C, using the C Major scale. The three notes we want to use are the tonic, the third, and the fifth—C, E, and G. So let's start our melody with two half notes and a whole note, starting with C and progressing up to G on the whole note.

This gives us the first two measures of the melody:

The first two measures of our first melody.

Let's elaborate on these notes a bit. If you want to give the melody a little more of a flow, you can fill in the blanks between these three notes by adding notes in the step between each pitch. We'll do this by turning the half notes into quarter notes, and adding *passing tones* between the C and the E, and the E and G. (That means we'll go from C to D to E, and from E to F to G.)

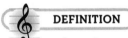

DEFINITION

A **passing tone** is a subsidiary tone you have to pass through to move from one important note to another. The passing tone is not part of the underlying chord structure, but is often situated between two of the notes in a triad.

The result looks like this:

The first two measures, with passing tones added.

We're still left with that single whole note sitting there. It's okay to leave it like that, but doing so makes this part of our melody sound like nothing more than a simple major scale—which it actually is! Fortunately, we can add a little more interest by using another technique called a *neighboring tone,* in which you land on the main note (in this case, the G), slide briefly to an adjacent note, and then return to rest on the main note (G, again). The result sounds a little like "doo-de-doo," which is slightly more interesting than a plain "doo."

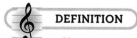

DEFINITION

You create a **neighboring tone** by starting on a pitch, moving up or down by a step (either half or whole) and then returning to the original pitch; the neighboring tone is the one that "neighbors" the original note. Like a passing tone, a neighboring tone typically is not one of the three notes in the underlying chord triad.

You can place neighboring tones above or below the main tone; for our little melody, we'll use the neighboring tone above the G—which happens to be an A. Keeping the rhythm simple, we'll now start the second measure with a quarter note on G; then follow it by a quarter note on A and a half note on G.

The result looks like this:

Embellishing the melody with a neighboring tone.

This is a nice little melody—but it's really only half of a melody. Ending on the fifth note of the scale, as it does, actually sets up some melodic tension. When you hear this melody, you want to resolve the tension, and somehow get things back to where they started—on C.

There's an easy way to do this, of course. All you have to do is create a sort of mirror image of the first two measures, but with a downward motion from G to C.

The first thing we'll do is copy the first measure into a new third measure—except we'll copy it with the first note starting on G, and with the quarter notes moving down in a G F E D progression. (Note that this progression puts two of the C Major triad notes—G and E—on the primary beats of the measure: one and three.) Then we'll end the run with a whole note in the fourth measure, positioned on the tonic note: C.

Your completed melody looks like this:

Your completed melody—play it loud and proud!

That wasn't so difficult, was it? Granted, this melody won't win any Grammy awards, but it is a legitimate melody, and it's quite singable. (Trust me, I've heard worse.) The key thing is that you've seen that creating a melody isn't hard, as long as you know the basic theory involved.

Now, there's certainly a lot more to learn about composing melodies, some of which you'll read about in Chapter 19. Skip to there if you want to continue along this melodic track, or continue on to Chapter 9 to learn about another important component of a song: chords.

Exercises

Exercise 8-1

Listen to a variety of popular songs and classical compositions, paying particular attention to the main melodies. Analyze the melodies in question and determine what qualities they have in common. Listen in particular for longer melodies made up of shorter melodic phrases or motifs. When you find a melody that is particularly appealing to you, try to determine what makes it so listenable.

Exercise 8-2

Using the techniques you've learned, take the 4-measure melody we created in this chapter and expand it into a 16-measure composition.

The Least You Need to Know

- Melody is the most important part of a composition; it's the part that people remember.
- A melody consists of a logical progression of tones and rhythms—a tune set to a beat.
- Longer melodies are built from simple motifs and short melodic phrases.

Chords

Lesson 6, Track 41

More often than not, music is more than a single melodic line. Music is a package of tones, rhythms, and underlying harmonic structure. The melody fits within this harmonic structure, is dependent on this harmonic structure, and in some cases dictates the harmonic structure.

The harmonic structure of a piece of music is defined by a series of *chords*. A chord is a group of notes played simultaneously, rather than sequentially (like a melody). The relationships between the notes—the intervals within the chord—define the type of chord; the placement of the chord within the underlying key or scale defines the role of the chord.

This chapter is all about chords—and it's a long one, because there are many, many different types of chords. Don't let all the various permutations scare you off, however; at the core, a chord is nothing more than single notes (typically separated by thirds) played together. It's as simple as that. If you can play three notes at the same time, you can play a chord.

In This Chapter

- Understanding major, minor, diminished, and augmented triads
- Extending chords to sevenths, ninths, and beyond
- Creating altered, suspended, and power chords
- Inverting the chord order
- Writing chords into your music

This chapter, then, shows you how to construct many different types of chords, with a particular emphasis on the type of harmonic structure you find in popular music. (This is important; the study of harmony in classical music is much more involved, with a slightly different set of rules.) And, when you're done reading this chapter, you can find a "cheat sheet" to all the different chords online at idiotsguides.com/musictheory, a quick yet comprehensive reference to every kind of chord imaginable—in every key!

Forming a Chord

Okay, here's the formal definition: a chord is a combination of three or more notes played together.

Let's do a little exercise: sit down at the nearest piano and put your right thumb on one of the white keys. (It doesn't matter which one.) Now skip a key and put another finger on the third key up. Skip another key and put a third finger on the fifth key up from the first. You should now be pressing three keys, with an empty key between each finger. Press down and listen—you're playing a chord!

Basic chords consist of just three notes, arranged in thirds, called a *triad*. The most common triads are constructed from notes plucked from the underlying scale, each note two steps above the previous note. So, for example, if you want to base a chord on the tonic of a scale, you'd use the first, third, and fifth notes of the scale. (Using the C Major scale, these notes would be C, E, and G.) If you want to base a chord on the second degree of a scale, use the second, fourth, and sixth notes of the scale. (Still using the C Major scale, these notes would be D, F, and A.)

Building a three-note triad.

Within a specific chord, the first note is called the *root*—even if the chord isn't formed from the root of the scale. The other notes of the chord are named relative to the first note, typically being the third and the fifth above the chord's root. (For example, if C is the chord's root, E is called the *third* and G is called the *fifth*.) This is sometimes notated 1-3-5.

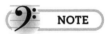 **NOTE**

The notes of a chord don't always have to be played in unison. You can play the notes one at a time, starting (usually, but not always) with the bottom note. This is called *arpeggiating* the chord, and the result is an *arpeggio*.

Different Types of Chords

Let's go back to the piano. Putting your fingers on every other white note, form a chord starting on middle C. (Your fingers should be on the keys C, E, and G.) Nice sounding chord, isn't it? Now move your fingers one key to the right, so that you're starting on D. (Your fingers should now be on the keys D, F, and A.) This chord sounds different—kind of sad, compared to the happier C chord.

You've just demonstrated the difference between *major* and *minor* chords. The first chord you played was a major chord: C Major. The second chord was a minor chord: D minor. As with major and minor scales, major and minor chords sound different to the listener, because the intervals in the chords are slightly different.

In most cases, the type of chord is determined by the middle note: the third. When the interval between the first note and the second note is a major third—two whole steps—you have a major chord. When the interval between the first note and the second note is a minor third—three half steps—you have a minor chord.

It's no more complex than that. If you change the middle note, you change the chord from major to minor.

Read on to learn all about major and minor chords—as well as some other types of chords that aren't quite major and aren't quite minor.

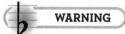

WARNING

You should always spell a triad using every other letter. So D♭-F-A♭ is a correct spelling (for a D♭ Major chord), but the enharmonic spelling of C♯-F-A♭ is wrong.

Major Chords

A major chord consists of a root, a major third, and a perfect fifth. For example, the C Major chord includes the notes C, E, and G. The E is a major third above the C; the G is a perfect fifth above the C.

Here's a quick look at how to build major chords on every note of the scale:

Major triads.

There are many different ways to indicate a major chord in your music, as shown in the following table.

Notation for Major Chords

Major Chord Notation	Example
Major	C Major
Maj	C Maj
Ma	C Ma
M	CM
Δ	CΔ

In addition, just printing the letter of the chord (using a capital letter) indicates that the chord is major. (So if you see C in a score, you know to play a C Major chord.)

TIP

When you play a chord based on the tonic note of a major scale or key, that chord is always a major chord. For example, in the key of C, the tonic chord is C Major.

Minor Chords

The main difference between a major chord and a minor chord is the third. Although a major chord utilizes a major third, a minor chord flattens that interval to create a minor third. The fifth is the same.

In other words, a minor chord consists of a root, a minor third, and a perfect fifth. This is sometimes notated 1-♭3-5. For example, the C minor chord includes the notes C, E♭, and G.

Here's a quick look at how to build minor chords on every note of the scale:

Minor triads.

There are many different ways to indicate a minor chord, as shown in the following table.

Notation for Minor Chords

Minor Chord Notation	Example
minor	C minor
min	C min
mi	C mi
m	Cm

Diminished Chords

A diminished chord is like a minor chord with a lowered fifth. It has a kind of eerie and ominous sound. You build a diminished chord with a root note, a minor third, and a diminished (lowered) fifth. This is sometimes noted 1-♭3-♭5.

 TIP

In this and other chord charts in this book, the accidentals apply only to the specific chord; they don't carry across to successive chords.

For example, the C diminished chord includes the notes C, E♭, and G♭.

Here's a quick look at how to build diminished chords on every note of the scale:

Diminished triads.

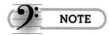 **NOTE**

Note the double flat on the fifth of the E♭ diminished chord.

There are many different ways to indicate a diminished chord, as shown in the following table.

Notation for Diminished Chords

Diminished Chord Notation	Example
diminished	C diminished
dimin	C dimin
dim	C dim
o	C°

Augmented Chords

An augmented chord is like a major chord with a raised fifth; thus an augmented chord consists of a root, a major third, and an augmented (raised) fifth. This is sometimes notated 1-3-♯5.

For example, the C augmented chord includes the notes C, E, and G♯.

Here's a quick look at how to build augmented chords on every note of the scale:

Augmented triads.

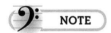 **NOTE**

Did you spot the double sharp on the fifth of the B augmented chord in the illustration of augmented chords?

There are many different ways to indicate an augmented chord, as shown in the following table.

Notation for Augmented Chords

Augmented Chord Notation	Example
augmented	C augmented
aug	C aug
+	C+

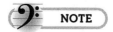

NOTE

Although it's important to learn about diminished and augmented chords, you won't run into too many of them, especially in popular music. If you base the root of your chord on the notes of a major scale, as you'll learn in Chapter 10, only the seventh degree triad forms a diminished chord. (Triads based on the other degrees of the scale form major or minor chords.) There is no augmented chord found on any degree of the major scale.

Chord Extensions

Chords can include more than three notes. When you get above the basic triad, the other notes you add to a chord are called *extensions*.

Chord extensions are typically added in thirds; so the first type of extended chord is called a *seventh chord* because the seventh is a third above the fifth. Next up would be the *ninth chord*, which adds a third above the seventh, and so on.

Chord extensions are nice to know, but you can simplify most pieces of music to work with just the basic triads. The extended notes add more color or flavor to the sound, kind of like a musical seasoning. Like a good meal, what's important is what's underneath—and you can always do without the seasoning.

So if you see a piece of music with lots of seventh and ninth chords, don't panic—you can probably play the music without the extensions and still have things sound okay. Of course, for the full experience, you want to play the extended chords as written. But remember, the basic harmonic structure comes from the base triads; not from the extensions.

That said, it helps to have a full understanding of extended chords, just as a good chef must have a full understanding of all the different seasonings at his or her disposal. That means you need to know how to build extended chords, so you can throw them into the mix when necessary.

Sevenths

The seventh chord is the most common chord extension—in fact, it's so common that some music theorists categorize it as a basic chord type, not as an extension. In any case, you need to be as familiar with seventh chords as you are with triads. They're that important.

Creating a seventh chord within a specific key or scale is normally as simple as adding another third on top of the fifth of the base triad. This gives you a 1-3-5-7 structure—the equivalent of playing every other note in the scale.

There are actually three basic types of seventh chords: major, minor, and dominant. Major and minor seventh chords are kind of sweet sounding; the dominant seventh chord has its own internal tension.

Dominant Sevenths

The dominant seventh chord—sometimes just called the "seventh" chord, with no other designation—takes a major triad and adds a *minor* seventh on top. In other words, it's a major chord with a lowered seventh; the chord itself consists of a root, major third, perfect fifth, and minor seventh. This is sometimes notated 1-3-5-♭7.

For example, a C7 chord includes the notes C, E, G, and B♭.

The dominant seventh chord is an especially important—and frequently used—extension, as this is what you get if you play a seventh chord based on the fifth (dominant) tone of a major scale. As you'll learn in Chapter 10, the dominant chord is frequently used to set up the tension leading back to the tonic chord; when you add a seventh to the dominant triad (with its mix of major triad and minor seventh), you introduce even more tension to the music. So when you want to get back home to the tonic, you set it up with a dominant seventh chord. (Although it's possible, of course, to also form dominant seventh chords on any note of the scale—it's not limited to the fifth tone.)

Here's a quick look at how to build dominant seventh chords on every note of the scale:

Dominant seventh chords.

There's really only one way to notate a dominant seventh chord: by placing a single 7 after the name of the chord. For example, you notate a C dominant seventh chord like this: C7.

Major Sevenths

The major seventh chord takes a standard major chord and adds a major seventh on top of the existing three notes. This gives you a chord consisting of a root, major third, perfect fifth, and major seventh. For example, a C Major 7 chord includes the notes C, E, G, and B.

Here's a quick look at how to build major seventh chords on every note of the scale:

Major seventh chords.

There are several ways to indicate a major seventh chord, as shown in the following table.

Notation for Major Seventh Chords

Major Seventh Chord Notation	Example
Major 7	C Major 7
Maj7	C Maj7
M7	CM7
Δ7	CΔ7

Minor Sevenths

The minor seventh chord takes a standard minor chord and adds a minor seventh on top of the existing three notes. This gives you a chord consisting of a root, minor third, perfect fifth, and minor seventh. (This is sometimes notated 1-♭3-5-♭7.)

For example, a C minor 7 chord includes the notes C, E♭, G, and B♭.

Here's a quick look at how to build minor seventh chords on every note of the scale:

Minor seventh chords.

There are several ways to indicate a minor seventh chord, as shown in the following table.

Notation for Minor Seventh Chords

Minor Seventh Chord Notation	Example
minor 7	C minor 7
min7	C min7
m7	Cm7

Other Sevenths

When I said there were three basic types of seventh chords, I left the door open for other types of less frequently used seventh chords. Indeed, you can stick either a minor or a major seventh on top of any type of triad—major, minor, augmented, or diminished—to create different types of seventh chords.

For example, a major seventh stuck on top of a minor triad creates a *minor major seventh* chord. (That is, the base chord is minor, but the seventh is major.) This is notated 1-♭3-5-7; a C minor Major 7 chord would include the notes C, E♭, G, and B (natural).

Other types of seventh chords.

A minor seventh on top of a diminished triad creates what's called a *half-diminished seventh* chord, like this: 1-♭3-♭5-♭7. It's sometimes notated as a minor 7 with a flatted fifth. (This is the chord you get if you play a seventh chord based on the seventh tone of a major key.) If you want a full diminished seventh chord, you need to double-flat the seventh, like this: 1-♭3-♭5-♭♭7.

Put a minor seventh on top of an augmented triad and you get an *augmented seventh chord,* like this: 1-3-♯5-♭7. A major seventh on top of an augmented triad creates a major seventh chord with a raised fifth (♯5), like this: 1-3-♯5-7 … and so on.

Other Extensions

Although the seventh chord is almost as common as an unadorned triad, other chord extensions are less widely used. That doesn't mean you don't need to bother with them; when used properly, sixths and ninths and other extended chords can add a lot to a piece of music.

Let's look, then, at the other extensions you can use to spice up your basic chords.

Sixths

I said previously that all chords are based on notes a third apart from each other. There's an important exception to that rule: the sixth chord. With a sixth chord (sometimes called an *added sixth* chord), you start with a basic triad; then add an extra note a second above the fifth—or a sixth above the root. You can have major sixth and minor sixth chords, as well as sixths above diminished and augmented triads, as shown in the following figure:

Different types of sixth chords.

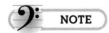 **NOTE**

Later in this chapter, you'll learn about chord inversions, where the order of the notes in a chord is changed. Interestingly, a sixth chord can be viewed as nothing more than the first inversion of a seventh chord. For example, the C Major 6 chord (C E G A) contains the same notes as the A minor 7 chord (A C E G), just in a different order. For that reason, you sometimes might see sixth chords notated as seventh chords with a separate note (the third) in the bass. (C Major 6 could be notated like this: Am7/C.) This is a little advanced—come back to this sidebar after you've read the section on inversions. It'll make sense then.

Ninths

A ninth chord adds another third on top of the four notes in the seventh chord. That makes for five individual notes; each a third apart. You can have ninth chords based on both major and minor triads, with both major and minor sevenths. Here's just a smattering of the different types of ninth chords you can build:

Different types of ninth chords.

Seventh, ninth, and eleventh chords see frequent use in modern jazz music, which often employs sophisticated harmonic concepts.

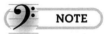 **NOTE**

When you get up to the ninth chord, you assume that the chord includes both the underlying triad and the seventh.

Elevenths ... and Beyond

An eleventh chord adds another note a third above the ninth, for six notes total: 1-3-5-7-9-11. You can set an eleventh on top of any type of triad, along with all sorts of seventh and ninth variations—although the most common eleventh chord always uses the unchanged note from within the underlying key or scale.

As with the ninth chord, you have to make a few assumptions with the eleventh chord. You have to assume the underlying triad, of course, but you also have to assume the presence of both the seventh and the ninth.

Different types of eleventh chords.

It's also possible to construct a thirteenth chord by adding another third above the eleventh. But that's as high as you can go because the new note for the next chord up—the fifteenth chord—is exactly two octaves up from the chord root. There's no point in calling it a new chord when all you're doing is doubling the root note.

Altered, Suspended, and Power Chords

To ensure that you have a comprehensive background in chord theory, there are three other chord types you need to know about. These are variations on the basic chord types that crop up from time to time—and can help you notate more complex musical sounds.

Altered Chords

When you get into seventh and ninth and eleventh chords, you run into the possibility of a lot of different variations. It's math again; the more notes in a chord, the more possible combinations of flats and sharps and such you can create.

This is why we have something called *altered chords*. Altered chords take standard, easy-to-understand chords and alter them. The alteration—a lowered fifth, perhaps, or maybe an added ninth—is typically notated in parentheses, after the main chord notation. (By the way, don't confuse altered chords with the *altered bass* chords discussed in Chapter 16. The names are similar but they're completely different beasts.)

For example, let's say you wanted to write a C Major seventh chord, but with a lowered fifth. (I know ... that's a really weird-sounding combination.) To notate this, you start with the basic chord—CM7—and add the alteration in parentheses, like this: CM7(♭5). Anyone reading this chord knows to start with the basic chord and then make the alteration shown within the parentheses.

Here's another example: let's say you have a C minor chord and want to add the ninth but without adding the seventh. Now, if you wanted to include the seventh, you'd have a Cm9 chord, which is relatively standard. But to leave out the seventh takes a bit more planning. Again, you start with the underlying triad—in this case, Cm—and make the alteration within parentheses, like this: Cm(add9). Anyone reading this chord knows to play a C minor triad and then add the ninth—not to play a standard Cm9 chord.

The difference between a ninth chord and a triad with an added ninth.

TIP

Added notes can be notated by the word *add* plus the number, or just the number—within parentheses.

There are an endless number of possibilities you can use when working with altered chords. You can even include more than one variation per chord—all you have to do is keep adding the variations onto the end of the chord notation. Just remember to start with the base chord and make your alterations as clear as possible. (And, if all else fails, you can write out the notes of the chord on a staff—just to make sure everybody understands.)

Suspended Chords

We're so used to hearing a chord as a 1-3-5 triad that any change to this arrangement really stands out like a sore thumb to our ears. (Not that you should put your thumbs in your ears, but you know what I mean.) This is what makes a *suspended chord* so powerful, especially when used properly.

A suspended chord temporarily moves the normal major third of a major chord up a half step to a perfect fourth. This suspension of the second note of the triad is so wrong to our ears, we want to hear the suspension resolved by moving the second note down from the fourth to the third—as quickly as possible.

For example, a C suspended chord includes the notes C F G—instead of the C E G of C Major. This sets up an incredible tension, as the fourth (F) sounds really out of place; your ears want the F to move down to the E to create the more soothing C Major triad.

In fact, most often you do resolve suspended chords—especially at the end of a musical phrase. You can use the suspended chord to set up the desired end-of-phrase tension, but then quickly resolve the suspended chord to the normal major chord, like this:

Resolving a suspended chord—the F in the first chord drops down to the E in the final chord.

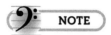

NOTE

As you can see from the example, you notate a suspended chord with the phrase *sus4*, or more simply *sus*.

The resolution from the perfect fourth to the major third is just a half-step movement, but that little half step makes a world of difference; until you make the move, you're sitting on the edge of your seat waiting for that incredible tension to resolve.

Power Chords

If you want a really simple chord, one with a lot of raw power, you can play just the root and the fifth, leaving out the third. This type of chord is called a *power chord*; it is noted by adding a "5" after the chord note. (For example, a G power chord is notated G5, and includes only the notes G and D.) Power chords are used a lot by guitarists in certain types of popular music, in particular the hard rock and heavy metal genres.

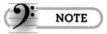

NOTE

In classical music theory, a power chord is called an *open fifth,* and is technically an interval, not a chord.

Here's one bad thing about power chords: if you use a bunch of them in a row, you create something called *parallel fifths.* As you'll learn, parallel fifths are frowned upon, especially in classical music theory. So use power chords sparingly and—if at all possible—not consecutively.

Power chords, up and down the scale.

Inverting the Order

Although it's easiest to understand a chord when the root is on the bottom and the fifth is on the top, you don't have to play the notes in precisely this order. Chords can be *inverted* so that the root isn't the lowest note, which can give a chord a slightly different sound. (It can also make a chord easier to play on a piano, when you're moving your fingers from chord to chord; inversions help to group the notes from adjacent chords closer together.)

When you rearrange the notes of a chord so that the third is on the bottom (3-5-1), you form what is called the *first inversion.* (Using a C Major chord as an example, the first inversion is arranged E G C.) The *second inversion* is where you put the fifth of the chord on the bottom, followed by the root and third (5-1-3). (Again using C Major as an example, the second inversion is arranged G C E.) The standard triad form, with the root on the bottom, is called the *root inversion.*

The first and second inversions of a C Major chord.

If you're working with extended chords, there are more than two possible inversions. For example, the third inversion of a seventh chord puts the seventh in the bass; the fourth inversion of a ninth chord puts the ninth in the bass.

The particular order of a chord's notes is also referred to as that chord's *voicing.* You can specify a voicing without writing all the notes by adding a bass note to the standard chord notation. You do this by adding a slash after the chord notation, and then the name of the note that should be played on the bottom of the chord.

For example, if you want to indicate a first inversion of a C Major chord (normally C E G, but E G C in the first inversion), you'd write this: C/E. This tells the musician to play a C Major chord, but to put an E in the bass—which just happens to be the first inversion of the chord. If you wanted to indicate a second inversion (G C E), you'd write this: C/G. This tells the musician to play a C Major chord with a G in the bass.

You also can use this notation to indicate other, nonchord notes to be played in the bass part. For example, Am7/D tells the musician to play an A minor seventh chord, but to add a D in the bass—a note that doesn't exist within the A minor seventh chord proper.

An A minor seventh chord with a D in the bass—not your standard seventh chord.

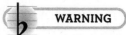

WARNING

Don't confuse the chord/bass notation with the similar $\frac{chord}{chord}$ (like a fraction with a horizontal divider, as opposed to the chord/bass diagonal slash). The $\frac{chord}{chord}$ notation tells a musician—typically a pianist—to play one chord over another. For example, if you see $\frac{Cm}{Dm}$ you should play a Cm chord with your right hand, and a Dm chord with your left.

Adding Chords to Your Music

When you want to indicate a chord in your written music, you add the chord symbol above the staff, like this:

Write the chord symbol above the staff.

The chord applies in the music until you insert another chord. Then the new chord applies—until the next chord change. For example, in the following piece of music you'd play a C Major chord in measure 1, an F Major chord in measure 2, a C Major chord in the first half of measure 3, a G7 chord in the second half of measure 3, and a C Major chord in measure 4.

Changing chords in your music.

If you're writing a part for guitar, or for a rhythm section (bass, piano, and so forth) in a pop or jazz band, you don't have to write out specific notes on the staff. A guitarist will know to strum the indicated chords, a piano player will know to *comp* through the chord progressions, and the bass player will know to play the root of the chord.

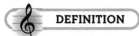

DEFINITION

Comping is a technique used by jazz and pop musicians to play an improvised accompaniment behind a particular piece of music. A piano player might comp by playing block or arpeggiated chords; a guitarist might comp by strumming the indicated chords.

You write a comp part by using slashes in place of traditional notes on the staff. Typically, you use one slash per beat, so a measure of 4/4 will have four slashes, like this:

Writing chords for a rhythm section.

You can indicate specific rhythms that should be played by writing out the rhythm, but with slashes instead of note heads. The result looks something like this:

Indicating a specific rhythm for the chord accompaniment.

If you're writing specifically for guitar, you also have the option of including guitar *tablature*. (A guitar part with tablature is sometimes called guitar *tab*.) Tablature shows the guitarist how to fret the chord, and is very useful for beginning-level players. More advanced players probably don't need this assistance, unless you're indicating a particularly complex chord.

A guitar part with tablature added.

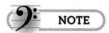 **NOTE**

If you go to idiotsguides.com/musictheory, you'll find a comprehensive reference to just about every kind of chord you can think of—major chords, minor chords, extensions, you name it. You'll find out how to construct each chord, learn the guitar tablature, and discover alternate ways to describe the chord. Keep this website bookmarked—you'll get a lot of use out of it!

Exercises

Exercise 9-1

Name the following major chords.

Exercise 9-2

Name the following minor chords.

Exercise 9-3

Write the following major chords on the staff.

Exercise 9-4

Write the following minor chords on the staff.

Exercise 9-5

Name the following extended chords.

____   ____   ____   ____   ____   ____   ____   ____   ____

Exercise 9-6

Write the following extended chords on the staff.

A 7   E♭m7   C 6   D Maj7   B♭m9   F 11   G 7   Gm(maj7)   E Maj7   F m7

Exercise 9-7

Write the first and second inversions of the following chords.

G sus4   D sus4   F sus4   F♯sus4   B♭sus4

Exercise 9-8

Resolve the following suspended chords by lowering the suspended note (the middle note of the chord) to the note a half step below.

G sus4   D sus4   F sus4   F♯sus4   B♭sus4

The Least You Need to Know

- A chord consists of three or more notes (called a triad) played simultaneously— with each note typically a third above the previous note.

- A major chord includes the root note, a major third, and a perfect fifth.

- A minor chord includes the root note, a minor third, and a perfect fifth.

- Extensions above the basic triad are typically added in thirds, and can be either major or minor.

- A minor seventh chord is a minor triad with a minor seventh; a major seventh chord is a major triad with a major seventh; a dominant seventh chord is a major triad with a minor seventh.

- When you play a chord with a note other than the root in the bass, you're playing a chord inversion.

- When you write for guitar, piano, or bass, you don't have to write out all the notes; all you have to do is specify the chord, along with rhythmic slashes on the staff.

Chord Progressions

In Chapter 9, you learned how to group notes together to form chords. Individual chords alone are interesting, but they become really useful when you string them together to form a succession of chords—what we call a *chord progression*. These chord progressions provide the harmonic underpinning of a song, "fattening out" the melody and propelling the music forward.

Of course, to create a chord progression that sounds natural, you can't just string a bunch of chords together willy-nilly. Certain chords naturally lead to other chords; certain chords perform distinct functions within a song. You have to use your chords properly, and arrange them in the right order, to create a piece of music that sounds both natural and logical.

Chord progressions don't have to be complex, either. The simplest progressions include just two or three chords—which are easy enough for any beginning guitarist to play. How many songs, after all, do you know that use only the G, C, and D chords? (A lot, I bet.) Those three chords comprise one of the most common chord progressions—which should show you how easy all this is.

In This Chapter

- Understanding scale-based chords

- Learning the rules of chord leading

- Figuring out how to end a progression

- Discovering the most common chord progressions

- Fitting chords to a melody—and a melody to a chord progression

Chords for Each Note in the Scale

To better understand the theory behind chord progressions, you need to understand that you can create a three-note chord based on any of the seven notes of a major key or scale. You start with the note of the scale (one through seven) as the root of the chord; then build up from there in thirds—using only the notes within the scale.

Let's use the key of C as an example, because it's made up of only the white keys on a piano. When you play a triad based on C (the tonic of the scale), you play C E G—a C Major chord. Now move up one white key on the keyboard, and play the next triad—D F A, or D minor. Move up another key, and you play E G B, the E minor chord. Move up yet another key, and you play F A C—F Major. Keep moving up the scale and you play G Major, A minor, and B diminished. Then you're back on C, and ready to start all over again.

This type of chord building based on the notes of a scale is important, because we use the position within a scale to describe the individual chords in our chord progressions. In particular, we use Roman numerals (I through VII) to describe where each chord falls in the underlying scale. Uppercase Roman numerals are used for major chords; lowercase Roman numerals are used for minor chords. To indicate a diminished chord, you use the lowercase Roman numeral plus a small circle (a degree sign: °). To indicate an augmented chord, use the uppercase Roman numeral plus a small plus sign.

Thus, within a major scale, the seven chords are notated as follows:

I	ii	iii	IV	V	vi	vii°

If you remember back to Chapter 2, each degree of the scale has a particular name—tonic, dominant, and so on. We can assign these names to the different chords, like this:

I	ii	iii	IV	V	vi	vii°
Tonic	Supertonic	Mediant	Subdominant	Dominant	Submediant	Leading Tone

Of these chords, the *primary chords*—the ones with the most weight—are the I, IV, and V. These also are the only major chords in the major scale—and often the only chords used within a song.

When describing chord progressions, we'll refer to chords by either their Roman numerals or their theoretical names (tonic, dominant, and so forth). You can figure out which specific chords (C Major, D minor, and so forth) to play, based on the designated key signature.

To make things easier, you can refer to the following table, which lists the seven scale-based chords for each major key signature.

Scale-Based Chords

Key Signature	Chords
C	
C#	
Db	
D	
Eb	
E	
F	
F#	

continues

Scale-Based Chords   (continued)

Key Signature	Chords
G♭	G♭ A♭min B♭min C♭ D♭ E♭min Fdim I ii iii IV V vi vii°
G	G Amin Bmin C D Emin F♯dim I ii iii IV V vi vii°
A♭	A♭ B♭min Cmin D♭ E♭ Fmin Gdim I ii iii IV V vi vii°
A	A Bmin C♯min D E F♯min G♯dim I ii iii IV V vi vii°
B♭	B♭ Cmin Dmin E♭ F Gmin Adim I ii iii IV V vi vii°
B	B C♯min D♯min E F♯ G♯min A♯dim I ii iii IV V vi vii°
C♭	C♭ D♭min E♭min F♭ G♭ A♭min B♭dim I ii iii IV V vi vii°

Creating a Progression

Let's see how you can use these Roman numerals to create a chord progression. For the time being we won't pay attention to the underlying harmonic theory; we'll just concentrate on the mechanics of creating a progression.

I mentioned earlier the popularity of the G, C, and D chords. In the key of G Major, these chords happen to fall on the first (G), fourth (C), and fifth notes of the scale. This makes these the I, IV, and V chords—or, more technically, the tonic, subdominant, and dominant.

If you've ever played any rock, country, or folk songs, you know that one of the more common chord progressions goes like this:

     G / / /   C / / /   G / / /   D / / /

(Naturally, the progression repeats—or ends with a final G chord.)

 NOTE

These examples use *slash notation,* where each slash (/) equals one beat. Measures are separated by spaces.

Because you know that the G = I, C = IV, and D = V, it's easy to figure out the Roman numeral notation. It looks like this:

     I   IV   I   V

There—you've just written your first chord progression!

The benefit of using this type of notation is you can apply the chord progression to other keys. Let's say you want to play this I-IV-I-V progression in the key of C. Referring back to the Scale-Based Chords table earlier in this chapter, you can translate the progression to these specific chords:

     C / / /   F / / /   C / / /   G / / /

This definitely makes things simpler.

It's All About Getting Home

The goal of most major chord progressions is to get back to the home chord—the tonic chord, or I. All the other chords in the progression exist as part of a roadmap to deliver you back to the I chord. The route can be simple (just a chord or two) or complex (lots and lots of different chords), but ultimately you want to end up back on I.

As you'll learn in the next section, certain chords naturally lead to the I chord. In addition, you can employ multiple-chord progressions to get you back to I—these are called *cadences* and are also discussed later in this chapter.

One Good Chord Leads to Another

Although you can write a song using any combination of chords that sounds good to your ears— even chords from other keys—in most cases chord progressions are based on a few simple rules. These rules come from a concept called *chord leading,* which says that certain chords naturally lead to other chords.

You can hear chord leading for yourself by playing some chords on the piano. To keep it simple, we'll stay in the key of C—so you don't have to play any of the black keys.

Start by playing a C Major chord (C-E-G). This is the I chord, which doesn't necessarily lead anywhere because, based on chord-leading rules, the I chord can be followed by any chord in the scale.

Now play a G Major chord (G-B-D). This is the V chord in the scale, and it definitely wants to go somewhere. But where? You could follow it with an F Major chord (F-A-C), but that isn't fully satisfying. Neither is D minor (D-F-A) or E minor (E-G-B) or even A minor (A-C-E). The only chord that sounds fully satisfying—the chord that V naturally leads to—is the I chord, C Major.

The rule here is that the V chord naturally leads back to the I chord. Although you can write another chord after a V, the best resolution is to follow the V with the I.

Other chords also have related chords that they naturally lead to. Some chords can even lead to more than one chord. To learn which chords lead where, take a look at the following table.

Chord Leading Reference

These Chords ...	Lead to These Chords ...
I	Any chord
ii	IV, V, vii°
iii	ii, IV, vi
IV	I, iii, V, vii°
V	I
vi	ii, IV, V, I
vii°	I, iii

Although there are exceptions to these rules, you can create a pleasing chord progression by following the order suggested by this chart. This means if you have a iii chord, you follow it with either a ii, IV, or a vi chord. Or if you have a vi chord, you follow it with either a ii, IV, V, or I chord, and so on.

Let's put together some of these combinations. We'll start, of course, with the I chord. Because I leads to any chord, let's go up one scale note and insert the ii chord after the I. According to our chart, ii can lead to either IV, V, or vii°. We'll pick V. Then, because V always leads to I, the next chord is a return to the tonic.

The entire progression looks like this:

```
I              ii             V              I
```

When you play this progression in the key of C, you get the following chords:

```
C / / /     Dm / / /     G / / /     C / / /
```

Sounds good, doesn't it?

Let's try another example. Again, we'll start with the tonic, but this time we'll use the vi chord as the second chord. According to the chart, vi can lead to either ii, IV, V, or I; let's pick IV. Then, because IV can lead to either I, iii, V, or vii°, we'll pick V as the next chord—which leads us back to I as our final chord.

The entire progression looks like this:

```
I         vi         IV         V         I
```

When you play this progression in the key of C, you get the following chords:

```
C / / /     Am / / /     F / / /     G / / /     C / / /
```

You should recognize that progression as the chords that drove thousands of doo-wop tunes in the 1950s and 1960s.

Let's return to that progression, and make an alternate choice for the third chord—ii instead of IV. Because ii also leads to V, we can leave the rest of the progression intact, which creates the following alternate progression:

```
I         vi         ii         V         I
```

This, when played in the key of C, results in these chords:

```
C / / /     Am / / /     Dm / / /     G / / /     C / / /
```

TIP

When you're playing a chord progression, the number of beats or measures allotted to each chord isn't set in stone. For example, you could play the I-IV-V progression with a single measure for each chord. Or you could play two measures of I, and a measure each of IV and V. Or you could play three measures of one and then two beats each of IV and V. It all depends on the needs of the song—and helps provide an almost infinite variety of possible chord combinations.

You can also work backward from where you want to end up—your final chord. Because in most cases you want the final chord to be the tonic (I), all you have to do is work through the options that lead to that chord. Consulting the Chord Leading Reference table, you find that four chords can lead to the I: IV, V, vi, and vii°. The obvious choice is the V chord, so that's what we'll use. Now we have to pick a chord to lead to V; the choices are ii, IV, vi, and I. Let's pick ii. Now we pick a chord that leads to the ii; the choices are I, iii, and vi. Let's pick iii. Now we pick a chord that leads to the iii; the choices are I, IV, and vii°. Let's pick I, which is also a good chord with which to start our phrase. When you put all these chords together, you get the following progression:

```
I          iii         ii         V          I
```

Play this progression in the key of C, and you use these chords:

```
C / / /     Em / / /     Dm / / /      G / / /      C / / /
```

Pretty easy, isn't it?

Ending a Phrase

When you come to the end of a musical phrase—which can be anywhere in your song, even in the middle of your melody—you use chords to set up a tension, and then relieve that tension. This feeling of a natural ending is called cadence, and there are some accepted chord progressions you can use to provide this feeling of completion.

Perfect Cadence

The most common phrase-ending chord progression uses the V (dominant) chord to set up the tension, which is relieved when you move on to the I (tonic) chord. This progression, called a *perfect cadence*, is notated V-I. In the key of C, it looks like this:

```
G / / /    C / / /
```

You could probably see this cadence coming, from the chord leading shown in the table named Chord Leading Reference earlier in this chapter. There's no better way to get back home (I) than through the dominant chord (V).

TIP

The V-I progression can be enhanced by using the dominant seventh chord (V7) instead of the straight V. This progression is notated V7-I.

Plagal Cadence

A slightly weaker ending progression uses the IV (subdominant) chord in place of the V chord. This IV-I progression is called a *plagal cadence;* in the key of C, it looks like this:

```
F / / /     C / / /
```

Although this is an effective cadence, it isn't nearly as strong as the perfect V-I cadence. For that reason, you might want to use a plagal cadence in the middle of your song or melody, and save the stronger perfect cadence for the big ending.

Imperfect Cadence

Sometimes, especially in the middle of a melody, you might want to end on a chord that isn't the tonic. In these instances, you're setting up an unresolved tension, typically by ending on the V (dominant) triad.

This type of ending progression is called an *imperfect cadence,* and you can get to the V chord any number of ways—I-V, ii-V, IV-V, and vi-V being the most common. In the key of C, these progressions look like this:

```
I-V:      C / / /      G / / /
ii-V:     Dm / / /     G / / /
IV-V:     F / / /      G / / /
vi-V:     Am / / /     G / / /
```

Interrupted Cadence

Even less final than an imperfect cadence is an ending progression called an *interrupted cadence.* In this progression, you use a V chord to trick the listener into thinking a perfect cadence is on its way, but then move to any type of chord except the tonic.

V-IV, V-vi, V-ii, and V-V7 progressions all are interrupted cadences—and, in the key of C, look like this:

V-IV:	G / / /	F / / /
V-vi:	G / / /	Am / / /
V-ii:	G / / /	Dm / / /
V-V7:	G / / /	G7 / / /

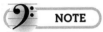

NOTE

In classical music theory, an interrupted cadence is more often called a *deceptive cadence*.

Common Chord Progressions

Given everything you've learned about chord leading and cadences, you should be able to create your own musically sound chord progressions. However, just in case you get stuck, let's take a look at some of the most popular chord progressions used in music today.

I-IV

It doesn't get much simpler than this, just the tonic (I) and the subdominant (IV) chords repeating back and forth, over and over. This is a cyclical progression, good for songs that don't really have a final resolution point.

In the key of C, the progression looks like this:

C / / /   F / / /

I-V

If you can cycle between the tonic and the subdominant (IV), why not the tonic and the dominant (V)? Like the first progression, the simplicity of this one makes it quite common in folk and some forms of popular music.

In the key of C, the progression looks like this:

C / / /   G / / /

Unlike the I-IV progression, this one has a bit more finality, thanks to the V-I relationship. But since you keep going back to the V (and then the I, and then the V again, and then the I again, and on and on), it still is very cyclical sounding.

I-IV-V

You can't get any more popular than the old I-IV-V progression. This is the progression (in the key of G) you're playing when you strum the chords G, C, and D on your guitar.

There are many different variations on the I-IV-V progression. You can leave out the IV, insert an extra I between the IV and the V, and even tack on another I-V at the end to wrap things up with a perfect cadence. You also can vary the number of beats and measures you devote to each chord.

One example of I-IV-V in a four-measure phrase might look like this, in the key of C:

```
C / / /     C / / /     F / / /     G / / /
```

You could also bunch up the IV and the V into a single measure, like this:

```
C / / /     C / / /     C / / /     F / G /
```

The progression also could be used over longer phrases, as in this eight-measure example:

```
C / / /     C / / /     C / / /     C / / /
F / / /     F / / /     G / / /     G / / /
```

TIP

This progression is often played with a dominant seventh chord on the fifth (V7), which provides increased tension before you return to the tonic.

The point is, these three chords are used in a huge number of modern songs—and make up the core of what many refer to as "three-chord rock and roll." They're not limited to rock, of course; many folk, country, jazz, rap, and even classical and show tunes are based on these three chords.

It's an extremely versatile progression.

I-IV-V-IV

This progression is a variation on I-IV-V. The variation comes in the form of a shift back to the subdominant (IV), which then forms a plagal cadence when it repeats back to the tonic. In the key of C, the progression looks like this:

```
C / / /     F / / /     G / / /     F / / /
```

It's a nice, rolling progression—not too heavy—without a strong ending feeling to it—which makes it nice for tunes that repeat the main melody line again and again.

I-V-vi-IV

This progression is another rolling one, good for repeating again and again. (That's because of the ending plagal cadence—the IV repeating back to I.)

In the key of C, it looks like this:

```
C / / /      G / / /      Am / / /     F / / /
```

I-ii-IV-V

This progression has a constant upward movement, resolved with a perfect cadence on the repeat back to I. In the key of C, it looks like this:

```
C / / /      Dm / / /     F / / /      G / / /
```

I-ii-IV

This is a variation on the previous progression, with a soft plagal cadence at the end (the IV going directly to the I, no V involved). In the key of C, it looks like this:

```
C / / /      Dm / / /     F / / /
```

As with all progressions that end with a plagal cadence (IV-I), this progression has a rolling feel, and sounds as if it could go on and on and on, like a giant circle.

I-vi-ii-V

This was a very popular progression in the 1950s, the basis of a lot of doo-wop and jazz songs. It's also the chord progression behind the song "I've Got Rhythm," and sometimes is referred to (especially in jazz circles) as the "I've Got Rhythm" progression.

In the key of C, it looks like this:

```
C / / /      Am / / /     Dm / / /     G / / /
```

I-vi-IV-V

This is a variation on the "I've Got Rhythm" progression, with a stronger lead to the V chord (IV instead of ii). It looks like this, in the key of C:

```
C / / /      Am / / /      F / / /      G / / /
```

This progression was also popular in the doo-wop era and in the early days of rock and roll. The defining factor of this progression is the descending bass line; it drops in thirds until it moves up a step for the dominant chord, like this: C-A-F-G. You've heard this progression (and that descending bass line) hundreds of times; it's a very serviceable progression.

I-vi-ii-V7-ii

This is another variation on the "I've Got Rhythm" progression, with an extra ii chord squeezed in between the final V and the return to I, and with the V chord played as a dominant seventh. In the key of C, it looks like this:

```
C / / /      Am / / /    Dm / / /      G7 / Dm /
```

By adding the ii chord between the V7 and the I, almost in passing, it takes the edge off the perfect cadence and makes the progression a little smoother.

IV-I-IV-V

As this progression shows, you don't have to start your chord progression on the tonic. In the key of C, it looks like this:

```
F / / /      C / / /      F / / /      G / / /
```

This progression has a bit of a rolling nature to it, but also a bit of an unresolved nature. You can keep repeating this progression (leading from the V back to the IV), or end the song by leading the progression home to a I chord.

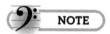

NOTE

The IV-I-IV-V progression is also frequently played at the end of a phrase in many jazz tunes. Used in this manner, it's called a *turnaround*. (See Chapter 16 to learn more.)

ii-V-I

This progression is quite popular in jazz, often played with seventh chords throughout. So you might actually play a ii7-V7-I progression, like this (in the key of C):

```
Dm7 / / /   G7 / / /    CM7 / / /
```

Sometimes jazz tunes cycle through this progression in a variety of keys, often using the circle of fifths to modulate through the keys. (That's the term you use any time you change the key within a song.)

Circle of Fifths Progression

There's one more chord progression that's fairly common, and it's based on the circle of fifths you learned about back in Chapter 4. Put simply, it's a progression where each chord is a fifth above the next chord; each chord functions as the dominant chord for the succeeding chord. The progression circles back around on itself, always coming back to the tonic chord, like this: I-IV-vii°-iii-vi-ii-V-I.

Here's what the progression looks like in the key of C:

```
C / / /   F / / /   Bdim / / /   Em / / /   Am / / /   D / / /   G / / /   C / / /
```

You can also play this progression backward, creating a circle of fourths, but that isn't nearly as common as the one detailed here.

Chromatic Circle of Fifths

The circle of fifths progression we just discussed is a simple one you can use without getting into nonscale chords. But there's also another, longer, circle of fifths progression, based on chromatic chords, that you might want to play around with.

This progression is a little too complex to write out in Roman numeral notation, but it works by having each chord function as the precise subdominant of the next chord—that is, the chords move in perfect fifths around the chromatic scale. Even more fun, each chord is turned into a dominant seventh chord, to make the dominant-tonic relationship more explicit.

Here's how it looks, in the key of C:

```
C / / /    C7 / / /    F / / /    F7 / / /    Bb / / /    Bb7 / / /
Eb / / /   Eb7 / / /   Ab/ / /    Ab7 / / /   Db / / /    Db7 / / /
Gb / / /   Gb7 / / /   B / / /    B7 / / /    E / / /     E7 / / /
A / / /    A7 / / /    D / / /    D7 / / /    G / / /     G7 / / /    C
```

You can jump on and off this progression at any point in the cycle. Kind of neat how it circles around, isn't it?

Singing the Blues

There's a unique chord progression associated with the genre of music we commonly call the *blues*. This blues form isn't relegated solely to blues music, however; you'll find this form used in many jazz and popular tunes, as well.

The blues progression is a 12-measure progression. (It's sometimes called a "12-bar blues.") This 12-measure progression repeats again and again throughout the melody and any instrumental solos.

The form is essentially a I-IV-I-V7-I progression, but spread over 12 measures, like this:

```
I  / / /        I  / / /        I  / / /        I  / / /
IV / / /        IV / / /        I  / / /        I  / / /
V7 / / /        V7 / / /        I  / / /        I  / / /
```

In the key of C, the blues progression looks like this:

```
C  / / /        C  / / /        C  / / /        C  / / /
F  / / /        F  / / /        C  / / /        C  / / /
G7 / / /        G7 / / /        C  / / /        C  / / /
```

Although these are the basic blues chords, you can use lots of variations to spice up individual songs. (Turn to Chapter 16 to see some of these variations.)

 NOTE

The blues progression is sometimes played with a V7 chord in the final measure.

Chords and Melodies

Although chords fill out a tune and provide its harmonic underpinning, you still need a melody to make a song.

The relationship between chords and melody is complex—and works a little like the proverbial chicken and the egg. You can start with one or the other, but in the end you have to have both.

This means you can write a melody to a given chord progression, or you can start with the melody and harmonize it with the appropriate chords. There's no set place to start; whether you start with the melody or the chords is entirely up to you.

Fitting Chords to a Melody

If you write your melody first, you then have to figure out which chords fit where. In many cases, it's a simple matter of applying one of the common chord progressions to your melody; more often than not, you'll find one that's a perfect fit.

To demonstrate, let's look at the chords behind some of the melodies we first examined back in Chapter 8.

"Michael, Row the Boat Ashore"

We'll start with "Michael, Row the Boat Ashore," which is a great example of a progression that relies heavily on the I, IV, and V chords—but with a few twists. Here's the song, complete with chords:

The chords to "Michael, Row the Boat Ashore."

The first twist in the chord progression comes in the fifth full measure (the start of the second phrase), which uses the iii chord (F#m) instead of the expected I. The second twist is the sixth measure, which moves down to the ii chord (Em). From there the melody ends with a perfect cadence (I-V-I), just as you'd expect.

So, if you started your hunt for the perfect progression for this melody by applying a standard I-IV-V progression, you'd be in the right neighborhood.

Bach's *Minuet in G*

Next, let's examine Bach's *Minuet in G*. Again, if you apply the standard I-IV-V progression, you'll be pretty much on the mark, as you can see here:

The chords to Bach's Minuet in G.

Old Johann was able to wring the most out of a very simple chord progression; in this case nothing more than I-IV-I-IV-I-V-I. Of course, this shows that you don't need a complex chord progression to create great music.

Dvořák's *New World Symphony*

Dvořák's *New World Symphony* uses another relatively simple chord progression, as you can see here:

The chords to Dvořák's New World Symphony.

The chord progression is basically I-V-I, with a neat little ii-V-I imperfect-to-perfect cadence at the end. There's also a unique non-scale twist in the second half of the third measure, where the I chord (D♭) suddenly gets a raised fifth and goes augmented. (In the orchestral score, the fifth is in the bass in this measure, for a very dramatic effect.) The use of the augmented tonic sets up an unexpected tension, without messing up the harmonic structure by throwing in something like a IV or a V chord where it wouldn't really belong.

Pachelbel's *Canon in D*

Even more simple is the chord progression behind Pachelbel's *Canon in D*, as you can see here:

The chords to Pachelbel's Canon in D.

Note how the chords flow, one into the next, based more or less on established chord leading rules—I-V-vi-iii-IV-I-IV-V—and then back to the I, again and again. You can play this progression all night long and not get tired of it; that's what makes it such a classic.

"Mary Had a Little Lamb"

Finally, let's figure out the chords to "Mary Had a Little Lamb." Just as the melody is a simple one, so is the accompanying chord progression—nothing more than I-V-I, repeated once. Sometimes the simplest progressions are the best!

The chords to "Mary Had a Little Lamb."

Chord Writing Tips

When it comes to fitting a chord progression to an existing melody, here are some tips to keep in mind:

- Try some common chord changes first. You'd be surprised how many melodies fit with the I-IV-V progression!

- The main notes in the melody (typically the notes that fall on the first and third beats of a measure) are the first, third, or fifth note of the underlying chord.

- Try to simplify the melody by cutting out the passing and neighboring tones (typically the shorter notes, or the notes not on major beats); the main notes you have left often will suggest the underlying chord.

- Make sure you're in the right key. In most cases, the "home" note in the melody is the tonic note of the underlying key.

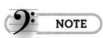
NOTE

Jazz musicians sometimes refer to chord progressions as chord changes—as in, "Dig those crazy changes, man!"

- Generally, the slower the tempo, the more frequent the chord changes. (So if you have a long whole note, or a note held over several measures, expect to find several different chords played behind that single note.)

- Work backward from the end of a melodic phrase, remembering that melodies almost always end on the I chord. You then can figure out the cadence leading to the I, and have half the song decoded fairly quickly.

- Chord changes typically fit within the measure structure, which means you're likely to see new chords introduced on either the first or third beat of a measure.

Writing a Melody to a Chord Progression

You don't have to start with a melody; you can base your tune on a specific chord progression and compose a melody that best fits the chords.

If you prefer to work this way, it helps to get a good feel for the chord progression before you start writing the melody. Play the chords again and again on either a piano or guitar. In many cases, you'll find a melody forming in your head; if this type of natural melody comes to you, you only have to figure out the notes and write them down.

If no natural melody occurs, it's time to roll out the theory. You don't want to work totally mechanically, but there are some basic approaches you can use. Take a look at these tips:

- Stay within the notes of the chords—at least for the main notes in the melody. If you're holding an A minor chord in a specific measure, work with the notes A, C, and E for your melody.

A simple melody for the popular I-IV-V chord progression—note the heavy use of chord notes in the melody. The notes indicated with a (p) are passing tones.

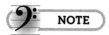 **NOTE**

In this example, the C in measure 3, beat 4 is technically an *anticipation,* not a passing tone. An anticipation is, in effect, an "eager" note—a note from the next chord that is sounded just a little earlier than the chord itself.

- Try to find a logical line between the main notes in different measures. For example, if your chord progression goes C-Am-F, realize that these chords have one note in common—the C. So you can base your melody around the C note. Conversely, if your chord progression goes C-F-G, you might want to pick three notes (one from each chord) that flow smoothly together—E to F to G, for example; or G to F to D.

- Use notes that emphasize the quality of the underlying chords. For example, when you're writing to a V7 chord, emphasize the tension by using either the root or the seventh of the chord in the melody.

- Once you pick your main tones, fill in the gaps with passing tones.

- Come up with an interesting rhythmic motif, and repeat that rhythm throughout the melody.

I wish there were a more complete set of rules for adding a melody to a chord progression, but we're getting into an area that is more art than science. As it should be! The best way to hone your skill is simply to work at it—play a lot of chord progressions, and practice writing different types of melodies over the chords. (And remember to read my companion book, *The Complete Idiot's Guide to Music Composition,* for lots more advice and instruction.)

Over time, you'll figure out your own rules for writing melodies—and develop your own melodic style.

Exercises

Exercise 10-1

Write the following chords in the key of F.

I   V   ii   vi   IV   iii   V7   vii °   IVM7   iim7

Exercise 10-2

Write the following chords in the key of D.

ii   IV   iii   vi   vii°   I   V7   iiim7   IM7   V

Exercise 10-3

Write the following chords in the key of E♭.

Exercise 10-4

Write the chords that lead from the following chords, in the key of C.

Exercise 10-5

Create the following types of cadences in the key of A.

Exercise 10-6

Figure out which chords go with the following melody. (Hint: there are two chords in every measure.)

Exercise 10-7

Write a melody to the following eight-measure chord progression.

The Least You Need to Know

- Every note of the scale has an associated chord, notated by a Roman numeral (uppercase for major; lowercase for minor).
- Chord progressions naturally lead back to the tonic, or I, chord of the underlying scale.
- Every chord naturally leads to at least one other chord; for example, the V chord naturally leads to the I.
- The final chords in a progression—the ones that ultimately lead back to I—are called a cadence.
- The most common chord progressions include I-IV, I-V, I-IV-V, I-IV-V-IV, I-V-vi-IV, I-ii-IV-V, I-ii-IV, I-vi-ii-V, I-vi-IV-V, I-vi-ii-V7-ii, IV-I-IV-V, and ii-V-I.

Phrases and Forms

Now that you know all about melodies and chord progressions, it's time to think about the entire piece of music, from start to finish. A piece of music, after all, is more than just an eight-measure melody (and accompanying chords) played once. Most pieces repeat a melody several times, and often contain more than one melody.

When you're constructing a song (or a longer piece of music), you have to consider the overall form of the piece. If you have a main melody, do you need to repeat that melody—and if so, where, and how many times? Do you need to add a second, contrasting melody? What about some sort of buffer or break between the two melodies? And how do you work your way into the main melody? How do you wrap things up at the end?

All these questions pertain to what we call *song form*. Song form is the sum of all the parts that make up your song, usually in some sort of logical order. Think of song form as the grammar you use when writing music. Just as you can analyze the pieces and parts of a sentence, you can also analyze the pieces and parts of a song and, not surprisingly, there are some common parts you probably want to use.

In This Chapter

- Understanding the parts of a piece of music
- Analyzing song structure
- Discovering head tunes

Parts of a Song

When you're writing popular music, there are accepted parts of a piece of music you have to work with. Not that you have to use each song part in each and every song you write; these parts are more like building blocks you can use (at your discretion) to construct your own individual piece of music.

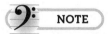

> **NOTE**
>
> In popular music, most any piece of music is typically called a *song*. In other types of music, such as classical music, the word "song" has more specific connotations regarding length and form and use of instruments and voices. To be more universal, you could use the word *composition,* or (less formally) the words piece or tune. Since this book, however, deals primarily with popular music, we'll use the word song—as long as you realize we're talking about any formal musical composition, not just something played by four guys with guitars.

Introduction

The introduction to a piece is typically (but not always) some sort of instrumental lead-in. The introduction can be of any length and doesn't even need to exist—a song can start cold on the first note of the first verse. The introduction may include a theme based on the song's main melody, played by one of the instruments, or maybe just a chord progression from either the verse or the chorus. In any case, the introduction is used to set up the first verse of the song and then is quickly forgotten.

Verse

The verse is the first main melody of the piece. It's an important melody, and often is repeated several times throughout the course of the song. Harmonically, the melody might end on the tonic chord (I), or it might end on the dominant (V), creating a tension that is resolved when you proceed to the chorus.

If your song has words, each instance of the verse typically has a different set of lyrics. The lyrics to the first verse are sometimes repeated in the final verse. In all cases, the verse should relate to and lead into the song's chorus.

Chorus

The chorus is the second main melody of the song, and the emotional high point of the piece. It should contain the main melodic theme, as well as any hook you might include to grab the listener. The hook can be in the melody, chords, rhythm, or lyrics—something unique and memorable that sets this song apart from all others. Choruses are often shorter than verses, often lasting just four or eight measures.

Bridge

The bridge is kind of a break in the middle of the piece. Most bridges sound completely different from the verse and chorus and are often based on a different harmonic structure. For example, a bridge might be based around the IV chord instead of the I chord. Bridges typically are short—only about eight measures. (That's why a bridge is sometimes called the "middle eight" of a song.)

Ending

The ending isn't necessarily a separate section of the song. Sometimes you end the song after the last chorus, either by stopping on the I chord or fading out the volume. More sophisticated songs have unique ending sections tacked on to the end of the song, which typically use some sort of cadence or turnaround (explained in Chapter 16). You might even want the ending to mirror the song's intro, or otherwise reflect the melodic or harmonic nature of the piece.

Putting It All Together

Most popular and jazz music is based on eight-measure phrases. Your verse might be one eight-measure phrase and your chorus, another. We keep track of the different parts of a song by assigning them letters—which shouldn't be confused with the letters we used to label the notes in a scale. (These letters have nothing to do with individual notes or pitches.)

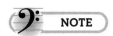

> **NOTE**
>
> The eight-measure phrase rule isn't hard and fast, although the concept of being divisible by 8 is somewhat rigidly followed. So in addition to the standard 8-measure phrases, you can have 16- and 32-bar phrases, both of which are divisible by 8. (Although if a phrase gets to be 32 bars long, it's probably more of a section than a phrase.)

The very first eight-measure phrase in your song—which is typically the first verse—is labeled "A." If the verse is repeated anywhere in the song, it retains its "A" labeling. The second eight-measure phrase—typically the chorus—is labeled "B." If the chorus repeats later in the song, the repeated chorus is still labeled "B." The third eight-measure phrase—the bridge, if you have one—is labeled "C." Additional phrases build on this lettering scheme.

Let's look at a song that has a verse, a chorus, a verse, and another chorus. The form of this song would look like this:

A   B   A   B

Note that when the verse repeats, we don't give it a new letter; it keeps the "A" designation—even if the lyrics change. Same thing with the chorus: the B section is always B, no matter how many times it repeats.

Now let's look at a song that has two verses, a chorus, and a final verse. The form of this song looks like this:

    A   A   B   A

Things get more interesting when you add a bridge to the mix. Consider a song with two verses, a chorus, a bridge, and a final chorus:

    A   A   B   C   B

It's not really that hard to follow, once you know what letters stand for what.

Incidentally, some songs are all A. This is fairly common in folk music, where you have one melodic phrase repeated over and over, each time with a different set of lyrics. Think of "If I Had a Hammer," or "Where Have All the Flowers Gone?" as good examples. Neither song has a chorus, per se; they're all verses, and lots of them.

 TIP

When you have variations of a single section like this, you can label each instance of the section by a number after the letter, as in A1, A2, A3, and so on.

Exercise

Exercise 11-1

Compose a 32-measure song in the ABCA form: verse, chorus, bridge, and verse. Use the key of G, in 4/4 time, and label each section of the piece.

The Least You Need to Know

- Most popular songs consist of a short instrumental intro, one or more verses, a chorus, a bridge, and an ending.
- Each part of the song is assigned a letter; the form of the song is notated by a combination of letters.

Accompanying

In Part 4, you learn how to train your ears so you can write down the music you hear. Then you discover how to create simple accompaniment parts on piano or guitar. Finally, you learn how to transpose a song in one key to a totally different key—no math required!

Transcribing What You Hear

In an ideal world, everything you need is served up to you on a silver platter. As a musician, that means you'll always get perfectly noted pieces of sheet music from which to read, with all the chords and melodies and rhythms clearly and correctly written out.

Unfortunately, we don't live in an ideal world: you won't always get sheet music for the songs you have to play; sometimes you'll be expected to "play by ear" and figure out the music on your own.

How do you write down a piece of music, note for note, based on a few listens to a recording? It's a particular skill, that's for sure; one that involves a technique called *ear training*. That means you have to train your ears to recognize certain rhythms and intervals, and be able to transfer what you hear to the written page.

In This Chapter

- Understanding why ear training is important
- Discovering how to actively listen
- Developing your tonal memory
- Learning how to transcribe songs from recordings

Training Your Ear

Consider the following: you're in a band that plays the latest hit songs, and the band leader points you to an online playlist or hands you a CD and asks you to learn a new tune—by tomorrow night. No sheet music, no one to answer your questions, no one to practice with you and help you figure it out—you're completely on your own, just you and the recording.

Or you're working with a songwriter who doesn't read music. Your friend sings a melody, and asks you to write it down so he can send it to a music publicist. He doesn't know what key the song is in, or what notes he's singing; he leaves those details up to you to figure out.

Maybe you're playing organ in the church choir. The guest vocalist this week approaches you just before Sunday's service, and says she'll be singing "Amazing Grace," in the key of G. She doesn't have any sheet music for you—"You know the song," she says—and if you don't, you'll have to learn it, fast.

Perhaps you're playing saxophone in a pickup band at your local bar. It's open mic night, and the next performer wants you to add some horn accompaniment to his tune. "It's a 12-bar blues," he says, "in the key of A. You have a solo after the second chorus." No music, no nothing—just you, onstage, winging it.

All of these situations require you to think on your feet—or, more properly, to play by ear. You need to be able to hear a song and figure out what chords and notes are being played, without the benefit of any written music.

This might sound daunting, but it's a skill you need to develop. You have to be able to hear a melody or chord progression, and then *transcribe* what you hear. With practice, you'll be able to do this quickly and accurately; it can even become second nature. All you have to do is train your ears.

 DEFINITION

Transcribing is the art of writing down melodies and chords by ear, without the benefit of any other written notation.

Transcribing music involves three distinct steps:

1. Listen

2. Process

3. Document

You begin by listening to the music—not for passive enjoyment, but more actively, so that you clearly hear every note. Then you process what you've heard, figuring out what notes and chords and rhythms are being played. Finally, you document the music you've processed, either by writing down the notes on paper, or using the processed music as a basis for live playing or improvisation.

With practice, you'll move through the listen-process-document system almost subconsciously; the notes will come to you automatically when you hear them, without a lot of work on your part. So warm up your ears—it's time for the training to begin!

 NOTE

Ear training is a difficult skill to learn. Developing listening skills takes time and guidance, and for most people is best accomplished in a classroom setting or with an experienced teacher. If you're serious about training your ears, a good place to start is with this book's online audio files. You can then check your progress against the answers provided in Appendix B. You also can pick up a copy of Ron Gorow's *Hearing and Writing Music: Professional Training for Today's Musician*. Even better, head down to your local community college or university and sign up for an ear-training class. The personal feedback and guidance you'll receive from the instructor will be worth the effort.

Listening—Actively

Before we get into ear training proper, you need to learn how to actively listen to music. This isn't listening for enjoyment; it's listening to remember, and to analyze.

Start by isolating yourself from the hurly-burly of your day-to-day life. Turn off the TV, close the windows, and block out all extraneous noises—the air conditioner, the refrigerator, the hum of the air pump in your fish tank. Create an environment in which you can focus on the music, without any distractions.

Prepare the music. This means setting up your computer or audio system with a good pair of speakers, or even a quality set of headphones. Make sure the music source can be easily accessed; you'll be doing a lot of clicking backward and forward.

Now get yourself comfortable. Find a comfy chair, or a couch, or even a place on the floor, surrounded by pillows. Get comfortable, but don't get relaxed; instead, remain alert and ready for input. When you're fully prepared, it's time to listen. Select a song, one of your favorites; then click or press the play button … and listen.

Begin by listening to the overall form of the song. Determine where one phrase ends and another begins. Figure out where the verses are, and the chorus, and even the bridge, if there is one. Get a feel for how the song is constructed, for its internal logic, for the way it flows from one point to another.

Now listen to the song again, but this time focus carefully on the melody line. Listen hard, and listen critically. Note where the melody goes up, and where it goes down. Note where the melody changes, where the verse ends and the chorus begins, and where any variations occur. Listen to it as many times as you need, until you're sure you can sing it back, verbatim.

Return to the start of the song, and this time don't listen to the melody. Instead, listen to the bass line. Listen to the tones played, and to the rhythms. Note how the bass notes relate to the melody, and to the other parts. Listen to the bass part and memorize the bass part; then play the song back again and sing along with the bass, from memory.

Again, return to the start of the song. This time listen to another part—the lead guitar, or the piano, or the saxophone. It doesn't matter; pick a part, and follow it from start to finish. Listen critically, and hear how this part fits with the bass and the melody and all the other parts. Listen until you have the part memorized.

Repeat this process until you *know* all the parts of the song. Get to the point where you can sing back any given part, without prompting. Let that song get inside your brain; become one with the music.

When you're isolating the bass line, you might want to turn up the bass (and turn down the treble) on your audio system, to better hear the low notes.

Finally, listen to the entire song again and try to figure out where the chord changes are. There might be a new chord every 4 beats, or 8, or even 16. Figure out the time signature (probably 4/4), and then try to lay a map of the chord changes over the form of the song.

This is how you actively listen to a song. You're not listening for enjoyment (you can do that separately); you're listening to *learn*—and to remember. Once you can recall a part exactly, from memory, you're one step closer to figuring out the notes behind the part, and transcribing it to paper.

Developing Super Hearing

As part of your active listening, you have to be able to discern the component parts of the music. You have to be able to hear discrete pitches and intervals, hear different rhythms, and even hear the individual pitches within each chord. Sound difficult? It is—which is why you need to *practice!*

Hearing Pitch

 Lesson 1, Track 2

The first part of the music you need to hear is the pitch. You need to be able to listen to a pitch, isolate it, and then replicate it. In plain English, that means you need to be able to sing back any specific pitch you hear in a song. To do this, you have to develop what is called *tonal memory*, or *pitch memory*. This is simply the ability to recall a specific pitch, outside the context of the song or melody.

You can develop your tonal memory with this simple exercise. Take a half-full glass of water and hit it (gently!) with the edge of a spoon. The glass will produce a distinct pitch. Listen to the pitch, and fix it in your head. Wait until the glass stops ringing, then wait a few seconds more, then sing or hum the note that you heard. While you're singing (or humming), hit the glass again; if your tonal memory was on target, the second tone generated by the glass will be the same as the tone you're singing. If not, try it again—and pay more attention this time.

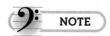 **NOTE**

When you hear notes or melodies inside your head (in your inner voice), you're *internalizing* the music.

Repeat this exercise, adding more time between hitting the glass and singing the note. The longer you can hold the note in your head, the better developed your sense of tonal memory will be.

Next, try to find that pitch on an instrument. (Use whatever instrument you like—piano, guitar, trumpet, whatever—it doesn't matter.) Hit the glass, wait a minute, sing the pitch, and then try to play that pitch on your instrument. Don't worry if you can't find the pitch right off. You might need to poke around a few related notes until you find the one that matches what you're singing. That's natural. With practice, you'll be able to more quickly identify individual tones.

Obviously, you want to verify the note you're playing with the source—the ringing glass. Play the note on your instrument while you hit the glass; if you have the right note, they'll be in unison.

You can extend this exercise by generating different notes with different objects. (You can also fill the glass to different levels to produce different pitches.) When you're comfortable with your progress, fire up a track and pick a single note from the melody. Repeat the exercise, this time trying to reproduce that melody note. Replay the track to check your accuracy.

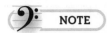

NOTE

Interestingly, about 5 percent of musicians (just musicians—not the general population) have something called *absolute pitch* or *perfect pitch,* which means they can, with no prompting or assistance, correctly sing or identify any given pitch in the scale. Some people claim to be able to help you develop this skill, but in general it is virtually impossible for anyone over the age of five or so to "learn" perfect pitch. (Not 100 percent impossible, but almost.) In any case, you don't really need this kind of long-term pitch memory to transcribe music. You can get along fine with the short-term pitch memory that we all possess, along with a good interval memory, which we'll discuss next.

Hearing Intervals

    Lesson 2, Track 11

If you can hear and reproduce a single note, what about two of them?

That's right: the next step is to develop your tonal memory to decipher and reproduce pitch intervals.

Before you begin your exercises, you need to develop an internal database of relative interval relationships. That means internalizing all the different intervals within a given object—remembering what each interval sounds like.

The best way to do this is to sit down at your instrument and play each interval until it's burned into your brain. Play a minor second, and a major second, and a minor third, and a major third, and so on, until you have each interval committed to memory. Can you sing a minor third? If not, you need to study some more.

Of course, there are shortcuts you can take. If you can remember specific snatches of melody, you can associate those melodies with particular intervals. The following table provides some melodic shortcuts for your interval training.

Intervals Found in Popular Melodies

Interval	Song-Specific Phrase	
Ascending		
Minor second	Theme from *Jaws*	Dum-dum … (bass line)
	"As Time Goes By" (from *Casablanca*)	YOU MUST remember this …
Major second	"Frere Jacques"	FRE-RE Jacques …
	"Happy Birthday"	Hap-PY BIRTH-day to you …

Interval	Song-Specific Phrase	
Minor third	"To Dream the Impossible Dream"	TO DREAM the impossible dream …
	Brahms Lullaby	LULLA-BY and goodnight …
Major third	"Have Yourself a Merry Little Christmas"	HAVE YOUR-self a merry little Christmas …
	"When the Saints Go Marching In"	OH WHEN the saints …
Perfect fourth	"Here Comes the Bride"	HERE COMES the bride …
	"Amazing Grace"	A-MAZ-ing grace …
	"We Wish You a Merry Christmas"	WE WISH you a merry Christmas …
Tritone	"Maria" (from *West Side Story*)	MA-RI-a …
Perfect fifth	Theme from *Goldfinger*	GOLD-FIN-ger …
	"My Favorite Things" (from *The Sound of Music*)	RAIN-DROPS on roses …
	"Twinkle Twinkle Little Star"	TWINKLE TWINKLE little star …
	Chant of the Wicked Witch's guardsmen in *The Wizard of Oz*	YO-EE-oh …
Minor sixth	"Sunrise, Sunset" (from *Fiddler on the Roof*)	IS this THE little girl …
Major sixth	"NBC" chime	N-B-C (first two notes)
	"Jingle Bells"	DASH-ING through the snow …
	"It Came Upon the Midnight Clear"	IT CAME upon the midnight clear …
Minor seventh	"There's a Place for Us" (from *West Side Story*)	THERE'S A place for us …
	Theme from *Star Trek*	Doo-doooo … (first two notes)
Major seventh	"Cast Your Fate to the Wind"	(first two notes of the melody)
	"Somewhere Over the Rainbow"	SOME-where O-ver the rainbow …
Octave	"Somewhere Over the Rainbow"	SOME-WHERE over the rainbow …
	"A Christmas Song"	CHEST-NUTS roasting on an open fire …

continues

Intervals Found in Popular Melodies   (continued)

Interval	Song-Specific Phrase	
Descending		
Minor second	"Joy to the World" (Christmas carol)	JOY TO the world, the Lord is come …
	"Spinning Wheel" (Blood, Sweat and Tears)	RIDE A painted pony …
Major second	"Three Blind Mice"	THREE BLIND mice …
	"Mary Had a Little Lamb"	MA-RY had a little lamb …
	"Yesterday" (The Beatles)	YES-TERDAY, all my troubles seemed so far away …
Minor third	"Jesus Loves Me"	JE-SUS loves me this I know …
	"Hey Jude" (The Beatles)	HEY JUDE …
Major third	"Swing Low, Sweet Chariot"	SWING LOW, sweet chariot …
	"Good Night Ladies" (from *The Music Man*)	GOOD NIGHT ladies …
	"Summertime" (from *Porgy and Bess*)	SUM-MER-time, and the livin' is easy …
Perfect fourth	"Born Free"	BORN FREE …
	"My Girl" (The Temptations)	MY GIRL, talkin' 'bout my girl …
Tritone	European police siren	
Perfect fifth	Theme from *The Flintstones*	FLINT-STONES, meet the Flintstones …
	"Feelings"	FEEL-INGS, whoa, whoa, whoa, feelings …
Minor sixth	Theme from *Love Story*	WHERE DO I begin …
Major sixth	"Over There"	O-VER there …
	"Nobody Knows the Trouble I've Seen"	NO-BOD-y knows …
Minor seventh	"Watermelon Man"	Water-MEL-on MAN …
Major seventh	"Have Yourself a Merry Little Christmas"	And HAVE YOUR-self a merry little Christmas now …
Octave	"Salt Peanuts" (Dizzy Gillespie)	Salt PEA-NUTS, salt peanuts …

Exercise your interval memory the same way you did your tonal memory. Start by listening to a song and picking two adjacent notes in the melody—the first two notes are often the best to work with. Wait a few seconds; then try to sing the two notes. Verify your accuracy by playing the song again.

Once you can internalize the interval, try to determine what interval you're singing. Is it a second? A third? Is it major or minor? Determine the interval, and then try to reproduce the interval on your instrument. Once you can accurately play the interval, you can verify the specific interval you guessed. (For example, if you find yourself playing a G and then a B, you know you're playing a major third.)

 TIP

> When you first start listening to intervals, you should focus on the relative distance between the two notes. Is it a wide span between the pitches? If so, the interval is a larger one; maybe a fifth or a sixth or something even larger. Is it a narrow span between the pitches? If so, the interval is a smaller one; maybe some sort of second or third. Narrow the possibilities down as much as possible before you determine the precise interval.

Hearing Rhythms

 Lesson 4, Track 27

We'll set aside pitches for a moment and instead focus on note durations—in other words, your *rhythmic memory.* Use the same technique as you did before, but this time listen to the rhythm of a song's melody. Start by figuring out the time signature of the song and breaking the melody (in your head) into measures. Now pick the first few beats of the melody's first measure. Stop the playback, fix that rhythm in your head, and then pound it out with your hand on a table. Repeat this process until you can hold the rhythm in your head for half a minute or longer.

Once you can repeat a short rhythmic phrase, it's time to up the ante. Try repeating the rhythm for an entire measure; then two, then four, then for the entire melody. Always check your accuracy by pounding the table in time to the original song.

With the entire rhythm of the melody committed to memory, use the theory you've learned and try to transcribe the rhythm. Start small, a beat or two at a time. Make sure the rhythm you write is mathematically sound; for example, if the song is in 4/4, all the notes have to add up to a full whole note. (That means four quarters, or eight eighths, or two quarters and four eighths, or whatever.)

Once you've written down the entire rhythm, play back the song again, this time reading the rhythm you've written. If you notice a discrepancy, correct it; otherwise, repeat the exercise with another song, this time one that is more rhythmically complex.

Hearing Melodies

Lesson 5, Track 36

Now that you can hear individual notes, intervals, and rhythms, you should be able to hear and transcribe complete melodies. All you have to do is put together everything you hear, in the right order, to develop your melodic memory.

Although you can piece together a melody one note or interval at a time, it's easier if you try to grasp the big picture first. That means figuring out how many measures long the melody is, and how it's broken up into phrases. Once you can disassemble a melody into its component parts, you should focus on each part separately.

On what pitch does this part of the melody start? On what pitch does it end? On what pitch does the middle of the phrase end? If you try to pinpoint individual parts of the melody, it should be relatively easy to connect the dots and fill in the empty spaces with the proper passing and neighboring tones.

Once you've written out the entire melody—including both pitches and rhythmic notes—remember to verify your accuracy by playing back the melody you've written. Compare the melody you play with the melody you first heard; the better you get, the closer they'll match up.

Hearing Keys

Once you can notate a melody, you should be able to determine what key the song is in. For example, if your melody incorporates a B♭—but no other flat or sharp notes—it's a good guess that the song is written in the key of F. (As you probably remember from Chapter 4, the key of F has a single flat.) If the melody has an F♯ and a C♯, you're probably in the key of D.

Another way to determine the key is to fix the home pitch of the melody. If the melody keeps resolving to G, chances are you're in the key of G. (Unless, that is, the melody is minor—in which case, you could be in the key of G minor.)

Test your guess by using your instrument to play a major scale in the designated key, while the original song is playing. If all the notes fit, you've guessed right. If not, try a related key—a key one or two steps away on the circle of fifths.

Hearing Chords and Chord Progressions

 Lesson 6, Track 41

The last piece of the puzzle concerns the underlying chord structure. You need to hear when the chords change, and what they change to.

When determining chords, it helps to listen to the song's bass line. If you listen to the notes the bass is playing, 9 times out of 10 the main notes—all embellishment aside—will be the root notes of the underlying chords. For example, if you know the song is in the key of C and the bass player plays, in successive measures, C, A, F, and G, it's a good guess that the chord progression is C-Am-F-G.

You should also listen carefully to determine whether you're hearing a major or a minor chord. Remember, major chords are happy sounding; minor chords are a little sad.

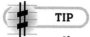 **TIP**

If you're having trouble hearing the chords, you can always try to figure out the chords from the notes of the melody, which you learned how to do in Chapter 10.

Once you've figured out the chords in the song, you should test your chord transcription against the melody you've previously transcribed. Make sure the notes of the melody fit within the chord structure; if not, you probably need to rethink a few chords.

The real test comes when you play your chords against the original recording. Be especially careful to match where your chords change with where the chords change in the original song. It's not uncommon to accidentally skip a chord change or two, so listen closely to make sure you picked up on all the changes.

Writing It All Down

If you've followed the exercises carefully, you've ended up with a complete transcription of the melody and chords for a specific song. Congratulations! It's a lot of work, I know, but this new-found skill is one you'll use again and again as you progress in the music field.

You can further develop this skill by transcribing other parts of the song, not just the melody. If the song has a horn section, try to figure out and transcribe each individual horn part. If there's an orchestral backing, work on transcribing the string parts. If there's a fancy rhythm section, isolate and transcribe the rhythms played by each individual percussionist.

Further developing your transcribing skill is especially important if you choose to pursue the fields of composing or arranging. You can certainly challenge yourself by transcribing an entire big-band arrangement for your high school jazz band, a full choral arrangement for your church choir, or a string quartet for your community orchestra. There's value in this skill—and a great sense of accomplishment when you get it right.

Exercises

Exercise 12-1

Play each of the following notes on your instrument, wait for 30 seconds, and then sing them back.

Exercise 12-2

Sing each of the following ascending intervals, starting on any note you like.

- Major third
- Perfect fifth
- Perfect fourth
- Major second

- Minor second
- Minor third
- Octave
- Tritone

Exercise 12-3

Sing each of the following descending intervals, starting on any note you like.

- Minor third
- Major second
- Perfect fifth
- Major sixth

- Perfect fourth
- Major seventh
- Major third
- Minor sixth

Exercise 12-4

Sing all the notes of the following chords, one after another. (Start on any root note you like.)

- Major chord
- Minor chord
- Diminished chord
- Augmented chord

- Major seventh chord
- Minor seventh chord
- Dominant seventh chord
- Major ninth chord

Exercise 12-5

Transcribe the rhythm (only) of "I Got Rhythm."

Exercise 12-6

Transcribe the melody of "This Land Is Your Land."

Exercise 12-7

Transcribe the melody and chords of one of your favorite popular songs.

Exercise 12-8

Listen to and complete all of this book's online ear training exercises, and check your answers in Appendix B.

The Least You Need to Know

- Ear training is necessary for those times when you don't have written music to work with—or when you want to figure out a song you've recently heard.
- The key to transcribing a song is to listen, process what you've heard, and then document what you've processed.
- To accurately analyze a piece of music, you have to learn how to actively listen—to isolate and then remember the individual parts of the song.
- As part of the ear training process, you must develop your intrinsic tonal, interval, and rhythmic memory, so that you can remember and replicate the pitches, rhythms, and melodies you hear.
- Once you've transcribed the entire melody, you can more easily figure out the song's key signature and its underlying chord structure.

CHAPTER 13

Accompanying Melodies

If you play piano or guitar, at some point you'll be asked to accompany another musician or group of musicians. Maybe it's playing behind a singer at church, or backing up your children's choir at school, or even vamping behind a harmonica soloist in a blues band. Whatever the situation, you'll be expected to provide at least rudimentary backing to the primary musicians.

If, along with this request, you also are handed a page of detailed sheet music, you're set. All you have to do is read your part, play the notes, and take your bows.

However, if there's no written music accompanying the request, you have your work cut out for you. Depending on the gig, you might have to transcribe the melody, figure out the chords, and compose your own part—all of which you can do, if you have the proper grounding in music theory.

In This Chapter

- Working with a lead sheet
- Figuring out what to play
- Understanding different types of accompaniment
- Adding a more interesting bass part
- Accompanying on guitar

What's the Score?

When you're asked to accompany someone on piano (or guitar, for that matter), you should first figure out how much homework you need to do. This is determined by the amount of written music you're given.

The best of all possible situations is that you receive a complete musical score. If this is the case, you don't need to read any further in this chapter—you're set!

However, it's more likely that you'll be provided with only sketchy written information—or none at all. If this is the case, you need to apply the skills you've learned in the previous chapters to figure out just what to play.

Working from a Lead Sheet

Here's the 411: you're given a sheet of music that includes the melody and the chords—what musicians call a *lead sheet*. It will look something like this:

A typical lead sheet—melody and chord symbols.

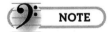 **NOTE**

Learn more about lead sheets and other types of arrangements in Chapter 21.

With this lead sheet in hand, what do you play?

The temptation for many novice musicians is to play the melody with your right hand and form the chords with your left hand. You should resist this temptation.

When you read a lead sheet, the melody (also known as the lead) is provided for your reference only. Unless you're playing solo piano in a cocktail bar, you're not expected to play the melody, except maybe during instrumental breaks.

No, what you're expected to play are the *chords*—along with any kind of embellishment or harmony you can create to play behind the melody.

NOTE

If you play in a cover band, jazz band, or other casual ensemble, you'll see lots of lead sheets. The so-called "fake books" many musicians use contain hundreds of lead sheets for popular songs in a variety of genres.

But the main thing you need in this situation is to play the chords, which you have—printed in big, bold letters on your lead sheet. Play the chords themselves with your right hand, while you play the root note of the chord (the bass line) with your left hand.

That's all you have to play, and it isn't hard at all.

 TIP

When you're playing chords with your right hand, try to avoid playing every chord in the standard 1-3-5 inversion. Try different inversions–different *voicings*–to better group the notes from adjacent chords together. (Turn back to Chapter 9 for more information on chord inversions.) For example, if you're alternating between the C and the F chord, you might play the C chord C-E-G, but then play the F chord C-F-A (first inversion), which lets you leave your thumb on the C note for both chords.

Working from a Chord Sheet

A chord sheet is like a lead sheet, but without the melody written out. Sometimes you'll see slash notation for each beat, other times the chords will be placed over a song's lyrics. Working from a chord sheet is just like working from a lead sheet—play the chords with your right hand and the root of the chord with your left. A typical chord sheet looks like this:

A chord sheet—no melody.

Working from a Melody

Sometimes you get the melody (in the form of a lead sheet) *without* chords. All you have to go on is the melody—no chords, no bass line, no anything else.

A melody sheet—no chords.

What do you do now?

First, don't panic. Second, remember back to Chapter 10, in which you learned how to create a chord progression based on a melodic line. That is the skill you need to draw on now.

Take the melody you were given and go off by yourself for a half hour or so. Play the melody on the piano, and try to figure out what chords sound good with that melody. If it's a familiar song, the chords might come easily to you; if you've never heard the song before, you have your work cut out for you. In any case, apply the rules you learned back in Chapter 10, and write out your own chord progression for this melody.

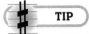

TIP

When you're trying to figure out the chords behind a melody, you can take several different approaches. The best, as you learned in Chapter 10, is to try some common chord progressions. See if I-IV-V fits the melody; if not, try I-ii-V, or I-vi-IV-V, or the "circle of fifths" progression. Chances are, one of the common chord progressions will fit or at least come close.

The key thing here is that the chords you write are now *your* chords. Even if they're not quite the established chords for this melody, you can get away with it by claiming that this is your unique harmonization. You're at the piano, and you're in charge, so what you play must be right!

Now, if you're playing along with other musicians—perhaps a bass player or a guitarist—you don't want to end up with three different sets of chords to this single melody. If you're playing in a group, put your heads together and work out the chord progressions as a group. Heck, maybe one of you actually knows the chords already! In any case, three heads are better than one, and together you should be able to come up with just the right chord progression for this song.

Working from Nothing

Now we visit the worst-case scenario. You're asked to play piano accompaniment and you're given no music at all. All you have are your ears and your fingers, and all the skills you've picked up from reading this book.

Now you can panic!

In this situation, it's okay to ask for help. Ask the person in charge if he or she has *anything* to give you—a lead sheet, a lyric sheet, an old trumpet part—anything at all. (Anything is better than nothing in this scenario.) Ask what key the song is in. Ask if there's anyone who knows the chords and can either teach them to you or write them down for you. Ask if anyone has a recording of the song you can take home and listen to.

In short, ask for all the help you can get.

Whatever meager help you get, you're now on your own. It's time to fall back on the ear-training skills you learned back in Chapter 12. You'll need to figure out the melody, figure out the key, and figure out the chords. In short, you have to reconstruct the song from memory and hope you get it right.

Then, when you start to play and the vocalist says "Those aren't the right chords!" make sure you have something small but heavy nearby—because you'll want to throw it!

Working the Form

Once you get the chords written down, you'll need to write down some sort of "cheat sheet" to help you remember the form of the song. Do you play one or two verses before the first chorus? How long is the introduction? Is there an instrumental break in the middle—and for how many measures? Do you fade out at the end, or stop cold?

You'll need to figure all this out and write it down, so you'll remember when to start, when to stop, and what to do in between. Use the form notation (AABA, ABCA, and so forth) you learned back in Chapter 11 to help you keep your place.

Playing the Part

Once you have the chords written down, you have to play the song. Because there's no formal piano part, you're on your own in terms of figuring out what type of part to play. Fortunately, you can employ some common accompaniment techniques; you don't have to reinvent the wheel.

Block Chord Accompaniment

The easiest type of accompaniment to play is the *block chord* accompaniment. This approach is exactly as it sounds: whenever there's a chord change, you put all your fingers on the keyboard (at the same time) and play the chord.

That's it. You don't play any special rhythms, you don't arpeggiate the chord, you don't do anything except *plunk!* the notes of the chord all at once.

All you have to do is put the three (or more) notes of the chord in your right hand and double the root of the chord with your left hand, like this:

Accompanying a melody with block chords.

The primary benefit of playing a block chord accompaniment is that it's easy—for you, anyway. The drawback is that it's a rather sparse accompaniment; it really doesn't add anything to the music, except to provide the most basic harmonic underpinning to the melody.

Still, if block chords are all you can master, that's what you should play. No one will ever accuse you of getting in the way or covering up the melody!

Rhythmic Accompaniment

There's another way to play chords that isn't quite as boring as the block-chord approach. You play the block chords, but with a more interesting rhythmic pattern.

What kind of pattern am I talking about? There are several you can choose from, including these:

Rhythmic accompaniment in quarter notes.

Rhythmic accompaniment with a syncopated rhythm.

Rhythmic accompaniment with a syncopated dotted quarter note rhythm—kind of a Latin feel.

You can even break up the rhythm slightly by playing your left hand (the bass) on beats one and three, and your right hand (the chords) on two and four, like this:

Playing the chords on the backbeat.

Or, if you want a more lively sound, play the bass on each beat and the chords as eighth notes on each upbeat (plus the downbeat of one), like this:

Playing the chords on the upbeat.

The benefit of this approach is that it provides a driving pulse for the song. The drawback is that you have to pick the right kind of pulse, which requires you to have some sense of rhythm.

If you don't have any natural rhythm, you might want to stick to block chords.

Arpeggiated Accompaniment

If you're playing a slower song, you might want to break up the chords and play the individual notes in a sequence, like an arpeggio. You can create a simple *arpeggiated accompaniment* by playing straight eighth notes over two beats, with the root of the chord on beat one, the third of the chord on the first upbeat, the fifth on beat two, and the third (again) on the second upbeat. (An arpeggiated accompaniment is often called a *broken chord accompaniment* because you break the chord apart and play each note separately.)

Written out, it looks something like this:

Playing an arpeggiated accompaniment.

You can vary this accompaniment by changing up the order of the chord tones, varying the rhythm, or even adding passing notes, like this:

An arpeggiated accompaniment with passing tones in addition to the main chord tones.

If you make sure you play the root of the chord in the bass, you have a quick and easy accompaniment for all types of music.

Moving Bass

Once you get good at these simple types of accompaniment, you can spice things up by playing a more complex bass part.

So far, all you have to do is play the root of the chord—in time!—with your left hand. However, if you listen to just about any song from the pop era, starting with the Beatles and the Motown sound, you'll hear a lot more in the bass than just the root. That's because bass guitarists in the '60s upped the ante and started playing some really interesting bass parts.

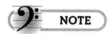 **NOTE**

> James Jamerson, the great Motown bassist, was one of the pioneers of this new style of bass playing. One of the most influential bass parts ever recorded was on the Four Tops' hit "Bernadette"—which is James Jamerson at the top of his form.

If you want to add more bass to your piano accompaniments, start by adding passing tones between the root notes of consecutive chords, like this:

Passing notes in the bass.

You're not limited to the root in the bass, either. Many bass parts provide interest by stopping on the third or the fifth of the chord, instead of on the root. If you expand on this concept you end up with a *walking bass line*, such as that found in a lot of jazz music. A walking bass line goes beyond simple passing tones by "walking" up and down the scale, like this:

A walking bass line.

As you develop your accompanying skills, you can elaborate on the bass or the chords in lots of different ways. Just remember to listen to the song and play a part that's appropriate.

One Good Strum Deserves Another

Pianos aren't the only accompanying instruments, of course. If you play guitar, you have to face many of the same challenges a piano player does when asked to provide accompaniment to others.

Chief of these challenges, of course, is figuring out what chords to play—which, you now know, is within your grasp. All you have to do is use the skills you learned previously in this book.

Once you've figured out the chords, you have to play them. In most instances, you can get by with simple strumming. You can strum on the first beat of every measure, you can strum on every beat, you can strum a backbeat on two and four, or you can strum in a more complex rhythm. Depending on the song, you can even break up the chords by playing one string at a time in an arpeggiated pattern. The important thing is to use your ears and play what fits the music.

And make sure you keep up with the changes!

Exercises

Exercise 13-1

Play a block-chord accompaniment based on the following lead sheet.

Exercise 13-2

Play a rhythmic accompaniment based on the following lead sheet.

Exercise 13-3

Play an arpeggiated accompaniment based on the following lead sheet.

Exercise 13-4

Play an accompaniment with a moving bass part, based on the following lead sheet.

The Least You Need to Know

- If you're given a lead sheet with chord notation, play the chords as written.
- If you're given a melody sheet with no chords noted—or no music at all—you have to figure out the chords before you play.
- When accompanying other musicians, play the chord with your right hand and the root of the chord with your left.
- You can play many different types of accompaniment—block chords, simple rhythms, broken chords, and so on—depending on the mood and tempo of the song itself.
- Before you play a new song, make sure you sketch out the form of the song (verse, chorus, and so forth) so that you don't get lost in the middle of things.

Transposing to Other Keys

You're sitting at your piano, on stage, ready to play the next tune, when the female vocalist walks over to you.

"This song's a little high for me in B♭," she says. "Take it down to A."

Huh?

Or maybe you're just starting to play guitar, don't know all the chords yet, and just got the sheet music for one of your favorite songs. You blanch when you discover that the song is in the key of G♭. G-flat! Who plays in G-flat? You don't know any chords in G-flat—not a one!

But you *do* know all your chords in G; maybe there's a way to change the song from G♭ to G.

Perhaps you're arranging a Christmas carol for your church choir, which will be accompanied by a solo trumpet. You hand the trumpet player his part, he plays what you thought was supposed to be a C, but it comes out as a B♭ instead, according to the notes on your piano.

What gives?

All three of these examples are situations in which you need to know how to *transpose* a piece of music from one key to another—which is what this chapter is all about.

In This Chapter

- Understanding transposition
- Discovering when you need to transpose a song
- Learning different methods of transposition
- Using computerized music notation programs to transpose your songs automatically

Move Your Notes Around

Transposition is the art of translating a note or chord from one key to another. It's really a math exercise—this note in this key equals that note in that key. When you transpose a note or a melody or a chord, you take it from one key, and instead play the equivalent note, melody, or chord in another key.

For example, let's say you're playing the note C in the key of C—the key's tonic note. When you transpose that note to the key of F, you now play an F—which is the tonic note for the key of F.

Sounds easy enough, doesn't it?

Let's look at a more complex example: say you're in the key of C and you play a melody that moves from C to D to E—the first three notes of the C Major scale. When you transpose that melody to the key of F, the new notes (the first three notes of the F Major scale) are F, G, A.

Getting the hang of it yet?

Here's another example: say you're in the key of C, and you're playing the I-vi-IV-V chord progression—C-Am-F-G. When you transpose that chord progression into the key of F, the new chords are F-Dm-B♭-C. It's still I-vi-IV-V; just in a different key.

You can transpose from any one key to any other key. That means you could move the notes anywhere from a half step to a major seventh up or down from where you started. (You also can move notes up or down by whole octaves—what is called *octave transposition*—but you're really not altering any notes; you're just changing octaves.)

Why You Need to Transpose

As you saw in the introduction to this chapter, there are many different reasons you might need to transpose a song. Here are some of the most common:

- The song, as written, is out of the range of a vocalist or instrumentalist. If a singer can't hit the high notes in the key of C, maybe the key of B or B♭, or even A might be friendlier.

- You or another musician don't know how to play the song in the given key. This is especially a problem with casual guitarists who don't always know the chords in some of the more extreme flat or sharp keys—but they do know the chords for G and A and C and E. If you can transpose the song to one of these keys, everyone can play their parts. (You have the same problem with any instrument that has to deal with a lot of sharps and flats in the key signature; it's easier to play in C, G, D, F, and B♭ than it is to play in the other, more complex, keys.)

- You're writing or arranging for one of the many instruments that don't play in what we call *concert key*. For example, trumpets always sound one whole note lower than what is written—so you have to transpose all trumpet players' music up a step so they'll be in the same key as the other musicians. (So if the concert key is C, you write the trumpet part in D; when a trumpet plays a D, it actually sounds as concert C.) These instruments are called *transposing instruments* because you have to transpose their parts for them.

These scenarios are more common than you'd think—which means you better learn how to transpose—and fast!

DEFINITION

Concert key or *concert pitch* is the underlying key of a piece of music—that is, the actual pitches that sound when played. The piano is always in concert key. (Many instruments do not play in concert key. See Chapter 20 to learn which instruments play in what keys.)

Four Ways to Transpose

When you have to transpose a song from one key to another, there are four ways to go about it. You can …

- Put your math skills to work and manually move each note up or down the required number of half steps.

- Put your music theory skills to work and utilize degree-wise Roman numeral notation.

- Use your music theory skills again and mechanically transpose each note based on the interval from the previous note.

- Put technology to work and let a computerized music notation program do the job for you.

Step-Wise Transposition

Step-wise transposition is the grunt work of the arranging and composing world. In this method, you count the half steps between the first key and the second, and then move each note and chord up or down the necessary number of steps.

For example, let's say you have the following melody in the key of D:

Your original melody, in the key of D.

You need to transpose this melody to the key of F. When you do the counting, you find that F is three half steps above D. So you have to move all the chords and notes up three half steps.

Start by changing the key signature from D (two sharps) to F (one flat). Then move the melody up three half steps, one note at a time, like this:

1. Take the first note of the melody—an A. If you move this note up three half steps, it becomes a C.

2. Move to the second note of the melody—a B. If you move this note up three half steps, it becomes a D.

3. Move to the third note of the melody—a C♯. If you move this note up three half steps, it becomes an E.

And so on, and so on. You do the same thing with the chords:

1. The first chord is D Major. If you move this chord up three half steps, it becomes an F Major chord.

2. The second chord is a G Major. If you move this chord up three half steps, it becomes a B♭ Major chord.

When you get done transposing all the notes and chords, you get this:

The same melody, transposed to the key of F.

It's grunt work, that's for sure—but it gets the job done.

Degree-Wise Transposition

If you've done a good job reading this book—and developing your music theory skills accordingly—there's another approach you can take to transposition. This approach requires you to break all the chords and notes down to their degrees of the underlying scale; you can then apply those degree representations to the new key.

The easiest way to understand this approach is to look at chords—in this case, the chords from our previous key-of-D melody:

The original chord progression, in the key of D.

To get the ball rolling, we've noted the chord type above each chord—I, IV, V, and so forth. For the next few minutes, we're going to work strictly with this degree notation and forget (for the time being) about the original chords.

The chord progression in Roman numerals only.

With the chord progression broken down by Roman numeral, you can write out each of the chords in your new key—in this case, the key of F. When you write out the new chords, you get this:

The chord progression transposed to the key of F.

Voilà! You've just transposed the entire chord progression—and you didn't have to count any half steps to do it.

If you're not sure which chords to use, refer to the Scale-Based Chords table in Chapter 10.

You can apply this same technique to the notes in the melody. Work through the original key-of-D melody and put the degree of the scale (1, 2, 3, and so forth) under each note of the melody, like this:

Marking up the original melody, write the degree of the scale under each note.

Now get a blank sheet of music paper and, in the key of F, write out the scale degrees below the staff. If you fill in the actual notes for each scale degree, you end up with the completed melody:

Your transposed melody, by the numbers.

This method is a little more work for melodies than it is for chords, but it definitely works.

Interval-Based Transposition

In interval-based transposition, you have to transpose the first note from one key to another, but then you ignore the key change and work completely in the new key. You do this by noting the intervals between each note in the melody, and then using those intervals to "compose" the transposed melody on the fly.

Let's turn again to our original melody, and note the intervals between each note in the melody, like this:

The original melody, marked up with intervals.

Now, you start composing your "new" melody in the new key. The first note in the new key (which you have to manually figure out) is a C, and the interval between that note and the second note is a major second—which makes the second note a D. The next interval is another major second, which makes the next note an E. The next interval is a major second down, which makes the next note a D. And so on, until you're done.

Transposing your melody one interval at a time.

This method doesn't work as well when you're transposing chords, because it doesn't tell you what type of chord comes next—major, minor, or other. I suppose you could augment this interval-based approach by noting the chord type from the original version, but that gets a tad complex; there are easier ways to transpose chord progressions.

Software-Based Transposition

Thanks to modern computer technology, you may be able to avoid manual transposition completely. Almost all computerized music notation programs, such as Finale and Sibelius, let you enter your music in concert key; all you have to do is click a button or select a menu item to automatically transpose one or more staves to another key.

For example, the Finale program has a drop-down menu option that lets you determine whether a given part is noted in concert key or the instrument's native key. Depending on the option you select, your score can show all instruments in concert key, or the specific keys for each instrument. The nice thing about this option is that you can do your original composing in concert key and then automatically transpose the parts to their own keys when you're done writing—which is easier than trying to manually transpose all the parts while you're composing.

Finale also lets you transpose a part from any one key to any other key, just by selecting a few options in a dialog box. When you want to change keys, you can instruct the program to transpose the original notes up or down, as appropriate, or hold to their original pitches. It's a lot easier than trying to transpose each part on your own! (Learn more about music notation programs in Chapter 21.)

Finale's Key Signature dialog box; the Transposition Options section lets you choose between transposing the notes when you change keys and holding the notes to their original pitches.

Exercises

Exercise 14-1

Use the step-based method to transpose this melody from the key of F to the key of G. (Watch the change from flats to sharps!)

Exercise 14-2

Use the degree-based method to transpose this chord progression from the key of A♭ to the key of E.

Exercise 14-3

Use the interval-based method to transpose this melody from the key of B♭ to the key of A.

Exercise 14-4

Use whatever method you like to transpose the following chords and melody from the key of C to the key of E.

The Least You Need to Know

- Transposition is the art of moving notes and chords from one key to another.

- You need to learn transposition for those times when a singer requests a song in a different key, you or other musicians can't play in the original key, or you're composing or arranging for instruments that don't play in concert key.

- You can transpose a melody by counting the half steps from one key to another, noting the scale degrees of the original melody and chords, or using the intervals between the notes of the melody.

- Many computerized music notation programs will automatically transpose your music for you with the click of a mouse.

Embellishing

Part 5 teaches you how to fill out your music with lush harmonies and interesting counterpoint as well as how to jazz up a tune with fancy chord substitutions. As a bonus, I share a chapter with more fiddly notation marks!

CHAPTER 15

Harmony and Counterpoint

A song doesn't have to be anything more than a melody and chords. Think of a folk singer and her guitar, or a solo violinist accompanied by piano. Melody and chords are all you need. However, when you turn on the radio you don't hear a lot of solo folk singers. What you typically hear is a full arrangement, complete with keyboards and bass and drums, background vocals, and other types of instrumental backing.

Of course, these background vocals and instruments are doing nothing more than playing the notes in the song's chord progression. But they also help to fill out the sound and make the piece of music more interesting.

To fill out your songs, you need to add harmony parts. These harmony parts can be either vocal or instrumental, and there can be any number of them. What they do is simple: they follow separate lines within the underlying chord progression, thus buttressing the harmonic structure of the song.

If you want to get really fancy, your backing parts can represent new and contrasting melodies when played against your original melody. When you create this type of complex harmony, it's called counterpoint; it's widely used in many forms of classical music.

In This Chapter

- Understanding the differences—and similarities—between harmony and counterpoint
- Creating pleasing background harmonies
- Using different chord voicings
- Composing interesting two-part counterpoint
- Learning effective voice-leading technique

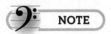

NOTE

This chapter presents harmony and counterpoint from a popular music perspective. Classical musicians have a much different—and more formal—take on these concepts.

Two Ways to Enhance a Melody

Two notes sounded together make a harmonic interval; three or more notes sounded together make a chord; and two or more melodies sounded together make counterpoint. Intervals and chords are used to construct harmony; counterpoint exists as separate melodic lines.

Another way to think of it is that harmony is a vertical (up and down) combination of notes, whereas counterpoint operates horizontally (side to side).

Harmony is vertical.

Counterpoint is horizontal.

In reality, harmony and counterpoint are related concepts; both involve "vertical" combinations of notes and both involve a "horizontal" movement of individual voices or instruments. Still, harmony is more about singing or playing parts of a chord; counterpoint is more about creating a second (or third or fourth) melody line—albeit one that adheres to the underlying harmonic structure.

NOTE

Technically, the study of harmony includes chords and chord progressions—basically, anything that combines two or more notes simultaneously. Because we already covered this
basic material in Chapters 9 and 10, in this chapter we're covering the use of multiple
voices or instruments to enhance melodies, based on the underlying harmonic structure
(chord progression) of a piece of music.

Living in Harmony

Harmony is like playing chords behind a melody, but using other instruments or voices. In fact,
the art of adding chords to a melody is a harmonic exercise. We add harmony parts to our music
because harmony lends richness to a song. It fills out a single melody line and reinforces the
underlying chord structure.

A melody with backing harmonies is the difference between a solo vocalist and a full chorus.
It's the difference between a folk singer with an acoustic guitar and a pop singer with a group of
backup vocalists. It's the difference between a jazz trio and a big band. In other words, harmony
makes music bigger.

You create harmony parts by using the notes in the underlying chord progression. If all you do
is assign specific notes of a chord to specific instruments or voices, you've created harmony. It
doesn't have to be any harder than that. Harmony parts, whether vocal or instrumental, are
typically less rhythmically complex than the main melody. It's not uncommon to find harmony
parts consisting of whole notes or half notes while the melody maintains a more complex rhythm.

Harmony parts can also mirror the rhythm of the melody; in these instances, the harmony
resembles classical counterpoint—which you'll learn about later in this chapter. Harmony can
also be used to punctuate the melody, fill in breaks in the melody, and function as a kind of call-
and-response mechanism. (Think of the classic pop tune "Midnight Train to Georgia"; Gladys
Knight is the call and the Pips are the response—woo woo!)

In terms of harmonic complexity, you can have everything from a single accompanying voice to
choruses and string sections with two and three and more voices. The more voices you have, the
more challenging it is to create distinct harmony parts without doubling or duplicating other
parts. Of course, writing a single harmony part is also challenging, but in a different way; that
single part has to include just the right notes, suggesting the underlying chord without distracting
from the main melody.

For the purposes of learning basic theory, we're going to concentrate on simple two- and three-
part backing harmony, without a lot of rhythmic or melodic complexity. Once you master this
type of rudimental harmony, you can expand to include more complex types of vocal and instrumental backing.

Voicing and Inversions

The order of the notes of a chord (top to bottom) is referred to as the chord voicing. (It's also called the chord inversion, as you learned in Chapter 9.) Voicing is very important when you're writing harmony parts, because you have to employ different voicings to avoid parallel motion between parts.

Let's consider the harmony you play as piano accompaniment. If you recall, we used the following chord progression as an example back in Chapter 13:

A common chord progression that needs harmonized.

As learned back in Chapter 13, a simple block-chord piano accompaniment (right hand only) to this chord progression looks something like this:

Simple block-chord harmonies.

The triads you play as accompaniment represent three-voice harmony; you just happen to play all three voices with one hand. All the chords are in the root (noninverted) form of 1-3-5—which represents a problem. When you change from chord to chord, all the harmony notes move in parallel to each other. In terms of voice leading, this is often frowned upon.

It's also boring.

You can prove this by isolating the top note of this chord accompaniment. Now sing the succession of top notes as if you were singing backup vocals:

Isolating the top voice in the I-vi-IV-V chord progression.

Like I said, pretty boring—and not particularly melodic, either. A better approach is to vary the voicings of the chords so the harmony parts don't have to move in parallel. For example, you might keep the C chord in its normal root position but change the Am to the first inversion

(C-E-A), the F to the second inversion (C-F-A), and the G to the first inversion (B-D-G), like this:

Inverting the chords to vary the internal voicings.

 TIP

The succession of root position, first inversion, second inversion is fairly common—and one you can apply to any number of chord progressions. (Also common is the succession of first inversion, second inversion, root position.)

Not only does this make the chord progression easier to play (all the notes are closer together on the keyboard) it also makes any individual part easier to sing. Take the top note part again; instead of moving G-E-C-D as it did originally, it now moves G-A-A-G, like this:

The new top voice harmony part, thanks to revoicing the chords.

Now the voice is fairly consistent; it doesn't jump all over the place like it did before. And if you check out the other voices, you find that they're also a lot more singable. (The middle voice moves E-E-F-D, and the bottom voice moves C-C-C-B.)

When you write out each of these parts separately, you use three different staves, like this:

Three-voice harmony—on three different staves.

These principles apply when you're playing piano accompaniment; they also apply when you're writing vocal or instrumental harmonies. If you vary the voicings, you open up a lot of possibilities as far as which voice goes where.

TIP

It's helpful to think of a chord progression as nothing more than a group of simultaneous melodies. This will help you create singable harmony parts, as opposed to parts that correspond only to notes within the underlying chord structure.

Making Harmony Parts More Melodic

Of course, you're not limited to having your voices follow the strict chord pattern. What if we start swapping the top two notes of our harmony between two different voices? There are lots of ways to do this, but one particularly good-sounding one looks like this:

Swapping a few notes between the top two harmony parts.

See what we did here? We swapped the second and fourth notes between the parts, so that the first part now goes G-E-A-D, and the second part goes E-A-F-G. You're still representing all the notes in the chord, but you're making each individual line more melodically interesting.

A good tip when you're creating either vocal or instrumental harmony is to physically sing each part yourself. If the part is boring or hard to sing, consider different inversions or swapping notes between parts. The best harmony parts sound great on their own!

Voice Leading

Voice leading is what you get when you follow one harmony part from start to finish; the different intervals between the notes follow a set of conventions and act to create a pseudo-melody out of the harmony line. You have to make sure that one note properly leads to the next to avoid having the harmony line sound like a bunch of totally unconnected tones.

> **TIP**
>
> If you follow these voice-leading conventions, you'll create chord progressions that sound good in both popular and classical music. When you're working in the popular and jazz styles, however, you'll discover that you can be a lot freer with your voice leading; let your ear guide you to what works best.

When you're writing harmony, there are three key voice-leading conventions to keep in mind. When you follow these conventions, the creation of harmony parts becomes somewhat easy:

- In general, voices should move smoothly. That means moving each voice the shortest distance possible, and retaining common tones between successive chords in the same voice. How big of a leap is too much? Try to avoid leaps larger than a fourth, except in the lowest (bass) voice, which can accept larger leaps that move along with the chord progression.

- When at all possible, you should avoid moving all the voices in the same direction. If some of the voices move up over the course of a line, at least one voice should move down.

- Avoid moving voices in parallel "perfect" intervals—fourths, fifths, or octaves. Voices can move in parallel thirds and sixths.

Here's an example of bad voice leading. Notice how the two parts move in parallel, and how each voice has huge leaps from note to note?

Bad voice leading ...

The second example shows how to fix the voice-leading problems merely by swapping a few notes from voice to voice or by picking other notes within the chord. It isn't that hard when you realize that any note can be assigned to any voice; all you have to do is pick the right notes to create the best-sounding musical lines.

... corrected.

Making a Point—with Counterpoint

Counterpoint is the art of combining two or more simultaneous musical lines. Unlike the art of harmony, where the harmony parts are subsidiary to the main melody, both melodic parts in counterpoint have equal weight.

The two voices in traditional counterpoint must not only sound melodic when played separately; they also must fit together harmonically to suggest the chord structure of the song. That means if you play the underlying chords against the counterpoint, the melodic lines mustn't sound dissonant; it also means you should be able to deduce the underlying chord structure from the melodic lines alone.

Keys to Successful Counterpoint

The interaction of the different voices (and when I say "voices," I mean melodic lines; counterpoint can be used in both vocal and instrumental music) is essential to successful counterpoint. The two lines have to work together, not fight with each other. The second line has to be the melodic equal of the first, and neither line should dominate.

Classic two-part counterpoint, courtesy of Bach—notice the independence of the two melodic lines.

It's also important that both lines be singable. That means either melody should be able to stand on its own as a main melody against the underlying chord progression. A melody in counterpoint should not be just a combination of notes to fit the chords; it has to be melodic, it has to have its own internal musical logic, and it has to fit with the other melody.

When composing melodies for counterpoint, call upon the skills you learned back in Chapter 8. Make sure each melody has a shape and a destination, as well as a coherent form. Also make sure each melody makes sense within the song's general chord structure, it fits within a comfortable vocal or instrumental range (generally no more than an octave range), and the intervals within the melody are small and singable.

When you put your two melodies together, you should make sure they both fit within the notes of the underlying chord, and stay within the confines of the underlying scale. The two melodies should also not duplicate each other; if you have two identical melodies, you're writing in unison, not in counterpoint. That means each melody should have its own motion—which should complement, but not interfere with, the motion of the other melody. The notes within each melody also should not interfere or clash with the notes in the other melody; avoid dissonant vertical intervals.

It's okay for the two melodies to have their own rhythmic patterns. In fact, in classical music it's expected. (If your two melodies have identical rhythmic structure you have what is called a 1:1 rhythmic ratio, which in some ways is easier to work with than more rhythmically complex forms.)

Creating Your First Counterpoint

The best way to learn about counterpoint is to dive into the deep end—and start composing!

For our first counterpoint, we'll start by defining some parameters. These are not necessarily hard-and-fast rules for the contrapuntal form, but they do make it easier for beginners to create a working counterpoint.

Here are the parameters:

- Use a 1:1 rhythmic ratio; both melodies should use the same rhythmic patterns.
- Only consonant harmonic intervals are allowed; no dissonant harmonies.
- The lower part must begin and end on the tonic of the key.
- The upper part must begin on either the first or the fifth of the key, and end on the tonic—either in unison with the bass part or an octave above.

- Between the melodies, rely heavily on intervals of thirds and sixths. Avoid octaves and unisons, except for the final note.

- Move each voice the shortest distance possible.

Now let's get started.

Some composers like to write both melodic parts simultaneously; this enables them to employ various advanced techniques, such as sharing a contrapuntal melody between the two parts. However, for beginners it's a lot easier to write the first part first and then complete the puzzle by adding the counterpoint melody. Which is exactly what we'll do.

We'll start from the bottom up and create our first melody for the lower voice. (This is the staff labeled "2," in bass clef.) Our melody is in 3/4 time, in the key of F Major. Because counterpoint works best when both parts have a lot of rhythmic and melodic movement, the melody is fairly lively, with a lot of eighth notes; it also starts and ends on the tonic note, F.

Now things get interesting. We need to come up with a second, higher, melody that doesn't clash with the lower melody—in fact, it should complement the first melody. You can't create this second melody in a vacuum; counterpoint is more than just putting two unrelated melodies together. The two melodies have to fit together logically, and have to work together to suggest the underlying chords.

The lower voice—the first of two parts in counterpoint.

So let's start at the start. The lower part started on an F, which is the tonic of the underlying key. According to our parameters, the upper melody can start either on the tonic or the fifth. We don't want to get too fancy with our first counterpoint, so we'll start the upper melody (the treble clef labeled "1") on the F two octaves higher.

In the first measure, the lower melody has a slight upward progression. To distinguish the upper melody from the lower part, we'll give this second melody a slight downward progression. Remember, we want the intervals between the two voices to be pleasant-sounding, which means emphasizing the thirds and sixths, and avoiding dissonant intervals. We also want to avoid parallel movement, so we'll leave the second note of the upper melody on F, which sounds good against the D on the bottom. (It's a nice minor third.)

For the third note, it's time to introduce some motion—in this case, a downward motion, to contrast with the upward motion in the lower melody. We'll move down from F to C, which is a nice singable fourth. It also forms a pleasing minor sixth against the E in the lower melody.

The fourth and final note in the first measure also needs to show downward movement, so we'll continue down from C to A, an easily singable minor third. The A also creates a pleasing major third against the F in the lower melody.

Now, if you look closely, you'll see that not only did we introduce *contrary motion* in the upper melody (down, in contrast to the upward-moving lower melody), but we also used the upper melody to suggest the underlying chord (F Major). The downward melody is actually an arpeggiated F Major chord, in its first inversion (F to C to A). What we have so far is shown here:

Starting to add counterpoint to the first voice.

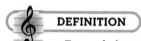

DEFINITION

Two melodies in counterpoint that move in opposite directions (one up; the other down) are said to have **contrary motion.**

As you can see, creating counterpoint requires a lot of logical thinking—it's a lot like thinking through the moves in a game of chess. The conventions are there and it's all very logical, but you have to work hard to make it all fit together as it should.

We'll continue adding to the upper voice line, following the conventions note by note. When we're finished, we have two complete melodies, in counterpoint to each other, like this:

Your first counterpoint!

Your first counterpoint is a good example of simple 1:1 rhythmic counterpoint. Of course, classical counterpoint requires that the rhythms differ between the two voices, so let's continue to work with this example to create some rhythmic variations.

How do you introduce different rhythms into the top melody? In this example, you can do it by essentially scooting all the notes to the left one beat. That is, you put the eighth-note figure on beat one instead of beat two of each measure, and extend the measure-ending quarter note into a half note.

Here's what this looks like:

Your first counterpoint—but with different rhythms in the top melody.

Note that this approach created eighth notes in the top part when the bottom part is using quarter notes, and vice versa. This provides a simple rhythmic variation without going whole-hog on complex interrelated rhythms.

What to Avoid

Whether you're writing harmony or counterpoint, there are certain combinations of notes that you want to avoid. In most cases, you'll avoid these combinations because they don't sound right; still, it's good to know the conventions in advance so you can keep from making rookie mistakes.

Here's what to avoid:

Extended parallel movement. Parallel movement is when two or more voices move in the same direction by the exact same interval. Parallel movement is frowned upon in some types of music—but perfectly acceptable in others. For example, in classical music you want to avoid parallel movement in perfect fourths or fifths and octaves; in popular music, however, parallel fourths and fifths are permitted and even somewhat common—even if they do sound a little boring if carried on for too long. In any case, if you try hard, you can generally come up with something that sounds more interesting than extended parallel voices. Go ahead and use a little parallel movement if you have to, but then vary things to keep from getting boring.

Big leaps. Whether you're writing harmony or counterpoint, you should follow one of the key conventions used when creating melodies—keep the intervals between notes as small as possible.

Avoid big leaps between notes; they not only sound disconnected, they're also hard to play and sing. As with standard voice-leading, any interval larger than a fourth or fifth is probably too big a leap.

Dissonant intervals—unless they resolve. In this case we're talking about the intervals between different voices—and this is as much a practical consideration as anything else. For example, if you're harmonizing an F Major seventh chord, don't put the seventh and the root (E and F) together on close voices. Instead, put one of the notes in a lower voice, so there's an octave or so of space between the two notes. That said, it's okay to introduce this kind of dissonance, if you then resolve it. That means you can include dissonance in passing tones, or even at the end of phrases, but only if one of the voices then resolves to a more pleasing interval. For example, in the F Major seventh chord, the voice with the E might resolve to F.

Exercises

Exercise 15-1

Find and correct the voice-leading errors in the following piece of harmony.

Exercise 15-2

Create two-voice harmony for the following melody, using half notes and quarter notes.

Exercise 15-3

Create a second melody part in counterpoint to the following melody.

Exercise 15-4

Based on the following chord progression, create a two-voice counterpoint.

The Least You Need to Know

- Harmony is a vertical combination of notes within the underlying chord structure; counterpoint is an integrated series of horizontal melodies relating to the underlying chords.

- Harmony is facilitated when you vary chord voicings throughout a progression.

- Each harmony part must be singable on its own and follow established voice-leading conventions.

- Each melody within a counterpoint should be able to function as a standalone melody, and at the same time complement the other melodies.

- Whether you're creating harmony or counterpoint, you should generally avoid extended movement in parallel fourths, fifths, or octaves—especially in classical music. (Popular music typically has fewer—and looser—conventions.)

Chord Substitutions and Turnarounds

This section of the book is all about embellishing your music. You can embellish your melody with harmony and counterpoint (as you learned in the previous chapter), embellish individual notes (as you'll learn in the next chapter), and embellish your chords and chord progressions. That's what this chapter is all about.

Even if you're stuck with a boring I-IV-V progression, there is still a lot you can do to put your own personal stamp on things. For example, you don't have to settle for precisely those chords; you can extend the chords, alter the bass line, and even substitute other chords for the originals. You'll still maintain the song's original harmonic structure—more or less—but you'll really jazz up the way things sound.

All this will impress your listeners and fellow musicians. A few key chord alterations and substitutions will make folks think you have the right touch—and that you really know your music theory!

In This Chapter

- Learning to spice up boring chord progressions with extensions
- Discovering how to alter a chord's bass note and play two chords simultaneously
- Mastering the art of chord substitution

Extending a Good Thing

The simplest way to spice up a boring chord progression is to use seventh chords, or even add a few extensions beyond that. As you learned back in Chapter 9, the basic chord is a triad consisting of the 1-3-5 notes. When you start adding notes on top of the triad—sevenths, ninths, and elevenths—you're extending the chord upward.

Chord extensions can make a basic chord sound lush and exotic. There's nothing like a minor seventh or major ninth chord to create a really full, harmonically complex sound.

Seventh chords—especially dominant seventh chords—are common in all types of music today. Sixths, ninths, and other extended chords are used frequently in modern jazz music—and in movie and television soundtracks that go for a jazzy feel. Pick up just about any jazz record from the 1950s on, and you'll hear lots of extended chords. There are even a lot of rock and pop musicians—Steely Dan comes to mind—who embrace these jazz harmonies in their music. So why not use this technique yourself?

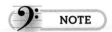

NOTE

Seventh chords have been part of the musical vocabulary from about the seventeenth century. There is a tendency to use the V7 and ii7 chords as much as or more than the triads on those degrees of the scale—even for the simplest musical genres, such as hymns and folk songs. In the blues, it is common to use seventh chords on every scale degree—even the tonic. Other extended chords (ninths, elevenths, and so forth) came into widespread use in the nineteenth century, and are still used in many forms of music today. For example, in many jazz compositions the ninth, eleventh, and thirteenth chords are used more often than triads and seventh chords.

Here's an example of how extended chords can make a simple chord progression sound more harmonically complex. All you have to do is take the standard I-vi-IV-V progression in the key of C (C-Am-F-G) and add diatonic sevenths to each triad. That produces the following progression: CM7-Am7-FM7-G7—two major sevenths, a minor seventh, and a dominant seventh. When you play this progression—and invert some of the chords to create a few close voicings—you get a completely different sound out of that old workhorse progression. And it wasn't hard to do at all!

The standard I-vi-IV-V progression (in C) embellished with seventh chords (and some close voicings).

You can get the same effect by adding ninths and elevenths to your chords while staying within the song's underlying key. The more notes you add to your chords, the more complex your harmonies—and the fuller the sound.

Altering the Bass

Here's another neat way to make old chords sound new—and all you have to do is change the note on the bottom of the chord.

Back in Chapter 9 we touched briefly on the concept of *slash chords,* more properly called *altered bass* chords. With an altered bass chord, the top of the chord stays the same, but the bass, as the name implies, is altered.

Some folks call these chords slash chords because the altered bass note is indicated after a diagonal slash mark, like this: G/D. You read the chord as "G over D," and you play it as a G chord with a D in the bass.

Examples of slash chords.

You can use altered bass chords to achieve several different effects, including the following:

- By putting one of the three main notes (but not the root) in the bass, you dictate a particular chord inversion.

- By treating the bass note as a separate entity, you can create moving bass lines with increased melodic interest.

- By adding a nonchord note in the bass, you create a different chord with a different harmonic structure.

Slash chords are used a lot in jazz, and also in more sophisticated popular music. Listen to Carole King's *Tapestry* album, and you'll hear a lot of altered bass (she's a big fan of the minor seventh chord with the fourth in the bass); the same thing with a lot of Beach Boys songs, especially those on the legendary *Pet Sounds* album.

Two Chords Are Better Than One

An altered bass chord uses a diagonal slash mark to separate the chord from the bass note. When you see a chord with a horizontal line between two different chord symbols, like a fraction, you're dealing with a much different beast.

This type of notation indicates that two chords are to be played simultaneously. The chord on top of the fraction is placed on top of the pile; the chord on the bottom is played underneath. For example, when you see $\frac{C}{G}$ you know to play a C Major chord on top of a full G Major chord.

Examples of compound chords.

When you play two chords together like this, you have what's called a *compound chord*. You use compound chords to create extremely complex harmonies—those that might otherwise be too complex to note using traditional extensions.

One Good Chord Can Replace Another

When you're faced with a boring chord progression, you may have no alternative but to substitute the chords as written with something a little less boring. The concept of *chord substitution* is common in jazz (those jazz musicians get bored easily!) and other modern music.

Chord substitution is a simple concept. You pull a chord out of the song, and replace it with another chord. The substitute chord should have a few things in common with the chord it replaces, not the least of which is its place in the song's underlying harmonic structure. So if you replace a dominant (V) chord, you want to use a chord that also leads back to the tonic (I). If you replace a major chord, you want to replace it with another major chord or a chord that uses some of the same notes as the original chord.

The key thing is to substitute an ordinary chord or progression with one that serves the same function, but in a more interesting manner.

Diatonic Substitution

The easiest form of chord substitution replaces a chord with a related chord either a third above or a third below the original. This way you keep two of the three notes of the original chord, which provides a strong harmonic basis for the new chord.

This type of substitution is called *diatonic substitution,* because you're not altering any of the notes of the underlying scale; you're just using different notes from within the scale for the new chord.

For example, the I chord in any scale can be replaced by the vi chord (the chord a third below) or the iii chord (the chord a third above). In the key of C, this means replacing the C Major chord (C-E-G) with either A minor (A-C-E) or E minor (E-G-B). Both chords share two notes in common with the C chord, so the replacement isn't too jarring.

Replacing the I chord (C Major) with the vi (A minor) and the iii (E minor)—lots of notes in common.

You can replace extended chords in the same manner, and actually end up with more notes in common. For example, you can replace CM7 with either Am7 or Em7, both of which have three notes in common with the original chord.

Major Chord Substitutions

Diatonic substitution is the theory; you'd probably rather know some hard-and-fast rules you can use for real-world chord substitution. Don't worry; they exist, based partially on diatonic substitution theory.

The following table presents three different substitutions you can make for a standard major chord. Remember that the root of the substitute chord must stay within the underlying scale, even if some of the chord notes occasionally wander about a bit.

Major Chord Substitutions

Substitution	Example (for the C Major Chord)
Minor chord a third below	Amin
Minor 7 chord a third below	Amin7
Minor chord a third above	Emin

The first substitution in the table is the standard "down a third" diatonic substitution. The second substitution is the same thing, but uses an extended chord (the minor seventh) for the substitution. The third substitution is the "up a third" diatonic substitution, as discussed previously.

Minor Chord Substitutions

Substituting a major chord is relatively easy. So what about substituting a minor chord?

As you can see in the following table, some of the same substitution rules work with minor as well as major, especially the "up a third" and "down a third" diatonic substitutions.

Minor Chord Substitutions

Substitution	Example (for the A Minor Chord)
Major chord a third above	C
Major chord a third below	F
Major 7 chord a third below	F Maj7
Diminished chord with same root	A dim

The last substitution falls into the "more of a good thing" category. That is, if a minor chord sounds good, let's flat another note and it'll sound even more minor. Some folks like the use of a diminished chord in this fashion; others don't. Let your ears be the judge.

Dominant Seventh Substitutions

Okay, now you know how to substitute both major and minor chords, but what about dominant seventh chords? They're not really major, and they're not really minor—what kind of chords can substitute for that?

The answer requires some harmonic creativity. You can do a diatonic substitution (using the diminished chords a third above or below the dominant seventh), but there are more interesting possibilities, as you can see in the following table.

Dominant Seventh Chord Substitutions

Substitution	Example (for the G7 Chord)
Major chord a second below	F
Minor 7 chord a third below	E m7
Diminished chord a third above	B dim
Minor 7 chord a fourth below—over the same root	D m7/G

The more interesting substitutions here are the first one and the last one. The first substitution replaces the V7 chord with a IV chord; the use of the sub-dominant (IV) chord results in a softer lead back to the I chord. The last substitution uses an altered chord, so that you're leading back to tonic with a iim7/V—what I like to call a "Carole King chord." (That's because Ms. King uses this type of harmonic structure a lot in her songwriting.) So if you're in the key of C, instead of ending a phrase with a G or G7 chord, you end with a Dm7/G instead. It's a very pleasing sound.

Functional Substitutions

Here's something else to keep in mind. Within the harmonic context of a composition, different chords serve different functions. The three basic harmonic functions are those of the tonic, subdominant, and dominant—typically served by the I, IV, and V chords, respectively. But other chords in the scale can serve these same functions, even if not as strongly as the I, IV, and V.

For example, the subdominant function can be served by either the ii, IV, or vi chords. The dominant function can be served by either the V or vii° chords. And the tonic function can be served by either the I, iii, or vi chords. All these functions are shown in the following table.

Chord Function	Chords
Tonic	I, iii, vi
Subdominant	ii, IV, vi
Dominant	V, vii°

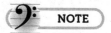

NOTE

Just in case you think you found a mistake in the preceding table, the vi chord can serve both the tonic and subdominant functions. It's a very versatile chord!

When you have a chord serving a specific function in a composition, you can replace it with another chord of the same type. So if you have a IV chord, serving a subdominant function, you can substitute any of the other subdominant-functioning chords—the ii or the vi. Along the same lines, if you have a ii chord, you can replace it with either the IV or the vi.

The same thing goes with the other functions. If you have a V chord, serving a dominant function, you can replace it with a vii° chord—or vice versa. And a I chord, serving a tonic function, can be replaced by either a iii or a vi chord—and also vice versa. It's actually a fairly easy way to make some simple chord substitutions.

Turnarounds

Chapter 10 also presented a concept of the phrase-ending cadence. Well, in the fields of jazz and popular music, you find a similar concept called a *turnaround*. A turnaround typically is a two-bar phrase, with two chords per measure, that functions much the same as a traditional cadence, "turning around" the music to settle back on the I chord at the start of the next phrase.

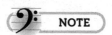

NOTE

Some jazz musicians refer to turnarounds as *turnbacks*.

There is a wide variety of chord combinations you can use to create an ear-pleasing turnaround, some of which go outside the underlying key to circle back around to the tonic.

The following table offers a few you might want to try.

Common Chord Turnarounds

Turnaround	Example (in C)
I-IV-iii-ii	
I-vi-ii-V	
iii-VI-ii-V	
I-vi-♭vi-V	
I-♭VII-iii-ii	
IV-iii-ii-♭ii	
I-vi-♭vi-♭II	
I-VI-♭V-♭III	
I-♭III-♭VI-♭II	
I-♭VII-♭III-♭II	

Note that some of these outside-the-key chords take traditionally minor chords and make them major, so pay close attention to the uppercase and lowercase notation in the table. (For example, the III chord is an E Major chord in the key of C, not the expected E minor.)

Also pay attention to flat signs before a chord; this indicates to play the chord a half step lower than normal. For example, a ♭vi chord in the key of C is a half step lower than the standard A minor vi chord, which results in the A♭ minor chord instead.

You can use these turnarounds in any of the songs you write or arrange. It's an easy way to add harmonic sophistication to your music, just by changing a few chords at the end of a phrase!

Exercises

Exercise 16-1

Write out the notes for the following slash chords.

Exercise 16-2

Write out the notes for the following compound chords.

Exercise 16-3

Write two substitute chords for each chord shown.

Exercise 16-4

Rewrite the following chord progression (on the second staff), using extended chords.

Exercise 16-5

Rewrite the following chord progression (on the second staff), using various types of chord substitutions.

Exercise 16-6

Add a two-measure turnaround to the following chord progression.

The Least You Need to Know

- When you don't want to play a boring old chord progression, you can use one of several techniques to make the chord progression sound more harmonically sophisticated.

- The easiest way to spice up a chord progression is to change triads to seventh chords or extended chords (such as sixths, ninths, elevenths, or thirteenths), and add sevenths and other extensions to the basic chords.

- Another way to change the sound of a chord is to alter the bass note—to either signal a different inversion, or to introduce a slightly different harmonic structure.

- Substituting one chord for another also can make a chord progression more interesting. The most common chord substitutions are diatonic, in which you replace a chord with the diatonic chord either a third above or below the original chord.

- You can also perform a chord substitution based on chord function. Any chord fulfilling a tonic, subdominant, or dominant function can be replaced by any other chord fulfilling the same function.

- You can add interest to a chord progression by introducing a two-measure turn-around at the end of the main phrase; these chords circle around and lead back to the I chord at the start of the next phrase.

CHAPTER 17

Special Notation

Some aspects of music theory just don't fit neatly within traditional categories. Still, you need to know about them, so I have to include them somewhere in this book.

That somewhere is this chapter. It's kind of a grab bag of more advanced techniques, mainly relating to notation, that you need to have at your fingertips—even if you won't use them every day.

So settle back and read about some of the oddball aspects of music theory, and that popular musical style we call swing.

In This Chapter

- Discovering how to notate phrasing with slur marks
- Writing and playing embellished notes, including turns, trills, and grace notes
- Learning how to play music with a swing feel
- Fitting words to music

Throwing a Curve

When you're writing music, you sometimes need to connect two or more notes together. You might literally connect them together to form a single, longer note, or you might simply want them played together as a smooth phrase. In any case, whenever you connect two or more notes together, you use a notation effect that looks like a big curve—and is called, alternately, either a tie or a slur.

Ties

You learned about ties back in Chapter 5. When two notes of the same pitch are tied together—either in the same measure, or across measures—the notes are played as a single note.

A tie is made with a small curve, either above or below the note, like this:

Two identical notes tied together equal one long note.

Slurs

A *slur* looks like a tie between two notes of different pitches, but really indicates that the notes are to be played together as a continuous group. Although you can't play two different tones as a continuous note, you can run them together without a breath or a space in between. This is called "slurring" the notes together; it looks like this:

Two different notes tied together are slurred together.

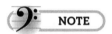 **NOTE**

The curved line used in a slur is called a *slur mark*.

There's a subtle difference between two notes that are slurred together and two notes that aren't. The notes without the slur should each have a separate attack, which ends up sounding like a slight emphasis on each note. The second of the two slurred notes doesn't have a separate attack, so the sound is much smoother as you play from note to note.

Phrases

When you see a curved line above several adjacent notes, it's not a slur—it's a *phrase.* You use phrase marks to indicate separate ideas within a longer piece of music. When one idea ends, you end the phrase mark; when a new idea begins, you start a new phrase mark.

Lots of notes grouped together are played as a smooth phrase.

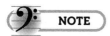 **NOTE**

Technically, a phrase mark indicates that a passage of music is played *legato*—which means to play smoothly.

Often, wind instruments (trumpets, clarinets, and so forth) base their breathing on the song's phrases. They'll blow during the phrase and breathe between the phrase marks.

Bowed instruments (violins, cellos, and so forth) use phrases to time their bowing. They'll use a single, continuous movement of the bow for the duration of the phrase; at the end of the phrase mark, they'll change the direction of their bowing.

The Long and the Short of It

Back in Chapter 7, you learned about some of the embellishments you can make to individual notes—accents, marcatos, and so on. There are a few more marks you can add to your notes; they're presented here.

Tenuto

A straight horizontal line over a note means to play the note for its full duration. In other words, stretch it out for as long as possible.

This mark is called a *tenuto* mark, and it looks like this:

The tenuto mark means to play a long note.

Staccato

The opposite of a long note is a short note; the opposite of tenuto is *staccato*. A dot on top of a note means to not play it for its full duration; just give it a little blip and get off it.

A staccato mark looks like this:

The staccato mark means to play a short note.

When Is a Note More Than a Note?

There are other marks you can add to your notes that indicate *additional* notes to play. These notes are kind of musical shorthand you can use in place of writing out all those piddly smaller notes.

Grace Notes

A *grace note* is a short note you play in front of a main note. In mathematical terms, a grace note might have the value of a sixteenth or a thirty-second note, depending on the tempo of the music. Basically, you play the grace note just ahead of the main note, at a slightly lower volume level. When you note a grace note, write it as a smaller note just in front of the main note, like this:

A grace note is like a little preview note before the main note.

Grace notes are typically written as small eighth notes, with a line drawn through the stem and flag. The grace note can be on the same tone as the main note, or on an adjoining tone. (You play whatever note the grace note is on.)

 NOTE

Drummers call a grace note a *flam*, because (on a drum) that's what it sounds like—"fa-lam!"

Turns

A *turn* is an ornament used primarily in Baroque and classical music. In a turn, the neighboring notes turn to the main note, "turning it around."

Let's look at how a turn works: when you see the turn mark (which looks like a line turned around on itself), you play the diatonic note above the main note, then the main note, then the note a step below the main note, and then the main note again. Here's how it looks on paper, and how you play it in practice:

A turn "turns around" the main note.

When you're playing a turn, you have a bit of latitude for how fast you actually play it. You can play a turn as written in the example, as a pure mathematical subset of the note's noted duration; or you can whip through the turn really quickly, landing back on the main pitch until the note is done. It's all a matter of interpretation.

 TIP

If you're unsure how to play a turn in a piece of music, ask your conductor for the proper interpretation.

Trills

A *trill* (*s*) is a way to extend a single note by alternating between two neighboring tones. In particular, you alternate between the main note and the note one step above, like this:

Play a trill with a whole bunch of neighboring notes.

As with turns, there are many different ways to play a trill. The most common approach is to alternate between the two notes as rapidly as possible, although technically a trill can have a *preparation* in which you play the main note straight before you enter into the "shake." (You can also terminate the trill—or just trill right into the next note.)

Glissandi

Whereas turns and trills alternate between two or three neighboring notes, a *glissando* packs a lot more notes into a short space. To be precise, a glissando is a mechanism for getting from one pitch to another, playing every single pitch between the two notes as smoothly as possible.

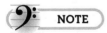   **NOTE**

> On the piano, you can also "cheat" a glissando by playing only the white keys between the top and bottom tones—which lets you play a glissando with a stroke of your hand.

Depending on the instrument, a glissando can be a continuous glide between the two notes (think trombone) or a run of sequential chromatic notes (think piano). Glissandi (*not* glissandos!) can move either up or down; typically, both the starting and ending notes are specified, like this:

Glissando up—and down.

Arpeggiated Chords

When you want an instrument to play a chord as an arpeggio, but you don't want to write out all the notes, you can use the symbol called the *role*. The role indicates that the instrument is to play an arpeggio—but a rather quick one. This squiggly line tells the musician to play the written notes from bottom to top, in succession, and to hold each note as it is played. The effect should be something like a harp playing an arpeggiated chord, like this:

The quick and easy way to notate an arpeggiated accompaniment.

Getting Into the Swing of Things

The last bit of notation I want to discuss concerns a feel. If you've ever heard jazz music, particularly big band music, you've heard this feel; it's called *swing*.

Traditional popular music has a straight feel; eighth notes are played straight, just as they're written. Swing has a kind of triplet feel; it swings along, all bouncy, percolating with three eighth notes on every beat.

What's that, you're saying—*three* eighth notes on every beat? How is that possible?

It's possible because swing is based on triplets. Instead of having eight eighth notes in a measure of 4/4, you have twelve eighth notes—four eighth-note triplets. So instead of the basic beat being straight eighths, the first and third beat of every triplet combine for a *spang-a-lang-a-lang-a-lang* kind of rhythm.

What's confusing is that instead of notating swing as it's actually played (with triplets), most swing music uses straight eighth notation—which you're then expected to translate into the triplet-based swing.

So if you're presented a swing tune and you see a bunch of straight eighths, you should play them with a triplet feel instead, like this:

In swing, straight eighths are played with a triplet feel.

Some arrangers try to approximate the swing feel within a straight rhythm by using dotted eighth notes followed by sixteenth notes, like this:

In swing, dotted eights and sixteenths are played with a triplet feel.

Whatever you do, don't play this precisely as written! Again, you have to translate the notation and play the notes with a triplet feel.

The swing feel is an important one, and you find it all over the place. Swing is used extensively in jazz music, in traditional blues music, in rock shuffles, and in all manner of popular music old and new. Learning how to swing takes a bit of effort; it's normal to play the stiff dotted-eighth/ sixteenth rhythm instead of the rolling triplets when you're first starting out. But that effort is worth it—a lot of great music is based on that swinging feel.

Getting the Word

Before we end this chapter, let's take a look at one other notation challenge: how to add *words* to your music.

Notating lyrics is something that all songwriters have to do, and it isn't that hard—if you think logically. Naturally, you want to align specific words with specific notes in the music. More precisely, you want to align specific syllables with specific notes.

This sometimes requires a bit of creativity on your part. You might need to split up words into awkward-looking syllables. You also might need to extend syllables within words where a note is held for an extended period of time. This requires a lot of hyphens in the lyrics, as you can see in the following example:

Notating lyrics; split words in syllables, and extended syllables.

Just remember to position your lyrics underneath the music staff. If you have multiple verses, write each verse on a separate line; then break each word into its component syllables and carefully match up each syllable with the proper musical note.

Exercises

Exercise 17-1

Write out how you would play each of these marked-up notes.

Exercise 17-2

Add grace notes to every quarter note in this melody.

Exercise 17-3

Add slurs to each pair of eighth notes in this melody.

Exercise 17-4

Use phrase marks to divide this melody into four natural phrases.

Exercise 17-5

Translate the following straight rhythm into a swing feel using triplet notation.

Exercise 17-6

Compose and play a four-measure melody with a swing feel, in the key of B♭.

Exercise 17-7

Write the following lyrics under the appropriate notes in the melody: "Tangerine elephants high in the sky, crocodile tears in my beer."

The Least You Need to Know

- Curved marks are used to tie identical notes together, slur neighboring notes together, and indicate complete musical phrases.
- A dot above a note means to play it short (staccato); a line above a note means to play it long (tenuto).
- You play grace notes lightly and quickly before the main note.
- Turns and trills ornament a main note by the use of rapidly played neighboring notes.
- A glissando indicates a smooth glide from one pitch to another.
- Swing music is played with a rolling triplet feel, not straight eighth notes.
- Lyrics must be broken down into syllables to fit precisely with notes in the music.

Composing and Arranging

In this final part, you learn how to create and arrange your own music, write for specific voices and instruments, and produce good-looking master scores and lead sheets.

CHAPTER 18

Musical Genres and Forms

Although basic music theory applies to all forms of music, it helps to know the different genres and forms out there. Yes, a quarter note is a quarter note is a quarter note, but how those notes are put together distinguishes jazz sounds from country or symphony sounds from today's pop songs.

In This Chapter

- Discovering classical music forms
- Turning on to blues and jazz
- Learning more about folk, rock, country, and other popular music

Classical Music

Our examination of musical forms starts with what most of us call "classical" music. It turns out there are a lot of different types of classical music, many of them associated with specific historical eras.

Classical Music Through the Years

Laypeople tend to refer to all serious music prior to the dawn of the twentieth century generically as "classical" music, no matter when it was written. That said, there *was* a distinct Classical era that ran from 1750 to about 1820, but that wasn't the only era in which so-called classical music was created.

The history of serious classical music is divided into the following major eras:

Medieval (also known as the Middle Ages; A.D. 500 to 1400). This early music is characterized by chants and other simple nonsecular forms of monophonic music. Notable Medieval composers include John Dunstable, Lionel Power, and Guillaume de Machaut.

Renaissance (A.D. 1400 to 1600). Music from the Renaissance era is characterized by a rise in polyphony, primarily within vocal forms. Notable Renaissance composers include Josquin des Préz, Guillaume Dufay, and Giovanni Pierluigi da Palestrina.

Baroque (A.D. 1600 to 1750). Baroque music is characterized by flamboyant, heavily ornamented melodies. Notable Baroque composers include Johann Sebastian Bach, George Frideric Handel, and Antonio Vivaldi.

Classical (A.D. 1750 to 1820). Music of this era is characterized by simple lyrical melodies, often expressed in majestic orchestral and choral works. The most important Classical composers include Ludwig van Beethoven, Wolfgang Amadeus Mozart, and Franz Joseph Haydn.

Romantic (A.D. 1820 to 1900). Romantic-era works are characterized by emotional musical expression and sophisticated harmonies, often employing chromaticism and a moving away from traditional tonality. Notable Romantic composers include Johannes Brahms, Antonin Dvořák, Franz Liszt, Felix Mendelssohn, Richard Strauss, Pyotr Tchaikovsky, and Richard Wagner.

Twentieth Century (1900 to present). Contemporary classical music adheres to no single style and is often wildly experimental in terms of tonality, rhythm, and form. Important composers of the twentieth century include Aaron Copland, Claude Debussy, Giacomo Puccini, Maurice Ravel, Arnold Shoenberg, and Igor Stravinsky.

Classical Forms

Each musical era is distinguished by its own unique musical forms. Here's a list of the most popular forms, in rough chronological order:

Plainsong. The earliest music of the Medieval period was an unaccompanied monophonic chant performed by the monks of the early Christian church. These chants were based on the seven so-called church modes—Ionian, Dorian, Phrygian, Lydian, Mixolydian, Aeolian, and Locrian.

Mass. This is the music of the Roman Catholic Mass, beginning in the fourth century A.D. Originally consisting of plainchant melodies, more modern Mass settings (modern being from the fifteenth century or so) utilize melodies from secular songs.

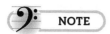
NOTE

> Around A.D. 600, Pope Gregory I moved to standardize the Mass and encourage a ritualized use of music by the church. The resulting chant eventually became known as *Gregorian chant.*

Motet and grand motet. The *motet* is a short, unaccompanied choral work for two or more voices, popular from the thirteenth through the sixteenth centuries. In Europe, the motet evolved into the *grand motet,* an expanded form that contrasts solo voices (accompanied by *continuo* instruments, such as bass viol or harpsichord) with a larger chorus.

Canon. This musical form dates to the Renaissance era. Its melody is imitated by various parts at regular intervals in contrapuntal fashion. Think of a canon as a type of "call and response"; the first voice is the call or statement, and the second voice is the response or imitation.

Madrigal. This piece of secular vocal music from the Renaissance period survives in Christmas traditions to this day. The typical madrigal is a polyphonic composition for four to six voices, typically unaccompanied, based on a poem or other secular text.

Ballet. This is an entertainment in which dancers perform to music to tell a story or, in some cases, to express a mood. Over the years, music for the ballet has proven a vital form for serious composers such as Mozart, Stravinsky, Tchaikovsky, Verdi, and Wagner.

Sonata. This piece of instrumental music is performed in several distinct and contrasting sections, called *movements.* Sonatas typically are written for a soloist and small ensemble.

Concerto. This piece of ensemble music is for voices and instruments, typically with a solo instrument or voice in contrast with an orchestral ensemble. It was developed by Vivaldi, Handel, Bach, and their counterparts in the early eighteenth century and continued onward into the Renaissance with important works by Mozart, Haydn, and others.

Suite. This longer instrumental form incorporates multiple contrasting sections, typically constructed from individual dance movements, often in the same key.

Opera. A long, complex dramatic work, the opera incorporates both voices and instruments. You can think of an opera as the classical equivalent of today's popular musicals, mixing music with a dramatic plot—kind of like a stage play with much of the plot being told via song.

Aria. A vocal piece (a song, operatic in nature) that can be either standalone or part of a larger vocal piece (a song, operatic in nature) that can be either standalone or part of a larger work, such as an opera. Over time, arias have become longer and more complex, serving as a type of showcase for the vocalist.

Operetta. A newer, less-ponderous type of opera, the operetta is a form of light entertainment that was a definite contrast to the often self-consciously "heavy" music of the times.

Oratorio. This dramatic musical setting of a sacred libretto is for solo singers, choir, and orchestra. An oratorio is like a religious opera but without the scenery or costumes; oratorios are typically performed in concert halls or churches.

Symphony. An extended work for an orchestra, a symphony typically is in three or four distinct movements. The modern symphony is a large-scale instrumental composition, much like a sonata for orchestra, usually in four movements.

Symphonic poem. This is a single-movement orchestral work on a symphonic scale. The symphonic poem is a type of Romantic-era *programme music*—an instrumental work that tells a story, illustrates a literary idea, or evokes a pictorial scene.

Chamber music. This work is for small instrumental ensembles designed to be played in small halls or private residences—the antithesis of majestic, concert-hall symphonies. One of the most popular forms of chamber music is the *string quartet*, consisting of two violins, a viola, and a cello.

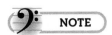

Learn more about the history of music in my companion book, *The Complete Idiot's Guide to Music History* (Alpha Books, 2008).

Blues and Jazz

Now let's move to two musical forms that have influenced and informed just about every type of popular music today—blues and jazz.

The Blues

When you think of the blues, you may think of an old black man singing with his acoustic guitar or wailing on an electric. Or you may think of a group of black singers singing a capella. Or you may think of a bar band cooking along to a boogie-woogie beat.

The blues is all of this, and more. In fact, the style commonly called the blues is actually an entire family of musical styles, all sharing similar roots in the African American slave community of the eighteenth and nineteenth centuries.

All the different blues styles are based on the concept of "blue notes," or the flattened notes of the normal major scale. These blue notes help distinguish what we call the *blues scale*. In the blues scale, several notes of the major scale—the third, the fifth, and the seventh—are flattened. This creates so-called *blue notes* between the normal scale notes. The resulting blues scale is a six-note scale (not counting the octave) that looks like this, in relationship to a major scale:

1 -♭3 - 4 -♭5 - 5 -♭7

This blues scale is unusual in that it doesn't have a second or sixth degree, but it does throw in a flatted fifth in addition to the regular perfect fifth. It's the flatted third, flatted fifth, and flatted seventh notes—the blue notes—that define the color of the blues scale. Here's how this looks in traditional music notation, in this instance the C blues scale :

The C blues scale.

Also distinctive are the chords played behind the melody, the unique *blues progression.* Most blues tunes follow a classic 12-bar chord progression. This 12-bar form is comprised of three phrases, each four bars long. Musically, the chords of the blues progression go like this:

I - I - I - I   IV - IV - I - I   V7 - IV - I - I

This blues progression is utilized in many forms of popular music, not just the blues. You'll find this progression used in many songs of the Great American Songbook, much rock and country music, and a whole lot of jazz. It's a uniquely versatile chord progression, with many popular variations. (You learned about the blues progression in Chapter 10.)

Jazz

Jazz is America's homegrown classical music. Derived from the blues, it is one of this country's truly indigenous musical styles. For a time, jazz was the country's popular music; audiences listened to and danced to jazz music just as they dance to rock or country or hip hop today.

So, what exactly is jazz? Some people might define jazz as music with improvised solos. Others might define it as music with a swing beat—a rolling *spang spang-a-lang spang-a-lang* kind of rhythm. But other types of music feature improvisation, and lots of jazz has a rock beat instead of a swing beat.

The truth is that jazz is a blend of several different musical styles and is itself represented by multiple stylistic variations. The first jazz music was born in New Orleans between 1885 and 1915. This type of jazz—call it *classic jazz, New Orleans jazz,* or *Dixieland jazz*—grew out of the existing blues, ragtime, and brass band traditions.

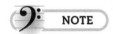 **NOTE**

> One name towers over all others in the history of early jazz: cornetist and vocalist Louis Armstrong. Armstrong's small ensemble recordings of the mid-1920s, famously known as the Hot Fives and Hot Sevens, revolutionized jazz music and introduced the era of the virtuosic leader/soloist. Armstrong also pioneered the vocal style of scat singing, improvising on nonsense syllables instead of actual lyrics. He was the first singer to *scat sing* on record ("Heebie Jeebies," 1926), when he purportedly dropped his lyric sheet while recording and was forced to improvise nonsense lyrics.

Dixieland jazz quickly morphed into *hot jazz,* which introduced full-blown improvisation into the mix. During the 1930s, hot jazz evolved into *swing,* and most jazz groups grew into big bands led by legends such as William "Count" Basie, Duke Ellington, Benny Goodman, and Artie Shaw.

Big bands became less fashionable after World War II, as jazz musicians began to explore more complex harmonic structures. This new music, called *bebop,* featured wildly inventive (and fast-paced) improvisation and became the dominant form of jazz for the next several decades.

Post-bop, jazz has become a bit of a niche genre, splintered into several different variations. There's *cool jazz* (a more melodic, more intellectual approach as practiced by Miles Davis, Dave Brubeck, and others), *modal jazz* (based on modes instead of chord progressions), *hard bop* (a less-frenetic offshoot of bebop), *soul jazz* (melding jazz improvisation with a contemporary rock/soul beat), *free jazz* (with fast tempos and complex chords and harmonies), *fusion* (merging jazz and rock), and even *smooth jazz* (laid-back jazz improvisation over simple beats and chords).

What all these variations have in common is a focus on improvisation. Jazz is, at the end of the day, all about solos and individual expression.

Popular Music

You might find it hard to believe, but classical music was the popular music of its day. So was jazz. But neither is all that popular with today's listening audience. Today's popular music is simpler and more accessible than the serious music of decades and centuries past. We're talking music, typically short songs, that are more easily grasped by listeners and more easily played and sung by performers.

In reality, there are lots of different types of popular music, including the following:

Folk. This is any music based on the folk tradition, typically played on traditional instruments such as acoustic guitars and banjos.

Country. Derived from a blend of Appalachian folk music and rural blues, country music is simple and folky, often performed with guitars and fiddles—and a distinct vocal twang. Over time, country evolved through and into a variety of related styles, including *Western swing* (country + jazz), *honky tonk* (electric + traditional country + blues), *bluegrass* (Western swing + traditional country + honky-tonk), *countrypolitan* (country + pop), *country rock* (country + rock), *alt country* (traditional country + honky-tonk + rock + folk), and *Americana* (country + folk). Then there's the *contemporary country* of today, which sounds pretty much like classic rock with a few steel guitars and fiddles thrown in (and with all the guys wearing cowboy hats).

The Great American Songbook. This consists of sophisticated pop songs written by professional songwriters between the years of 1900 and 1950, often for Broadway shows. These so-called Tin Pan Alley songwriters include giants like Irving Berlin, Cole Porter, and George and Ira Gershwin.

Rock. Rock and roll arrived in the mid-1950s, sanding off the rough edges of that era's black music to make it more palatable to white teenaged audiences. This new musical stew included elements of traditional country, honky-tonk, electric blues, jump blues, and R&B, all stirred together with a rolling straight eighth-note beat. From those initial country and R&B flavorings, rock evolved into myriad subgenres throughout the 1960s and beyond. There was the *surf music* of The Beach Boys, followed by the *British Invasion* of The Beatles and the Rolling Stones, followed by hippie-dippy *psychedelic rock* and Dylan-inspired *folk rock,* followed by *heavy metal* and *disco* and *punk rock* and *New Wave* and *progressive rock* and *grunge* and any number of related and unrelated variations.

Rhythm and blues (R&B). This is contemporary black music that evolved from the blues and jazz music of the 1940s. In its original form and in later incarnations as soul, funk, and contemporary R&B, this music brought black culture to white audiences across America.

Rap and hip hop. This music consists of spoken lyrics (that's the "rap") over a steady beat. Some rap songs incorporate snippets of melody, often sampled from other songs. That said, rap music is more about the beat and the words than anything else; there's still a basic verse-chorus form, but the focus is on the lyrics, not on the music.

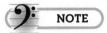

> **NOTE**
>
> Rock music arguably has been the most dominant type of popular music from the 1950s to today. The more generic term "pop music" refers to any type of popular music, typically using the same format but with a lighter beat and smoother instrumentation. For example, one might argue Katy Perry is more pop than rock, whereas Green Day is definitely more rock than pop. (Don't even ask about Barry Manilow and Pat Boone ....)

Exercises

Instead of traditional questions and answers, the exercises for this chapter are *listening* exercises. Your assignment, should you choose to accept it, is to seek out and listen to recordings that represent the various types of music you've just read about. Listen to the pieces with an ear toward what makes each type of music unique—think about the form, the level of complexity, the type of instrumentation, and so forth. Write down your impressions, if you like, and find someone equally interested to discuss them with. (Or just consider yourself more informed for doing the listening.) To get you started, I've created Spotify and YouTube playlists that include recordings that represent the music discussed in this chapter. You can link to these playlists from this book's web page, located at idiotsguides.com/musictheory.

The Least You Need to Know

- What we call "classical" music includes music from multiple musical eras, including the Medieval, Baroque, Renaissance, Classical, Romantic, and Twentieth Century eras.
- There are several important types of classical compositions, including Mass, motet, concerto, sonata, symphony, and opera.
- Blues and jazz music both derive from African American work songs and incorporate the blues scale and blues progression.
- Professional songwriters such as Irving Berlin and George Gershwin contributed sophisticated music and lyrics to the Great American Songbook of the early twentieth century.
- The world of popular music includes a variety of styles, including folk, country, rock, R&B, and rap.

CHAPTER 19

Composing Your Own Music

Whether you're writing a rock, country, or folk song, or composing a longer, more serious work (not that pop music isn't serious business), you work with the same elements. All musical compositions must include a melody and a series of chords. Now, you can write the melody first and then add chords, write the chords first and then add a melody, or write both melody and chords at the same time, but you need both of those elements.

How you put those melodies and chords together determines your final composition. And that's what this chapter is all about: composing music.

In This Chapter

- Discovering the tools you need to compose a piece of music
- Learning how to compose using chord progressions
- Finding out how to create strong melodies

How to Become a Composer

What is composition? In musical terms, composition is the art of creating a piece of music. That piece of music can be as short as an advertising jingle or as long as an opera. It can be instrumental or vocal; it can be "serious" or commercial, popular or avant garde, classical or contemporary. It can be a three-chord song for a rock or country band or a complex work for a full orchestra and chorus. In short, a musical composition can be anything you can hum or sing or play. There are no boundaries as to what you can create.

That said, you can't just jot down a bunch of random notes and call it a composition. (Well, you could, but nobody would want to listen to it.) A good composition has form and meaning; it tells a story, or invokes a mood, or takes you from one place to another. The best compositions create their own self-contained realities, where individual components relate to and with each other within the whole. There is a reason for each phrase and individual note, all of which combine to create a whole that is more than the sum of the parts.

I like to think of the process of writing a composition as being similar to telling a story. As you can tell many different types of stories, you can create many different types of compositions. Some stories relate a specific set of facts; others convey a general mood; still others exist merely to entertain. A good story takes you from point A to point B in a relatively efficient fashion, while containing enough extraneous elements to make the journey entertaining; there are often characters or places or other elements that provide both color and context. And, when the story is over, there's typically a point to the whole thing, something to remember and reflect upon.

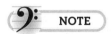 **NOTE**

> *Songwriting* is a particular type of composition with both music and lyrics. For the purposes of this book, we'll focus strictly on musical composition, which is kind of like songwriting without the words.

Different Approaches to Composition

As you learn how to write your own music, you'll discover that there are several different ways to approach a composition. They all start with a blank sheet of staff paper (or virtual page in your notation software), but require you to look at your pending composition in different ways.

There is no one "correct" way to begin a composition. Some composers take one approach, some another, some work both ways—often by creating the chords and melody simultaneously. Which method you choose is a personal decision. And you're not limited to just one approach; you can use different approaches for different pieces. Whichever way you start, the goal should be the same—to create an artistically viable piece of music. How you create each piece of music is a personal choice.

If you consider that a piece of music is typically constructed from a combination of chords and melodies (and, in the case of songwriting, lyrics), then you have a simple choice in front of you. You can start by creating a chord progression and fitting a melody to your chords, or you can start by creating a melody and then fitting chords to that melody. Consider:

Chords first: Also called *harmonic composition,* you start by creating a chord progression and then fit a melody to those chords. This approach is popular among many composers, especially those working within the framework of the popular song. That's because after you've created a chord progression, you essentially have a harmonic road map for the entire composition that helps to guide the melodies you create. Unfortunately, some composers tend to use a chord progression as a crutch, and often create melodies that simply outline the chords rather than standing on their own.

Melody first: Also called *melodic composition,* you start by creating a melody and then fit the appropriate chords to that melody. When you craft a melody on its own, it isn't subject to the harmonic constraints of an arbitrary chord progression; it's allowed to flow wherever it needs to. This approach is very respectful of the primacy of melody, with all other aspects of the composition taking a subsidiary role. If you go this route, you have to employ your knowledge of harmony to harmonize the melody—that is, to fit a chord progression to the melody.

Chords and melody together: If you can approach composition from either a chords-first or melody-first approach, why not combine both approaches and compose everything at once? That's the nature of *holistic composition,* where you progress measure-by-measure, creating the melodies and harmonies simultaneously. Since melodies and chords are intrinsically related, it makes sense to write them together—if you can. (This approach requires a thorough understanding of music theory, a very good ear, and a good feel for where you want your composition to go—and thus may not be the best way to go for beginners.)

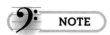 **NOTE**

Some composers prefer a *layering* approach, where you start by creating one vocal or instrumental part, and then you layer additional parts on top of that. The composition builds piece by piece, until you've built a layered whole. Layering is used to good effect with certain contemporary musical forms; it's also the approach used in loop-based music you create on your computer, where you build a composition by layering different musical loops on top of each other.

Learning How to Write Your Own Music

To be a successful composer, you need a certain set of skills. In particular, you need to be able to manipulate the building blocks of any composition—the notes and rhythms and chords that combine to create a piece of music. To this end, you must have a thorough grounding in music theory, as well as a good ear. It also helps to have some innate sense of melody and harmony, although this can be developed with proper training.

A successful composer must also have the ability to arrange and orchestrate the music he writes. Composition is seldom as simple as a melody and accompanying chords; most full-blown compositions are ultimately orchestrated for a range of instruments, whether that's a four-piece rock band or full symphonic orchestra. So you need to know at least a little bit about a lot of different instruments—not necessarily how to play each one, but rather how they sound and how they're written. (Learn more about arranging and orchestration in Chapter 20.)

Assuming you have (or learn) these basic skills, learning how to compose involves fitting the various building blocks together to express your musical vision. It's kind of like learning how to write prose or poetry; once you know the building blocks of written language, you then have to learn how to use those building blocks to tell your stories in print.

There's also the issue of creativity. Although you can, over time, learn the necessary compositional tools and techniques, you need to supply your own creativity and inspiration. Creating a melody really is more than just arranging notes in a certain order; the best melodies come from somewhere inside of you, and reflect your personality and experiences. Music is, after all, a creative endeavor—and composing music requires all the creativity you can muster.

Composing with Chords

Let's start with the approach that most beginning musicians and many songwriters employ—harmonic composition. That means coming up with a catchy chord progression and then fitting a melody to it.

When you're working with harmonic composition, you can work with any number and type of chords. You don't have to limit yourself to the natural chords within a scale or key (the diatonic chords) or with simple three-note triads, especially when you're working in more contemporary forms. You can explore all manner of chromatic chords and extended chords and the like, even chords that don't really look or sound like traditional chords—two-note harmonies, or note clusters with no discernable tonal center. In other words, the entire harmonic spectrum is available for your use.

That said, when you're first starting out, it's a good idea to work within some sort of structure, to help guide your creativity. Once you've learned how to compose within a traditional harmonic structure, you can begin to explore nontraditional harmonies; you use the structure to help hone your craft.

Using Chord Leading

One easy way to come up with a pleasant-sounding chord progression is to use chord leading. As you learned in Chapter 10, chord leading is the concept that certain chords naturally lead to other chords. For example, the V or dominant chord leads naturally back to I, the tonic. The IV, or subtonic, can lead naturally to the I, iii, V, or vii° chords. And so forth. (You learned about which chords lead to which in Chapter 10.)

The most common way to utilize chord leading is simply to use the chord-leading rules to move from one chord to the next. Let's say you start with a I chord, which can lead to any other chord. You choose the iii chord as the next chord, which then leads you to (among others) the IV chord. The IV chord leads you up to the V chord, and then back to I. And there's your chord progression:

```
I          iii          IV          V          I
```

In the key of C, that works out to:

```
C / / /    Em / / /    F / / /    G / / /    C / / /
```

And you can bend those chord-leading rules a bit too, as shown in this progression used in thousands of hit songs from "Let It Be" to "Don't Stop Believin'" to "Hey, Soul Sister." Start with the I, of course, but then jump up to the V. Now, the V *should* lead back to the I, but it can also lead in other directions, such as up one step to the vi chord. Move from the vi to the IV, then from there back home to the I. This is what you get:

```
I          V          vi          IV          I
```

Here's how that sounds, in the key of C:

```
C / / /    G / / /    Am / / /    F / / /    C / / /
```

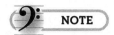

NOTE

Even easier, you can base your composition on one of the common chord progressions detailed in Chapter 10. Nothing wrong with a simple I-IV-V or ii-V-I progression for your tune!

Establishing a Harmonic Rhythm

Working with chord-based composition brings up an interesting question: just how often should you change chords? The pace of a chord progression, or where the chords are placed within a phrase, is called *harmonic rhythm*. In other words, the harmonic rhythm dictates how often you change chords—and when.

Obviously, the number of beats or measures allotted to each chord isn't set in stone. For example, you could write the I-IV-V progression with a single measure for each chord. Or you could write two measures of I and a measure each of IV and V. Or you could write three measures of I, then two beats each of IV and V in a fourth measure. Or you could write 16 measures of I, 16 measures of IV, and another 16 measures of V. It all depends on the nature of your composition and helps provide an almost infinite variety of possible chord combinations.

There are no rules for harmonic rhythm. You can extend a chord over any number of measures, or change chords frequently within a single measure. You can set your chord changes on the first beat of each measure or on any subsidiary beat. You can even change chords on the upbeat, if you want.

It's common to change chords more often at slower tempos than at faster ones. It's simply easier to fit two or four chords into one slower-moving measure than it is within a faster-paced tune. A fast-paced country song, for example, might have chord changes every two or four measures. A slower-tempo ballad, on the other hand, might change chords every two beats within a single measure. There's more space for each chord when the tempo is slower.

The harmonic rhythm is one factor that establishes the sound and feel of a particular composition. A rapid harmonic rhythm will dictate, more often than not, particular types of melodies—typically faster-moving melodies. A slower harmonic rhythm will let your piece breathe a little more. And varying the harmonic rhythm will provide contrast within your piece. Use harmonic rhythm to establish the mood and pace of your compositions.

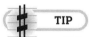

TIP

Although there are many notable exceptions, I find that a somewhat faster harmonic rhythm helps to create more interesting melodies. Whenever there's a chord change, there is impetus to make the melody move accordingly—and the more movement there is in a melody, the more interesting it is.

Fitting Melodies to Your Chords

When you employ a chord-based compositional approach, the chord progression you create becomes a framework on which you later construct a melody. But just how do you fit a melody to your chords? We discussed some of this back in Chapter 10, but let's go into more detail here.

A common approach is to base your melody on the notes of the chords. That is, you use the chord tones to define the main notes of your melody. For example, if you're holding a D minor for a few measures, you would work with the notes D, F, and A for your melody. You can then add passing and approach notes to connect these main chord tones.

A melody based on key chord tones.

You can also create a melody that utilizes the common notes in adjacent chords. For example, if you're using the popular C-G-Am-F progression, know that the first two chords have the note G in common, and the last two have the notes A and C in common. (The G and Am chords don't have any notes in common, sorry.) So you can base the melody in the first two bars around the note G, and in the last two bars around either A or C.

A melody based on common tones in the underlying chords.

Another approach is to use notes that emphasize the key quality of the underlying chords. For example, the dominant (V) chord gets its tension from the root, so emphasize that. Similarly, when shifting between major and minor chords, emphasize the changes by basing the melody on the thirds of each chord.

A melody that emphasizes the defining features of the underlying major and minor chords.

Whichever chord tones you use as the major notes in your melody, you can then use appropriate diatonic tones in a step-wise fashion to move from one major tone to another. For example, if the major melodic tone in measure one is a C and the major tone in the next measure is an F, use a D and E to smoothly move from one to the next. These passing tones make your melody more melodic, as opposed to just jumping from one chord tone to the next.

A melody that uses passing tones to move from one major tone to the next.

Making Memorable Melodies

Back in Chapter 8, we worked through the basics of what makes a melody a melody. As I hope you recall, a melody is a logical succession of tones and rhythms. Place the right notes in the right order, and you have yourself a melody.

A melody has to make harmonic sense—that is, the notes of the melody have to fit within the given key and the specific chords employed. Melodies can go up or down but they have to move somewhere, or else all you have is a single repeated note. The best melodies not only work within the chord structure but define and sometimes predict the song's chord progression. And the best melodies are not only singable (or at least hummable, if you're not a great singer) but also help tell a story or set a mood. (You learned about constructing simple melodies in Chapter 8.)

All of this brings us to the key question: how exactly can you create a memorable melody?

Center on a Pitch

You don't want your melodies wandering around all over the place, like a dog looking for a place to do his business. What you want is more of a hunting dog of a melody, one that knows where home is and, at the end of the day, finds its way back there.

The "home" of your melody needs to be a specific pitch. When you pick a home pitch, your melody can then revolve around the pitch. You can start on that pitch (although you don't have to), and you should end on that pitch. Equally important, the other notes in the melody can play around that pitch—and even land on it, occasionally.

Note that your home pitch doesn't have to be the tonic of the scale. You can make the third your home, or the fifth—but probably not the second or sixth or seventh, because they're less related to the tonic triad of 1-3-5.

For example, listen to the following melody. It's in the key of G, but revolves around the home pitch of B—the third of the scale.

A four-measure melody in the key of G, which hovers around the third of the scale (B).

What you want to avoid is having each measure of your melody center around a different pitch. If your melody wanders around in this type of fashion, with no central core, you won't know how to end it—you won't know where home is.

Make Sure You End Up at Home

Many of the most memorable melodies use the home pitch to lend logic to the melodic flow. In fact, it's good if your audience can listen to part of your melody and, based on the prominence of the home note, hum the end of the melody before they ever hear it.

When you don't end your melody on the expected note, you create an unresolved tension that can be unsettling to listeners. Although it's okay to insert that kind of tension in the middle of your melody, you don't want to end with that kind of tension. You want to resolve your melody so that there's a feeling of completion at the end.

What you want to avoid is a melody that wanders around aimlessly. Let your ear be your guide. Play over the melody and see if it holds together. It's a little bit like writing a good paragraph or a good stanza of a poem; when you're finished, the best thing to do is to read it aloud and see if it really works.

The wrong way to do it—you don't want to end your melody with unresolved tension.

Go Pentatonic

You can make things even simpler by sticking to five key notes within a given major scale—the first, second, third, fifth, and sixth of the scale. (In C Major, these notes are C, D, E, G, and A.)

These notes combine for what is called the pentatonic scale. (The word "penta" means "five"; five tones equal a pentatonic scale.) By using only these five notes, you avoid the two notes in the scale (the fourth and the seventh) that sometimes create harmonic tension.

On a piano, an easy way to see and play a pentatonic scale is to play strictly on the black keys. These five keys—G♭, A♭, B♭, D♭, and E♭—comprise the G♭ pentatonic scale.

When you use the five notes in the pentatonic scale, it's virtually impossible to insert a "wrong" note into your melody. However, you can overuse these notes and end up with a vaguely Asian-sounding tune—or even something that sounds a little bit like the theme to an old cowboy movie!

A melody based on the C pentatonic scale.

Find the Hook

For a melody to be truly memorable, there needs to be a piece of it that really reaches out and grabs the listener's attention. In pop music this is called the hook, because it's the part of the song that hooks the listener. In more traditional music, this piece of the song is sometimes known as the *motif*—and is repeated throughout the entire piece of music.

A motif is typically fairly short—a few notes (think of the five whistling notes in Sergio Leone's theme from the movie *The Good, the Bad and the Ugly*) or, at longest, one or two measures. When you hit on a good motif or hook, don't be afraid to use it—repeat it as often as you need, throughout your entire song.

A simple four-note motif, repeated throughout a longer melody.

Create Variations

You can create additional melodies in your music by varying your motif slightly, such as changing its rhythm or moving its tones up or down in the scale. You should retain enough of the main motif so that listeners can tell where it came from, but add enough variation so that you create a new—but related—melody.

How can you vary a motif? You can reverse the rhythm, simplify the rhythm, or make the rhythm more complex. You can reverse the notes (so that the melody goes up instead of down, or down instead of up), or change the middle notes in the motif, or shift the notes up or down a third or a fifth. In short, just about any variation is fair game, as long as the initial motif isn't completely obliterated by the variations.

Take a look at the following example, in which the simple four-note motif from the previous example is run through a number of variations—both rhythmically and melodically.

The same four-note motif, with variations.

Remember that you want your variations to relate to the original motif. If you get too far away from the original motif, it isn't a variation anymore—it's a brand-new melody!

Make It Move

A good melody doesn't just sit there; it goes someplace. You can propel a melody rhythmically, or tonally, through the "motion" of the tones. In this sense, motion refers to the progressive upward or downward direction of the pitches, or what some call the contour of a line of music.

A good way to think about the upward or downward motion of a melody is to look at the starting note and the ending note—while ignoring, for the time being, all the notes in between. To create an upward-moving melody, make sure the ending note is at least a third (and ideally a fifth or more) higher than the starting note. Same thing with a downward-moving melody; force the last note to be lower than the first one.

All the notes between the first and last notes help you move to that final note. The notes don't all have to go in the same direction, but they do have to gradually move up or down to where you want to end.

A melody with upward motion.

Note that it's okay to have a melody that starts and ends on the same note. What you can do is make the midpoint of the melody higher or lower than the starting/ending pitch. If you choose a higher midpoint, the first half of the melody will have upward movement, and the last half will use downward movement to return to the home pitch.

Take Small Steps

The most singable melodies progress in small steps, which means each note is only a step or two away from the previous note. The smaller the steps between the notes in your melody, the more lyrical your melody will sound.

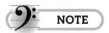

NOTE

A melody that progresses in half or whole steps uses what is called step-wise or conjunct motion. Melodies that progress by leaps larger than a whole step use what is called skip-wise or disjunct motion.

When you throw large jumps—of three or more steps—into your melody, it starts sounding random, and becomes much more difficult to play or sing. It's much better to use a series of passing notes within your chosen scale to move from one main note to another.

Obviously, this isn't a hard-and-fast rule. (And every rule is meant to be broken, anyway!) Think, for example, of "Somewhere Over the Rainbow," or "Moon River," or "When You Wish Upon a Star." All of these songs feature leaps of anywhere from a fifth to an entire octave in their melodies. So it's okay to leap, if you know what you're doing—although small steps are better suited for less-experienced songwriters.

Small steps and large leaps in a melody—the small steps sound more lyrical and are easier to sing.

Stay in Range

You don't want to cover too many notes in your melody. If the distance between the lowest note and the highest note is too wide, singers will have trouble singing all of your melody—and your melody will start to sound random and disjointed, without a home.

Consider, for example, America's national anthem, "The Star-Spangled Banner." Francis Scott Key put his words to one whopper of a tune, one that has a rather wide melodic range. Think of how hard this song is to sing—and how many well-trained vocalists have trouble hitting all the notes. The broad range in this song doesn't make it a bad song; it just makes it one of the more difficult songs to sing or play.

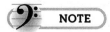

NOTE

Ironically, the melody of "The Star-Spangled Banner" comes from an English drinking song called "Anacreon in Heaven." Maybe the high notes are easier to hit after a few pints of British ale!

Thus, if at all possible keep the lowest and highest notes in your melody within an octave of each other (or at most, within an octave and a third). You should also consider the absolute range of the voice or instrument you're writing for, and try to stay within that range. (To learn more about voice and instrument ranges, turn to Chapter 20.)

A melody with too wide a range—really hard to sing!

Set Up—and Resolve—Tension

One of the most common melodic techniques is to divide your melody into two parts, and set up a harmonic tension in the first part that is then resolved in the second part. This gives your melody a distinct form, and its own internal logic; it also helps to propel the melody from the first part to the second.

One way to create tension is to end the first part of your melody on something other than the tonic of the scale. (When you factor in the chord structure, you find that tension is achieved by ending the first part of the melody on a IV or V chord instead of on the tonic.) Practically, you can create tension by ending a phrase with the second, fifth, or seventh notes of the scale—which correspond to the notes in the scale's V chord, if you're reading ahead.

The half note in measure two creates tension; the next two bars resolve the tension.

You then have to relieve this tension by manipulating the second part of your melody back to the tonic of the scale—or to one of the notes in the tonic triad (the I chord). The notes in the tonic triad are the tonic, third, and fifth of the scale, although the tonic and the third probably work better for relieving tension. (That's because the fifth is an ambiguous note, used both in the I chord and the V chord.)

In any case, you can hear the tension when you play a melody. Just look back to Dvořák's *New World Symphony* or "Michael, Row the Boat Ashore." For that matter, "Mary Had a Little Lamb" also has this type of internal tension, coming right after "Mary had a little lamb, little lamb, little lamb," and resolved with "Mary had a little a lamb, whose fleece was white as snow."

It's a popular technique—because it works!

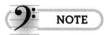

> **NOTE**
>
> Legendary songwriter Jimmy Webb, in his book *Tunesmith: Inside the Art of Songwriting* (Hyperion, 1998), says that the key to writing interesting melody is "to lead the ear on a path which is both *pleasant* and to some degree *unexpected*." (Emphasis his.) I agree wholeheartedly. The best melodies sound familiar yet still manage to surprise us somewhere along the line; they do a good job balancing repetition and variety.

Follow the Words

Another factor that can drive a melody is the presence of lyrics. If you're writing an instrumental, of course, you don't have to worry about following the words. But if you're writing a popular song, you have to deal with both music and words—and how they fit together.

You want your music to fit with your words. In the simplest sense, this means arranging the rhythm of the music so that it fits the natural rhythm of the words. You don't want your singers to be forced into awkward phrasing to fit all the syllables into a given space. Most words and phrases have a natural pace, and will suggest a rhythm to you. Make sure your music's rhythm fits this lyric rhythm—in particular, avoid putting an unaccented word or syllable on an accented part of the measure, like the downbeat.

Fitting Chords to a Melody

If you use the melodic approach to composition, you now have a melody that needs some chords. Just how do you find the right chords for a given melody? Here are a few things to try.

Try the Obvious

One quick way to add chords to an existing melody is to try to fit one or more common chord progressions to your melody. Examine the popular chord progressions presented back in Chapter 10, and see if any of them fit the melody you've written. You'd be surprised how many melodies fit with the I-IV-V progression!

For example, you can see how the downward progression of the following melody fits easily within the I-vi-IV-V progression. You can try other progressions (such as I-vi-ii-V), but when you find a good fit you're home free.

A melody made to order for the I-vi-IV-V chord progression.

Use the Melodic Outline

Guessing at the right chord progression isn't very sophisticated, even if it often gets you where you want to go. A more analytical approach is one that deconstructs your melody, looking for clues to an implied harmony. What you want to do, in essence, is strip out all the embellishing tones and create a melodic outline of the most important, or structural, tones. The structural tones of the melodic outline will quite often suggest the underlying chords.

In most cases each structural tone will be one of the notes of the underlying chord triad. You can try fitting chords around each structural tone, having that tone function as either the root, the third, or the fifth of the three possible chords.

For example, let's say you're in the key of C Major and one of the structural tones in your melody is a C. Working diatonically, you can fit that C into either a C Major chord (as the root), an A minor chord (as the third), or an F Major chord (as the fifth). So for any structural tone in your melodic outline, you have three possible diatonic chords that could fit. Play each of the three chords in the context of the melody, and see which one fits best.

Fitting three possible chords to a single structural tone.

Let's work through an example, starting with a full melody. When we reduce the melody to its structural tones, you can see that they create a framework for the underlying harmony. Through a process of trial and error, we choose those chords that, first, sound best and, second, make the most harmonic sense within the framework of the composition.

Start with your complete melody …

… then extract the embellishing tones to create a melodic outline …

… and fit the proper chords to each of the structural tones.

For example, once you get to the final measure, you have to determine which chord to fit with the C note. You could choose F the IV chord), Am (the vi chord), or C (the I chord). The question you have to ask is whether it's more likely that the preceding V chord (against the D) would lead to the IV, the vi, or the I?

If you remember your chord theory, you can be pretty sure that a V-I progression (the good old perfect cadence) makes more sense than any of the alternatives, so you harmonize that C with a C (I) chord. There's some guesswork involved, of course, but the theory should provide at least one possible way to proceed. You can test your harmonization by playing the chords against the entire melody; if it sounds good, you made the right choices. (If not, try again!)

Your chord choices, fit against the original melody.

Work Backward

Here's another trick for easier harmonization: work backward. That's right, you can often figure out the proper chord progression by working backward from the final chord in a phrase, using rudimentary chord-leading theory. Remember that most traditional melodic phrases end on the tonic harmony. This means that the final chord in your melodic phrase, more often than not, will be a I chord. You then can figure out the cadence leading to the I (probably a V chord), and work backward from there using the chord leading rules you learned in Chapter 10. With this approach you can have half the harmony decoded fairly quickly.

For example, if you assume that this melody ends on the I chord, then the penultimate chord should be the V chord. What chords best lead to a V chord? Try the ii (the dominant of the V), and you'll see that it works. Which chords lead to the ii chord? There are a few, but again try the dominate of the ii—the vi chord. This also works. And how do you get to the vi chord? There's nothing like a I to lead to a vi, and since that I would sit on the very first beat of the phrase, you know that's the best (if not the only) choice. By working backward, you've fit a I-vi-ii-V7-I progression to your melody.

Start at the end (with a V-I cadence) and use chord-leading theory to work backward from there.

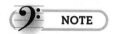 **NOTE**

When harmonizing a melody, don't make things more complicated than they have to be. This means starting with simple triads, rather than complex extended chords. You can always add extensions later, but working with simple three-note chords puts a limit on the available chords, which means you have to work through fewer options.

Exercises

Exercise 19-1

Write an eight-bar chord progression in the key of F that starts and ends with the I chord and includes both the IV and V chords.

Exercise 19-2

Write an eight-bar chord progression in the key of G that starts with the ii chord, ends with the I chord, and does *not* include the V chord.

Exercise 19-3

Compose an eight-bar melody in the key of C, using the C Major scale, in 4/4 time. Use whole notes, half notes, quarter notes, and eighth notes; and begin and end your melody on the C note.

Exercise 19-4

Compose an eight-bar melody in the key of G, using the G Major scale, in 4/4 time. Make this a rhythmically lively melody at a relatively fast tempo, using half notes, quarter notes, eighth notes, and sixteenth notes.

Exercise 19-5

Compose a melody to fit the chord progression you wrote for Exercise 19-1.

Exercise 19-6

Compose a melody to fit the chord progression you wrote for Exercise 19-2.

Exercise 19-7

Harmonize (add chords to) the melody you wrote for Exercise 19-3.

Exercise 19-8

Harmonize (add chords to) the melody you wrote for Exercise 19-4.

The Least You Need to Know

- You can create a composition by writing the chord progression first and then adding a melody (harmonic composition) or writing the melody first and then adding a chord progression (melodic composition).
- Use chord leading and other harmonic techniques to create a logical chord progression.
- The best melodies feature step-wise movement, a singable range, and some degree of repetition.
- To harmonize a melody, use structural tones and try some common chord progressions.

Arranging for Voices and Instruments

Unless you're writing for your own unaccompanied solo voice, you're going to eventually deal with how to have other voices and instruments play your music. This could be figuring out how to attack a song with a four-piece rock band, creating a simple vocal arrangement for your church choir, arranging a sophisticated piece for your high school jazz band, or orchestrating a multipart symphony.

Whatever size group you're working with, you have to deal with the same issues of theory, and call on the same set of skills. You also have to know a little bit about the ranges of each instrument or voice, and how each instrument will play the notes you write.

This chapter deals with the particular skills necessary for arranging vocal and instrumental music. I recommend you bookmark this chapter; if you do a lot of arranging, you'll find the information very useful!

In This Chapter

- Discovering the different voices in the choir—and all the instruments in the orchestra

- Uncovering the best—and the worst—keys to write in

- Finding out which instruments don't sound in concert pitch—and how to transpose their music

- Learning how to write for common vocal and instrumental ensembles

Vocal Arranging

A vocal ensemble is probably the easiest type of group to arrange for. That's because all the voices reproduce exactly what you write, with absolutely no transposition. (Well, except for the fact that the tenor voice sounds an octave lower than written—but that's an easy one to deal with.)

Voice Characteristics

When you're writing for a choir, you have to know the voices available. In general, you have two female voices and two male voices, with an optional third male voice to work with.

Soprano. This is the highest female voice. The soprano typically sings the lead part, as the highest voice naturally stands out from the rest. Some sopranos can sing quite high, although you might want to avoid the very upper reaches of the range; these high parts often sound shrill, especially with younger or less-experienced singers.

Alto. The alto is the lower female voice, with a deep and resonant tone. The alto range overlaps the soprano range, but know that an alto will sound strained at the top of her range—just as a soprano will sound strained at the bottom of hers.

Tenor. The tenor is the highest male voice; it overlaps significantly with the range of the female alto. Tenor parts are written in treble clef, but actually sound an octave lower than written.

Baritone. The baritone is an optional male part; most choruses don't have separate baritone lines. The baritone falls smack between the tenor and the bass, but typically has more of a basslike sound—without the very low notes.

Bass. The bass is the lowest male voice. It's natural to assign bass notes to the bass voice, which works out okay most of the time. At the low end of the bass range, the sound gets a tad rumbly.

The main voices (soprano, alto, tenor, and bass) combine into what is called SATB form, which is how most chorale works are arranged. If you have a younger or less skilled ensemble, you can always arrange a simple two-part score, with all the females singing one part and all the males singing the other.

Vocal Ranges

It's important that you write vocal parts that can actually be sung. It's no good to write a bass part that sounds forced—if the poor fellow can hit the note at all.

For that reason, pay close attention to the ranges listed in the following table and stick within these ranges when writing your vocal parts.

Vocal Ranges

Voice	Range (Concert Pitch)	Write It ...
Soprano		Concert pitch
Alto		Concert pitch
Tenor		One octave above concert pitch (unless sharing a staff with the basses)
Baritone		Concert pitch
Bass		Concert pitch

Instrumental Arranging

When you move on to instrumental arranging, you have a lot of different instruments at your disposal. You need to know a little bit about how each instrument works—in particular, the range of the instrument and whether it sounds in concert pitch or is somehow transposed.

Instrument Characteristics

Instruments are typically organized into several major groups. For our purposes, we'll look at strings (both bowed and plucked), brass, woodwinds, keyboards, and percussion.

Strings

When you think of stringed instruments, you typically think of the violin and its close cousins: the viola, cello, and double bass (sometimes called the *string bass* or *upright bass*). Each of these instruments works on the same principle, with four strings stretched over a hollow body. Music is made when a bow is pushed and pulled over the strings, or when the strings are plucked.

The highest string voice is the violin, followed (in descending order) by the viola, cello, and double bass. The violin is written with the treble clef; the cello and double bass use the bass clef; and the viola—the oddball of the group—uses the alto clef, as shown in the following figure. (Remember, the pointy part of the alto clef points at C.)

The alto clef, used primarily by the viola.

These are exceptionally versatile instruments, equally capable of both solo and ensemble work; especially useful is the fact that their tone color stays very constant over the entire range of the instrument. If you plan on writing a lot for strings, it behooves you to learn more about how the instruments work, in particular the various types of bowings.

Guitars and Other Plucked Instruments

The guitar is technically part of the string family, although most folks differentiate it from the violin-type instruments. That's because the guitar is never bowed; it's always plucked or strummed. (The guitar also has six strings, compared to the four strings of the violin instruments.)

Several other instruments fit within the guitar category. The mandolin and ukulele are smaller and higher pitched than the guitar, whereas the electric bass is more like a traditional double bass, but in a guitar-like configuration with just four strings.

Guitars, of course, can be either acoustic or electric—and the electric ones can have either solid or hollow bodies. The different configurations produce different types of sound, although the notation is the same for all the different guitars.

Guitar parts can be notated with notes on staves or, if you just want a strummed rhythm, by using chord notation. You can also spell out the fingering of each chord by using guitar tablature, as shown in the following.

Guitar tablature.

 TIP

Guitar tabs can be automatically derived from traditional chord notation when you use a computerized music notation program, such as those discussed in Chapter 21.

Oh, and while we're talking about plucking strings, we can't forget the harp. The harp isn't really a guitar (it's kind of like a piano, but vertical), but it does work when you pluck its strings.

Woodwinds

Some woodwind instruments are made of brass; some are made of wood. But all (except the flute) use a wooden reed to produce their sound; you put the reed in your mouth and blow until it vibrates.

The flute produces sound when you blow across an open hole—kind of like blowing across a soda bottle. But it's still classified as part of the woodwind family, probably because it has a similar valve structure and fingering for determining individual notes.

There are lots of different woodwind instruments. You have flutes and piccolos, at least four different types of saxophones, a variety of clarinets, those odd-sounding oboes and bassoons, and even the not-so-common English horn (which isn't a horn and isn't even English—it's an alto version of the oboe).

Woodwind instruments primarily use the treble clef, although the bassoon and contrabassoon both use the bass clef.

Brass

Brass instruments typically are made of brass; however, so are saxophones and cymbals and timpani, and they're not part of the brass family, so that really isn't a good indicator, is it? Nope, what makes brass instruments unique is that length of brass tubing wound up into a tight little package, the open mouthpiece you blow into (instead of the reed of a woodwind instrument), and the three or four valves you use (in conjunction with changing the shape of your lips) to create different tones.

The trumpet is the brash and annoying younger brother of the brass family, the trombone is the more stable older brother, and the tuba is the not-always-serious uncle. Also hanging around is the weird foreign relation, the French horn, and a few other unusual relatives, such as the baritone. All in all, it's a rather loud and brassy bunch—pun intended.

Brass instruments use either the treble or bass clefs, depending on their predominant pitch.

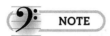 **NOTE**

> Although the trumpet is traditionally a B♭ instrument, many players today use C trumpets that sound in concert pitch.

Keyboards

Depending on whom you ask, keyboard instruments are really string instruments or percussion instruments. In reality, they're a little of both. The sounds are produced by internal strings, which are struck by tiny hammers—much like percussion instruments are struck.

There are many different types of keyboards, and they all have fairly wide ranges. The piano, of course, is the big dog, but you can't forget about organs, harpsichords, or any number of electronic synthesizers. A full piano has 88 keys; some smaller instruments can have shorter keyboards. Without exception, all modern keyboard instruments sound in concert pitch.

And let's not forget the newest category of keyboards, those electronic instruments known as synthesizers. Synthesizers can be either analog (creating new sounds via oscillators and other electronics) or digital (typically sampling and then reproducing the real-world sounds of other instruments). Digital synthesizers can be used to replace other instruments, especially when you're composing on a budget, or to create a virtually unlimited variety of wholly new sounds.

Percussion

When you talk percussion, you're talking about a lot of different instruments. Percussion instruments make noise when you hit them or shake them, so the family includes everything from snare drums and cymbals to marimbas and timpani. Most percussion instruments are of indefinite pitch—that is, although they make a noise when you hit them (or shake them), that noise isn't associated with a specific pitch. Other percussion instruments, such as timpani and the mallet family, do produce a definite pitch (or pitches).

When you're writing for an indefinite pitch instrument, you don't have to follow standard staff notation. For example, when you write for drum set, you assign different parts of the staff to different drums and cymbals in the set. In the following example, the bass drum is the bottom space on the staff; the snare drum is the third space up. Cymbals are at the top, notated by X-shaped note heads.

Writing for drum set.

Of course, you can save yourself a lot of time and trouble by just telling the drummer how many measures there are in each section of your song and letting him (or her) make up his (or her) own part. That's particularly common when you're arranging for a rock or jazz band.

Transposition

Many instruments read one note and play another—at least compared to concert pitch (the actual notes as played on a piano). For example, a trumpet reads a C but sounds a B♭. These so-called transposing instruments need to have their music transposed to a different key to play in the same concert key as all the other instruments.

Let's take the trumpet again. Because the trumpet always sounds a major second lower than written, you need to write the trumpet part a major second (two half steps) higher than the pitch you actually want to hear. So if you want the trumpet to play a concert C, you have to write a D; the trumpet reads D, sounds C, and everything is right with the world.

You learned about transposition back in Chapter 14, and you'll need to apply those skills here. That's because there are a lot of instruments that don't play in concert key; all the following instruments need their parts transposed.

Most transposing instruments fall into three groups and are named according to how they relate to C:

B♭ instruments, like the trumpet, sound a major second below their written pitch. That is, they're written a major second above the concert pitch. So if one of these instruments plays a C, it comes out sounding as B♭ in concert pitch.

E♭ instruments, like the alto sax, sound a major sixth below (or a minor third above) their written pitch. That is, they're written a major sixth above the concert pitch. So if one of these instruments plays a C, it comes out sounding as E♭ in concert pitch.

F instruments, such as the French horn, sound a perfect fifth below their written pitch. That is, they're written a perfect fifth above the concert pitch. So if one of these instruments plays a C, it comes out sounding as F in concert pitch.

The following table details which instruments fall into which group.

Transposing Instruments

Transposing Type	Sounds	Instruments
B-flat instruments	Major second lower than written	Bass clarinet (actually a major ninth lower)
		Bass saxophone
		Clarinet (B♭)
		Cornet
		Flugelhorn
		Soprano saxophone
		Tenor saxophone (actually a major ninth lower)
		Trumpet

continues

Transposing Instruments   (continued)

Transposing Type	Sounds	Instruments
E-flat instruments	Major sixth lower than written	Alto clarinet
		Alto saxophone
		Baritone saxophone (actually a major thirteenth lower)
		E♭ clarinet (actually a minor third higher)
F instruments	Perfect fifth lower than written	English horn
		French horn

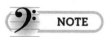

NOTE

There are actually many more transpositions than listed in this table, especially among the instruments used in classical music. For example, trumpets in D were often used by Mozart, Haydn, and other composers of their time. This is because early trumpets and horns had no valves, so there were only a limited number of notes available on them. A composer would then choose a transposition that gave him the best selection of available notes for each instrument.

With a few exceptions, instruments not listed here are nontransposing—that is, what they play sounds exactly as written, in concert pitch. The best example of a nontransposing instrument is the piano; you read middle C, you play middle C, the piano sounds middle C—no transposing necessary.

What does all this mean in terms of actual transposition? The next table details how each type of instrument transposes each of the possible concert keys. The key listed for each instrument is the key that you write for that instrument in order to sound the concert key. (For example, for the concert key of C, you would write a B♭ instrument in the key of D, an E♭ instrument in the key of A, and an F instrument in the key of G.)

Concert Key Transpositions

Concert Key	B♭ Instruments	E♭ Instruments	F Instruments
C	D	A	G
D♭	E♭	B♭	A♭

Concert Key	B♭ Instruments	E♭ Instruments	F Instruments
D	E	B	A
E♭	F	C	B♭
E	G♭ (F♯)	D♭ (C♯)	B
F	G	D	C
G♭	A♭	E♭	D♭
G	A	E	D
A♭	B♭	F	E♭
A	B	G♭ (F♯)	E
B♭	C	G	F
B	D♭ (C♯)	A♭	G♭ (F♯)

When you write a part for a transposing instrument, you do all the transposing up front, by changing the key of the piece. That is, you don't transpose each and every note individually; the transposition is done by shifting the key signature for the transposing instrument. For example, if a composition is in the concert key of C Major, you would write the trumpet part in D Major.

As you learned in Chapter 14, all of today's music notation programs will automatically perform this transposition for you, saving you the trouble of transposing all the instruments manually. With a program like Finale or Sibelius, you can write the entire piece in concert pitch and then have the program create individual output in the instruments' transposed pitch. Easy!

Good Keys and Bad Keys

Because of the need to transpose the nonconcert key instruments, you can end up with some instruments reading a whole bunch of sharps and flats, which of course is problematic. For example, the concert key of A has three sharps, and is relatively easy for nontransposing instruments to read. But for B♭ instruments, such as trumpets, the transposed key is B, which has five sharps and is a bear to read. For that reason, you probably want to avoid composing in the concert key of A—unless you want to give your trumpet section a real workout!

In general, you want to arrange things so no instrument is reading more than three sharps or flats. Taking this challenge into account, the following table shows the best—and the worst—keys to compose in.

Good and Bad Concert Keys

Good Keys	Acceptable Keys	Bad Keys
E♭	C	D♭
F	G	D
B♭	A♭	E
	G♭	A
		B

Each instrument has its own playable range, and it's important to know the lowest and highest notes possible for each instrument. To that end, check out the table of instrument ranges online at idiotsguides.com/musictheory—you'll use it!

Choosing Instruments for an Arrangement

Knowing how each instrument sounds (and is written) is just the first step in the study of orchestration. What's more important is using that information to create your own compositions and arrangements.

When composing or arranging a piece, one of the first things you need to do is determine for what instruments you're writing. A piece written for solo bassoon and piano accompaniment will sound quite different from one written for full symphonic orchestra. The characteristics and range of each instrument will influence the music you write. Conversely, the sounds you hear in your head will help determine the instruments you choose to write for.

This is why it's so very important to have fixed in your mind how each instrument sounds—both generally and across various parts of its range. If you have a particular sound in your head, you should be able to choose which instrument(s) can best produce that sound—or, in some instances, which combinations of instruments can do the job.

For example, you might know what a flute sounds like, and you might know what a flugelhorn sounds like, but do you know what they sound like when played together? It's actually a quite interesting sound, especially when they're played in unison. (They sound a little different when they're playing together in harmony, but still interesting.) Or how about paring a trombone in its high range with a cello? Or a baritone sax with a bassoon? Or a violin with a French horn? Or a piccolo with a xylophone?

You get the point. There's an entire world of musical colors out there for you to choose from, if you know how to choose.

And after you've chosen your instruments, you need to know how to best use those instruments within your composition. There are various ways to voice a saxophone section, for example, which produce entirely different sounds. Voice the saxes in nice open thirds, and you have a lyrical quality that sounds good in ballads and slow passages. Voice them in tighter blocks, and you get a buoyant sound that's good for fast passages.

I can't teach you all the possible combinations of instruments, or how to best use each combination—at least not in this book. For that, you have to embark on your own personal study of orchestration. It's definitely worth the effort.

Common Ensembles

Although you can compose and arrange for any combination of instruments and voices you like, you're likely to run into certain established ensembles over the course of your musical career. When asked to compose a piece for orchestra or string quartet, it helps to know precisely what instruments are involved—and how they're used.

For that reason, we'll look at a half-dozen or so of the most popular instrumental and vocal ensembles. Read on to learn more.

Choir

A choir can contain singers of any level of expertise, and can embrace music from a variety of genres, from the classical repertoire to the latest pop hits. Of course, to be accurate, there isn't a single ensemble type called "choir"; there are actually many different types of vocal ensembles for which you can arrange. Some of the more popular forms include:

Trio. A vocal trio is just what it says—three voices. In the classical genre, trio music is typically written for female voices (soprano, second soprano, and alto), although trios in pop music can consist of all female, all male, or mixed voices.

Quartet. A quartet is a four-voice ensemble. In classical music (and some pop and jazz) the breakdown is standard SATB—soprano, alto, tenor, and bass. Of course, you can have all-female or all-male quartets, like those in barbershop quartets. But the mixed-voice quartet is the most popular.

Chamber choir. A chamber choir is a small choir, normally with 12 to 24 singers, typically performing repertoire from the sixteenth and seventeenth centuries. There are also some modern chamber choirs that sing everything from Renaissance music to jazz.

Madrigal choir. Another common vocal chamber group is the madrigal choir. The madrigal is a form of choral music that was popular in Europe primarily in the sixteenth century. It is usually sung *a cappella*.

Swing choir. A so-called swing or show choir is a mid-sized, mixed-voice ensemble that performs various types of popular music, from Broadway show tunes to the latest pop songs. (This is the type of choir seen in the TV show *Glee.*) Swing choirs typically have a full rhythm section accompaniment—piano, bass, drums, and sometimes guitar.

Large choirs. This is the traditional large choir or chorus, encompassing everything from junior high or high school choirs to church choirs to community choirs and beyond. These choirs can be of any size and composition—while mixed-voice is most common, there are also many popular all-male and all-female choruses.

To make it simple, a high school or adult mixed-voice ensemble typically has four voice parts—soprano, alto, tenor, and bass. (Occasionally, each of these parts are split, so that you have first and second soprano, first and second alto, and so on.) Women's choirs have three or four voice parts: soprano I, soprano II, alto I, and alto II (optional). And men's choirs have three or four voice parts: tenor I, tenor II (optional), baritone, and bass.

TIP

When arranging for voices, remember that singers need to breathe. (So, for that matter, do woodwind and brass players.) Don't tie together four whole notes at a slow tempo, or the singers might pass out trying to make it to the end of a phrase. Try to arrange natural breathing places at the ends of phrases, and don't hesitate to insert a short rest after a few long notes.

Symphonic Orchestra

The modern orchestra is a very large ensemble. It's not necessary to have every instrument playing at all times, but you still have a large number of instruments to choose from for your orchestral arrangements.

A full symphonic orchestra can include virtually every instrument available, including a complete complement of strings, woodwinds, brass, and percussion. It's all hands on board, with multiple instances of most instruments, especially in the string sections.

The traditional orchestral string section consists of first and second violins, a single viola section, a cello section, and a section of double basses. In a large orchestra, you may have as many as 16 first violins, 14 second violins, 12 violas, 10 cellos, and 8 basses. Smaller orchestras use a similar ratio between sections, but with fewer individual instruments to start with—such as an 8-7-6-5-4 mix.

Woodwinds have an important but limited role in the modern orchestra. Orchestral instrumentation typically includes piccolo, first and second flute, first and second oboe, English horn, first and second B♭ clarinet, bass clarinet, first and second bassoon, and contrabassoon. (Note the total absence of the saxophone family.)

The orchestral brass section is actually quite large, at least in number of parts. Typical orchestral instrumentation includes four French horn parts, three trumpets, three trombones, and a single tuba. You may have one or two instruments per part—although one instrument per part is most common.

The orchestral percussion section includes a wide variety of instruments played by a small number of players; a single player typically plays multiple instruments, as the piece requires. Common orchestral percussion includes timpani, a range of mallet instruments (orchestra bells, chimes, xylophone, marimba, sometimes vibraphone), traditional percussion (snare drum, bass drum, suspended and crash cymbals), and a variety of hand percussion (sleigh bells, finger cymbals, triangle, tambourine, and so forth).

By the way, the symphonic orchestra is used for more than just symphonies. Many film and television soundtracks employ full orchestras, as do some videogame scores; some rock bands even call in an orchestra to fill things out on occasion. Because of all the instruments available, the orchestra is perhaps the most versatile type of instrumental ensemble available, and worthy of your studies.

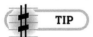

TIP

On a symphonic score (discussed in Chapter 21), the instruments are displayed in the following top-to-bottom order: woodwinds, brass, percussion, special instruments (like piano or harp), and, finally, strings.

Chamber Orchestra

A *chamber orchestra* is a stripped-down version of the full symphonic orchestra, typically playing chamber music in smaller halls. The typical chamber orchestra employs a small string section (first and second violin, viola, and cello), a handful of woodwinds and brass (flute, oboe, B♭ clarinet, bassoon, French horn, and trumpet), and the occasional piano and timpani. Chamber orchestras typically have fewer musicians on each part. Instead of an entire section of violins, for example, there might only be one or two violinists on each part.

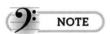

NOTE

Note the addition of the piano to the chamber orchestra (between the timpani and the strings); the piano is infrequently used in the full orchestra.

String Orchestra

A *string orchestra* is simply the five primary instruments of the string section (first violin, second violin, viola, cello, and double bass), sometimes accompanied by a piano. There are no brass, woodwind, or percussion instruments in this ensemble.

String Quartet

Another common ensemble in both classical and contemporary music is the *string quartet.* As the name implies, this is a grouping of four string instruments (one each—no doubling per part): first and second violin, viola, and cello. (There's no bass in a string quartet.)

Concert Band

A *concert band* is less like a marching band and more like an orchestra without the strings. A typical concert band contains virtually all the brass, woodwind, and percussion instruments from the larger orchestra, but more of them—and with saxophones added. Just no strings.

The concert band repertoire is symphonic in nature, like an orchestra, and the instruments play much the same roles as they do in orchestral works. You typically find multiple parts per section, and multiple players per part. There might be a little more use of the percussion section in a band arrangement, too, compared to the traditional orchestra.

 TIP

Since concert and marching bands don't have strings, you can tailor your arrangements for woodwind and brass instruments. That means selecting keys that are "band-friendly"—that is, keys that are easy to play for all the horn players, such as concert F, B♭, E♭, and A♭. You should avoid sharp keys, as well as keys with more than four flats.

Marching Band

Then there's the *marching band,* which has similar instrumentation to a concert band, minus the following instruments: oboe, English horn, bassoon, alto clarinet, cornet, and bass trombone. The percussion section is also different, with a lot more snare drums and bass drums and crash cymbals, less hand percussion, and (in many cases) a separate "pit" with nonmobile instruments, such as timpani, xylophones, and the like.

That said, there's really no such thing as a "standard" marching band these days. A band from a small school might have fewer than 20 members; a "pep" band organized for high school basketball games might have 30 to 40 members; a monster band from a large high school or college might have 200 members or more. Then there's the special category of *drum corps*, a streamlined band that consists solely of drums and brass instruments—no woodwinds.

There's also considerable variation in the ages and skills of the players. Writing for a middle-school marching band is going to be a lot different than writing for a high-school or college band. And the talent level (and interest) will vary depending on how focused the band is on competition, versus just playing at football games and a few local parades.

So you may need to keep your arrangements simple. That's also a good idea when you realize that many marching bands require their musicians to memorize their music—and then march their routine. Make it too hard to play and the kids won't be able to remember it!

Big Band (Jazz Band)

Another popular ensemble, especially in the jazz idiom, is the so-called *jazz band* or *big band*. A typical jazz band includes the following:

- Sax section with three to five players on alto, tenor, and baritone saxes

- Trumpet section with three to five pieces

- Trombone section with three to five instruments

- Rhythm section consisting of piano, bass, drums, and sometimes guitar

And that's it. Anywhere from 12 to 20 players, all capable of playing section parts or solos. It's amazing how versatile this combination of instruments really is.

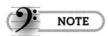
NOTE

Sax players sometimes double on flute. Trumpet players sometimes play fluegelhorn, especially on ballads.

Today's big bands can play in a variety of styles. The most common styles are classic 1940's swing (Benny Goodman, Glenn Miller, Artie Shaw), straight ahead jazz (Thad Jones/Mel Lewis, Woody Herman), hard driving jazz (Buddy Rich, Big Phat Band), blues (Count Basie), Latin/jazz (Stan Kenton, Dizzy Gillespie), jazz/rock (Maynard Ferguson), and ballads (any and all). A given band may specialize in a particular style, or may have a book that encompasses multiple styles.

Whatever the style, big-band music often adheres to an established-yet-flexible form. You start with some sort of an introduction, move into a series of verses and choruses (some of which are used as sections for improvisation), perhaps play through a short interlude, ramp it up for the shout chorus, and then drive through to the ending. Just remember to leave room for those instrumental solos—big bands do play jazz, and jazz is all about the improvisation.

Rock Band (Rhythm Section)

A typical rock band consists of one or more electric guitars, bass, and drums. You can add lots of other instruments, however; keyboards are common, as are acoustic guitars. This is also the basic instrumentation you'll see in most church praise bands, in many folk bands (but with acoustic instruments instead of electric ones, of course), and as the rhythm section in larger ensembles, such as big bands.

As you can see, it's a very versatile combination of instruments—and gets even more versatile when you augment the basic configuration with other instruments. Add a horn section with trumpet and a couple of saxes if you want a more soulful punch; add a cello or string quartet if you want a more orchestral sound; or add a pedal-steel guitar and fiddle if you want a country band.

The rock band's rhythm section is there to back the singer; in larger ensembles, the rhythm section's function is to back the other instruments. It provides not only the underlying beat (typically via repeated rhythmic patterns), but also the basic harmonic background to a piece.

And here's an important thing to know about arranging for a rock band or rhythm section—in most forms of jazz and popular music, you don't actually write out all the notes. That's right, most rhythm section parts are just sketches; you rely on the individual players to essentially ad lib their own parts.

In some cases, this means writing a single lead sheet that all the musicians read from. In other cases, you may need to write out individual parts for each of the instruments, notating specific passages you want played but elsewhere using slash notation and letting the musicians interpret as necessary. Seldom do you write out every note of every measure for every instrument.

Beyond this combination of both general and specific instructions, the individual players are free to improvise their own parts. This is actually a good thing, as it frees you from trying to come up with natural-sounding parts for instruments that you probably don't know how to play. After all, the specifics of creating a measure-long drum fill are probably best left to a drummer, who can do that sort of thing in his sleep.

Exercises

Exercise 20-1

Transpose the following melody for trumpet. (Remember to set the transposed key signature!)

Exercise 20-2

Transpose the following melody for alto sax. (Remember to set the transposed key signature!)

Exercise 20-3

Transpose the following melody for French horn. (Remember to set the transposed key signature!)

Exercise 20-4

Transpose the following trumpet melody back into concert pitch. (Remember to set the transposed key signature—and watch those accidentals!)

The Least You Need to Know

- In descending order, the four main voices in the choir are soprano, alto, tenor, and bass (SATB).
- The main families of instruments are strings (both bowed and plucked), woodwind, brass, keyboards, and percussion.
- Transposing instruments don't sound in concert pitch; they sound a specified interval above or below the written note. Their parts must be transposed so that the note they play is the proper note in concert pitch.
- B♭ instruments (trumpet, clarinet, and soprano and tenor saxes) sound a major second lower than concert pitch; E♭ instruments (alto and baritone saxes) sound a major sixth lower than concert pitch; and F instruments (English horn and French horn) sound a perfect fifth lower than concert pitch.
- Common vocal ensembles include the trio, quartet, chamber choir, madrigal choir, and large choir.
- Common instrumental ensembles include symphonic orchestra, chamber orchestra, string orchestra, string quartet, concert band, marching band, jazz big band, and rock band or rhythm section.

CHAPTER 21

Lead Sheets and Scores

Once you've written a piece of music, you need to present it in a way that other musicians can easily read. There are many different approaches to notating written music; which ones you use depends in part on the type of music you've written and who will be playing it.

If you've written a song for a rock or country band, the music you write can be fairly simple—chords and melody will generally suffice. If, on the other hand, you've written a piece for chorus or a full-blown symphony (good for you!), you'll need to create a detailed score containing the individual parts for each voice in the choir or instrument in the orchestra.

Whatever type of written music you create, you need to keep it neat and make it easily understandable. Musicians have to be able to read the music at first pass (called *sight reading*), which means it helps to follow certain established parameters. There's no point in being unique if nobody can read your music!

In This Chapter

- Creating clear and readable written music
- Understanding the differences between lead sheets, chord sheets, and scores
- Learning how to create a full score for choir, big band, or orchestra
- Exploring easy-to-use music notation software for your computer

Follow the Rules

Whatever type of music you prepare, you need to follow certain notation rules—guidelines, actually, since they're not set in stone. These guidelines include the following:

- The first instance of each staff for each instrument or voice must have its own clef sign, key signature, and time signature.

- Typically, the time signature is shown only in the very first measure—and wherever a time change appears.

- Each instrument should be clearly marked at the beginning of each staff. (The first instance typically has the full instrument name spelled out; subsequent staves can use abbreviations.)

- In band and orchestral *scores*, group like instruments together (all the trumpets together, for example).

- For instruments that use the grand staff (both bass and treble clef), group the two staves by using braces.

- Measure lines should be drawn through all the instruments belonging to the same section—but not through all the instruments in the score.

- If you want, you can combine all like instruments on a single staff (all the trumpet parts on one staff, for example).

- If an instrument or voice will be resting for an extended period of time, you don't have to include the staff for that instrument or voice during the rest period.

- Use letter markings to notate individual sections of the music. (For ease of reading, letter markings are typically enclosed in a box or circle.)

- Number your measures—or at least the first measure of every line. (Alternately, you can insert a number mark every 5 or 10 measures.)

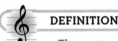

DEFINITION

The master piece of music—the one that contains all the individual parts—is called the **score**.

It goes without saying that the music you create should also be *readable*. If you're writing it all out by hand, make sure you produce clear and distinct notes that are easily distinguishable on the staff. If you have poor penmanship (like I do!), consider taking a calligraphy course to improve your handwriting, or use a computerized music notation program to create great-looking music on your computer printer. (See the "Use the Computer" section later in this chapter.)

These rules apply to the score you compose and that the conductor uses. As for the music that the musicians themselves read, you have to create individual parts for each instrument. (This is not a requirement for vocal scores.) So if you've written a piece for a big band, you have to create a separate first trumpet part, and a separate second trumpet part, and a separate third trumpet part, and so on. When you write out the individual parts, include only that instrument's part—the conductor is the only person who gets to see all the parts together on the master score.

Take the Lead

The most common form of written music is the *lead sheet*. A lead sheet doesn't include any individual instrumental parts; all you get is the song's melody, chords, and lyrics.

As you can see in the following example, a typical lead sheet consists of one staff for the melody line, with lyrics under the staff and chords above it.

Lead sheet.

Lead sheets are simple to create, and they're ideal for notating popular songs. If you play in a rock or country band (or even a jazz trio or quartet), you can use lead sheets to present much of the music you play.

WARNING

A lead sheet is not commercial sheet music. Sheet music typically includes full piano parts, whereas lead sheets contain melody and chords only. In addition, lead sheets are not available commercially, unlike sheet music.

Make It Simple

Even simpler than the lead sheet is a piece of music that contains only chords—no melody lines and no lyrics. There are two different approaches to this type of music, and we'll look at both.

Chord Sheets

The *chord sheet* is just what it sounds like: a sheet of music containing only the chords of a song. The chords are presented measure by measure, so that members of the rhythm section (piano, bass, and guitar) can play through the song with minimal effort.

TIP

If you prepare a chord sheet using a music notation program, you may choose to include guitar tablature in addition to the standard chord symbols. This is particularly useful if you're writing for beginning-level guitarists.

Chord sheet.

The Nashville Number System

In the field of country music, especially among studio musicians, a different type of chord sheet is used. This method of writing chords is called the *Nashville Number System*, and it uses numbers instead of letters.

In the Nashville Number System, everything revolves around the tonic chord of a given key. That tonic chord is assigned the number 1. The chord based on the ii of the key—a minor chord—is assigned the number 2m. (The m tells the musician it's a minor chord.) The chord based on the iii of the key—also a minor chord—is assigned the number 3m. And so on up the scale, up to chord number 7.

As you can see, major chords are distinguished by number only; minor chords have an m added. Extensions are added as superscripts to the right of the number, so that a dominant seventh chord based on the fifth of the scale is noted as 5^7.

A chord chart using the Nashville Number System looks something like the following example.

Chord chart using the Nashville Number System.

Because the Nashville Number System doesn't use traditional notes, it is ideal for musicians who don't know how to read music. It also makes it very easy to change key—just play the 1 or 2 or 3, or whatever chord in whatever key you want; it's as easy as that.

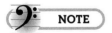 **NOTE**

The Nashville Number System is very much like the Roman numeral notation system, except it uses regular numbers (1, 2, 3) instead of Roman numerals (I, II, III).

Sing It Loud

Arranging for choirs is a bit more complicated than sketching out chords for a rock band. Choral music normally has four or five parts, and each part has to have its own line in the score.

Let's look at a typical four-part choral score. The parts are arranged with the highest voice (soprano) at the top, and the lowest voice (bass) at the bottom. The four vocal parts (soprano, alto, tenor, and bass) are grouped together with braces, and a piano accompaniment is included below the vocal parts. The top three parts use the treble clef; the bass line uses the bass clef. Lyrics are included below each staff.

SATB choral score.

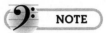

Charts for choruses are sometimes called *SATB scores*, for the soprano, alto, tenor, and bass parts.

When you create a choral score—or any score with multiple parts, for that matter—make sure a measure within one part aligns vertically with the same measure in all the other parts. In fact, the notes within each measure also should align between parts. If it helps, use a ruler to help keep the notes in alignment when you're writing the score.

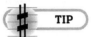

If there are additional backing instruments, they can also be included in the score—below the vocals, just like the piano part.

Jazz It Up for Big Bands

Another popular ensemble—particularly among high school and college musicians—is the *big band*, or *jazz band*. A typical jazz band includes a lot of instruments, which results in a fairly large piece of music. For example, whereas a choral score might get two groups of staves on a page, a jazz band score typically takes a whole page just to display all the different instruments.

When you create a big-band score, you have a choice of how you deal with transposing instruments. You can create a concert key score, with all instruments written in concert key; if you take this approach, you have to make sure you transpose the individual parts when you create them. Alternately, you can create a transposed score in which each instrument is written in its transposed key; this type of score might be harder for the conductor to read, but it more accurately represents what the musicians see on their individual parts.

Creating parts for the rhythm section is particularly interesting. In most cases you can use slash notation and indicate the chord changes, but you don't have to create fully realized parts. The big exception to this is when you have important rhythms that you want the rhythm section to reinforce; you can note these rhythms using slash notes, as shown in the fifth measure of the example.

Score for big band.

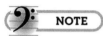

NOTE

In all band and orchestral scores, like instruments are typically grouped together in *systems*. In a system, the individual staves are joined together, to make it easier to view the instruments as a group.

Strike Up the (Concert) Band

An even bigger band to write for is the *concert band*. Unlike a jazz band, a concert band includes virtually all the brass and woodwind instruments, along with a full percussion section—snare drums, bass drums, timpani, marimba, and so forth. A concert band is almost like an orchestra, but without strings.

Concert bands evolved from traditional marching bands. The musicians get to sit down, and the instrumentation was augmented from the slightly more Spartan marching ensembles.

When you're writing a concert band score, you include the following groups of instruments, in top-to-bottom order:

- **Woodwinds:** Piccolo, flute, oboe, English horn, clarinet, alto clarinet, bass clarinet, bassoon, alto saxophone, tenor saxophone, baritone saxophone

- **Brass:** Cornet, trumpet, French horn, trombone, bass trombone, baritone horn, tuba

- **Percussion:** Timpani, percussion (with separate staves for snare drum, bass drum, and so on)

The example here shows a typical concert band score. As with jazz band scores, concert band scores can be in either concert key or transposed.

March Madness March

Michael Miller

(c) 2002

Score for concert band.

Make the Big Score—for the Symphonic Orchestra

Now we're in the big leagues. Creating a score for full orchestra is a major undertaking, if for no other reason than there are many instruments to deal with. Because of this, most orchestra scores are written on large sheets of paper—11 × 17 inches or so. Because of the sheer size of the beast, you'll probably get only four to eight measures on each page, which means the typical orchestral score also is fairly long.

TIP

You also can create a *condensed score,* in which individual parts are collapsed into single staves. This type of score is easier to read, even though it doesn't contain the part detail necessary for initial rehearsals. You have the option of cutting down the number of staves in the score during long sections of music where fewer instruments are playing.

As you can see from the example, instrument families are grouped together in the score in the following order:

- **Woodwinds:** Piccolo, flute (first and second), oboe (first and second), English horn, E♭ clarinet, B♭ clarinet (first and second), bass clarinet, bassoon (first and second), contrabassoon, French horn (first, second, third, and fourth)

- **Brass:** Trumpet (first, second, and third), trombone (first, second, and third), tuba

- **Percussion:** Timpani, percussion (including snare drum, bass drum, marimba, etc.)

- **Harp**

- **Piano**

- **Strings:** Violin (first and second), viola, cello, double bass

As with big-band scores, you can create orchestral scores in either concert key or transposed keys—whichever works better for you.

Because most orchestral pieces are fairly long, it's important to include proper road mapping in your scores. Number each measure, and designate each section with a new letter. This way musicians (and the conductor!) can easily find their places during the starting and stopping of the rehearsal process—or if they happen to fall asleep during a long rest in a live performance!

Score for full orchestra.

Use the Computer

In the old days, it was a real pain in the rear to create scores for large ensembles. Every part had to be written separately, by hand, and transposed as necessary. That was a lot of writing, and didn't always result in the most readable pieces of music—especially if your handwriting is as bad as mine!

Today, thanks to computer technology, a lot of this notation process can be automated. *Music notation software,* available for both Windows and Macintosh operating systems, enables you to create a complete piece of music—including full orchestral scores—from your computer keyboard. The result is a professional-looking piece of music, complete with proper note spacing and notation marks.

All music notation programs let you enter notes on the page with either your mouse or computer keyboard. All you have to do is click a position on the staff, and a note appears.

Many of these programs also let you connect a MIDI keyboard and input music directly from the keyboard to your computer. The notation program translates the notes you play on the keyboard into corresponding notes on a staff. You can then fine-tune the music onscreen as necessary.

 NOTE

> *MIDI* stands for "musical instrument digital interface," and is a computer protocol for passing audio information digitally from one electronic device to another.

The two most popular music notation programs today are Finale (finalemusic.com) and Sibelius (sibelius.com). Both programs work in similar fashion; Finale costs a flat $600, while Sibelius is sold on a subscription basis for $9.99/month. Fortunately for cost-conscious or outright starving musicians, both programs are also available in lower-priced and/or student versions, so you can get similar (but not identical) functionality at a bargain price.

If Finale and Sibelius are a little pricey or overpowered for you, other, lower-cost notation programs are available, too. Finale offers the $119.95 PrintMusic, $49.95 SongWriter, and free NotePad, each serving less-demanding needs. Sibelius offers the $119.95 Sibelius First program, similar in features and functionality to PrintMusic. Then there's the free MuseScore (musescore. org) and ScoreCloud (scorecloud.com), $24.00 Forte Basic (fortenotation.com), and $59.99 Notation Musician (notation.com). And if you have one of Microsoft's Surface Pro tablets, the $69.99 StaffPad app (staffpad.net) lets you write your scores directly onscreen with the tablet's stylus.

Exercise

Exercise 21-1

Use a blank piece of score paper or your music notation program of choice to create a simple eight-measure chart for big band. Base your piece on the chord progressions listed in the rhythm parts, and use the transposed keys for each instrument.

The Least You Need to Know

- Lead sheets present melody, chords, and lyrics.
- Chord sheets are used to present chords only—and can use standard chord notation or the simplified Nashville Number System of notation.
- Choral scores include individual parts for soprano, alto, tenor, and bass plus piano accompaniment.
- Band and orchestral scores include separate staves for each instrument—and can be written in either concert or transposed keys.
- The chore of creating written music can be made easier by computerized music notation programs, such as Finale or Sibelius.

Coda

Thus ends this book—and your first exposure to basic music theory. I hope you've found the information in these pages helpful, and that I've passed on some of my love and enthusiasm for how music gets created.

The key thing to remember (aside from all the notes and rhythms and such) is that these musical building blocks exist for you to use—however you like. We may say that there are rules and conventions, but when it comes to creating music, all the rules are made to be broken. What ultimately matters is how a piece of music sounds—to you, and to your listeners.

Theory is good, but it's just a guideline for what happens out in the real world. If you want to use parallel fifths in your harmony, go ahead. If you want to flat a fifth or resolve a turnaround to the ii chord instead of the I, do it. Some of the greatest pieces of music have broken all sorts of rules. As long as it sounds good, it's all okay.

Just because you're done with this book, however, doesn't mean that your music education has ended. In fact, if you choose to make music a part of your life, your education never ends. Every song you listen to, every piece of music you hear is an opportunity to learn more about the music you love. Keep your ears open and your mind free, and you'll continue to expand your knowledge and skills for the rest of your musical life.

You can also further your music education with more reading. If you're serious about becoming a better musician, I recommend you check out the following books:

Arranging and Composing (David Baker, Alfred Publishing, 1970; revised edition, 1988)

Arranging Concepts Complete (Dick Grove, Alfred Publishing, 1972; second edition, 1985)

Hearing and Writing Music: Professional Training for Today's Musician (Ron Gorow, September Publishing, 2000; second edition, 2015)

Melody in Songwriting: Tools and Techniques for Writing Hit Songs (Jack Perricone, Berklee Press, 2000)

Sounds and Scores: A Practical Guide to Professional Orchestration (Henry Mancini, Northridge Music Inc., 1973)

The Study of Orchestration (Samuel Adler, W.W. Norton & Company, fourth edition, 2016)

Tunesmith: Inside the Art of Songwriting (Jimmy Webb, Hyperion, 1998)

What to Listen for in Music (Aaron Copland, Mentor, 1939; softcover revision, 2011)

I'd be remiss if I didn't also mention some of the other music books that I have written. Like this book, they're all in Alpha Books' *Idiot's Guides* series, and (I hope) are equally easy to read and follow. These books include:

The Complete Idiot's Guide to Conducting Music (Michael Miller, Alpha Books, 2012)

The Complete Idiot's Guide to the Music Business (Michael Miller, Alpha Books, 2010)

The Complete Idiot's Guide to Music Composition (Michael Miller, Alpha Books, 2005)

The Complete Idiot's Guide to Music History (Michael Miller, Alpha Books, 2008)

The Complete Idiot's Guide to Playing Drums (Michael Miller, Alpha Books, 2000; second edition, 2004)

The Complete Idiot's Guide to Singing (Michael Miller and Phyllis Fulford, Alpha Books, 2003; second edition, 2014)

Of course, if you really want to learn about music, you need a good teacher. Whether you study one-on-one with a professional educator, or attend music classes at your favorite school or university, a teacher can provide the individual instruction that's necessary to develop your own unique musical skills.

There are also many music theory resources on the internet. These tend to change from year to year, so go to Google and do a search on "music theory" and see what you find. Among my favorite sites are Teoría Music Theory Web (teoria.com) and Musictheory.net (musictheory .net)—although a quick Google search will find even more sites to explore.

While you're online, make sure you check out my personal website (millerwriter.com). There you'll find information about my latest book projects and any updates or corrections to the information in this book. There's also a contact form you can use to send messages or questions my way. (You can also follow me on Twitter; my handle is @molehillgroup.)

If you love music, as I do, you'll want to experience as much of it as possible. The more you play, or sing, or just listen, the more you'll learn about the theory behind the music. So put down this book and listen to your favorite music—or pick up your instrument and start playing. The music is waiting for you!

Glossary

a cappella   Vocal music, without instrumental accompaniment.

a tempo   Return to the previous tempo.

accelerando   Gradually speed up. (Abbreviated as accel.)

accent   A note played louder or with more emphasis than regular notes.

accidental   A marking used to raise and lower the indicated pitch. Sharps raise the note a half step, flats lower the note a half step, and naturals return the note to the original pitch.

adagietto   Tempo marking for a moderately slow tempo, slightly faster than adagio.

adagio   Tempo marking for a moderately slow tempo.

allegretto   Tempo marking for a moderately fast tempo, not quite as fast as allegro.

allegro   Tempo marking for a fast, cheerful tempo.

altered bass chord   A chord with some note other than the root in the bass. The altered bass note is typically notated after a slash, like this: Am7/D.

alto clef   A clef, used primarily by the viola, that places middle C on the middle line of the staff.

alto voice   The lowest female voice.

andante   Tempo marking for a moderate, walking tempo.

andantino   Tempo marking for a moderate tempo, slightly faster than andante.

arpeggio   A chord that is broken up and played one note at a time.

articulation   The manner in which notes are struck, sustained, and released. One indicates articulation by the use of markings such as legato, staccato, tenuto, and so on.

atonality   Music that has no tonal center and no underlying key. In pure atonal music, the notes of the chromatic scale are used impartially and independently, with no home degree or tonic.

attack   The beginning part of a sound.

augmented chord   A chord with a major third and a raised fifth (1-3-♯5).

backbeat   In 4/4 time, beats two and four, typically played by the drummer on the snare drum.

bar   *See* measure.

bar line   The vertical line placed on the staff between measures.

baritone voice   A male voice pitched between the bass and tenor voices; not always isolated in choral music.

bass   The lowest pitch of a chord (not necessarily the root).

bass clef   A clef, used by lower-pitched voices and instruments, that places middle C on the first ledger line above the staff.

bass voice   The lowest male voice.

beat   Any pulsing unit of musical time.

big band   A large ensemble for playing jazz music, consisting of saxophones, trumpets, trombones, and a rhythm section.

block chord   An unbroken chord, where all the notes are played at once, typically along with the same rhythm as the melody.

blues   Music, originating in the African American community, that incorporates flatted notes and a specific chord progression (the *blues progression*).

blues progression   A 12-bar sequence of chords common in blues and jazz music, as follows: I-I-I-I-IV-IV-I-I-V7-V7-I-I.

blues scale   The scale used in blues music with the following scale tones: 1-♭3-4-♭5-5-♭7.

brass   The family of instruments, typically made of brass, that produces sound by blowing through a mouthpiece. The brass family includes the trumpet, trombone, tuba, and French horn.

broken chord   Another name for an arpeggiated chord, where the notes are played in sequence as opposed to all at once.

cadence   A pause or stopping point, typically a short chord progression inserted at the end of a phrase or piece of music.

canon   A musical form in which the melody is imitated by various parts in contrapuntal fashion.

choir   A large vocal ensemble.

chord   Three or more notes played simultaneously.

chord progression   A series of chords over a number of measures.

chord sheet   A sheet of music containing only the chords of a song.

chromatic   Pitches outside the underlying key or scale. The opposite of diatonic.

chromatic scale   A scale containing 12 equal divisions of the octave—all the white keys and black keys within an octave.

clef   A graphic symbol placed at the beginning of the staff to indicate the pitch of the notes on the staff.

coda   A short section at the end of a composition.

common time   The 4/4 time signature.

compound chord   Two chords sounded together. Typically notated with a vertical slash between the two chords.

concert key   *See* concert pitch.

concert pitch   The actual (nontransposed) pitch of a piece of music; some instruments (such as the trumpet) read their music transposed from concert pitch.

consonance   Harmonious combination of tones. The opposite of dissonance.

contralto   A lower subset of the alto voice, even lower than the traditional alto range; not used in all choral music.

contrapuntal   *See* counterpoint.

contrary motion   Where one voice moves in the opposite direction of another.

counterpoint   Two or more simultaneous, independent lines or voices. Some music theorists apply strict rules to the creation of contrapuntal lines.

crescendo   Gradually louder.

cut time   The 2/2 time signature.

D.C. al Coda   Navigation marking meaning to go back to the beginning and play to the Coda sign; then skip to the Coda section.

D.C. al Fine   Navigation marking meaning to go back to the beginning and play through to the end.

D.S. al Coda   Navigation marking meaning to go back to the Segno sign and play to the Coda sign; then skip to the Coda section.

D.S. al Fine   Navigation marking meaning to go back to the Segno sign and play through to the end.

decrescendo   Gradually softer.

diatonic   Notes or chords that are in the underlying key or scale. For example, in the key of C Major, the diatonic notes are C, D, E, F, G, A, and B; all other notes are chromatic.

diminished chord   A chord with a minor third and a diminished fifth (1-♭3-♭5).

dissonance   A combination of tones that sounds discordant and unstable, in need of resolution to a more pleasing and stable harmony. The opposite of consonance.

division   Fractional parts of a beat.

dominant   The fifth degree of a scale, a perfect fifth above the tonic. Also refers to the chord built on this fifth scale degree.

dominant seventh chord   A major chord with a minor seventh added (1-3-5-♭7). Typically found on the fifth degree of the scale, and noted as V7.

doppio movimento   Play twice as fast.

double bar   Two vertical lines placed on the staff to indicate the end of a section or a composition.

downbeat   The major beats in a measure; in 4/4 time, the downbeats are 1, 2, 3, and 4. (Some theoreticians hold that there is only one downbeat per measure—the very first beat.)

dynamics   Varying degrees of loud and soft. For example, forte signifies a loud dynamic, while piano signifies a soft dynamic.

enharmonic   Different notations of the same sound; for example, F♯ and G♭ are enharmonic notes.

extended chords   Chords with additional notes (typically in thirds) added above the basic triad. (Some theoreticians consider seventh chords extended chords; others don't.)

fermata   Symbol used to indicate that a note should be held indefinitely. Sometimes called a "bird's eye."

flag   The part of eighth notes, sixteenth notes, and all smaller notes dangling off the stem. The flag is always at the end of the stem, so if the stem is pointing up, the flag is above the notehead; if the stem is pointing down, the flag is below the notehead.

flat   The lowering of any pitch by a half step; signified by the ♭ sign.

forte   Loud. (Abbreviated as f.)

fortissimo   Very loud. (Abbreviated as ff.)

fortississimo   Very, very loud. (Abbreviated as fff.)

frequency   A scientific measurement of how fast the molecules of air are vibrating; the faster the vibrations, the higher the pitch.

fugue   A contrapuntal form that is built from a single subject.

glissando   A mechanism for getting from one pitch to another, playing every single pitch between the two notes as smoothly as possible.

grace note   One or more notes, played lightly and quickly, that precede a main note.

grave   Tempo marking for a very slow or solemn pace.

half step   The smallest distance between notes in a chromatic scale.

harmonic composition   Composing with the chords first and then fitting a melody to those chords.

harmonic interval   The interval between two notes sounded simultaneously to create harmony. (Contrast this with a melodic interval, which consists of two notes played one after another to create a melody.)

harmonic rhythm   The pace of a chord progression.

harmonization   The choice of chords to accompany a melodic line.

harmony   The sound of tones in combination. Also used to refer to the accompanying parts behind the main melody.

interval   The distance between two pitches or notes.

inversion   A chord in which the bass note is not the root of the chord.

jazz band   *See* big band.

key   A combination of a tonic and a mode. For example, the key of F Major has F as the tonic and major as the mode.

key signature   The sharps or flats that are placed at the beginning of a staff to indicate the key of the music.

larghetto   Tempo marking for a slow tempo, slightly faster than largo.

largo   Tempo marking for a slow and dignified tempo.

lead sheet   A piece of sheet music that contains a single staff for the melody, with the accompanying chords written above the staff.

leading tone   The note that is a half step below the tonic; thus leads up to the tonic.

lento   Tempo marking for a slow tempo.

major   The most common mode, consisting of the following intervals: whole-whole-half-whole-whole-whole-half.

major chord   A chord with a major third (1-3-5).

measure   A group of beats, indicated by the placement of bar lines on the staff.

mediant   The third degree of a scale, or a chord built on that degree (III).

melodic composition   Composing with the melody first and then fitting chords to that melody.

melodic interval   The interval between two notes played one after another.

melody   The combination of tone and rhythm in a logical sequence.

meter   The organization of beats and their divisions.

metronome   A device that precisely ticks off beat after beat at a specified tempo. Metronomes can be either pendulum-type affairs or computerized devices that emit an electronic beat.

mezzo forte   Medium loud. (Abbreviated as mf.)

mezzo piano   Medium soft. (Abbreviated as mp.)

microtone   An interval smaller than a semitone, prevalent in some non-Western music and twentieth-century art music.

minor   One of three modes, each with a flatted third of the scale. Natural minor is identical to Aeolian mode, with the following intervals: whole-half-whole-whole-half-whole-whole. Harmonic minor contains the following intervals: whole-half-whole-whole-half-whole-half-half. Melodic minor is different ascending and descending; ascending, the intervals are whole-half-whole-whole-whole-whole-half, whereas descending it uses the same intervals as natural minor.

minor chord   A chord with a minor third (1-♭3-5).

mode   (1) A series of notes that indicate the structure of a major or minor scale key or piece. (2) A set of scales, based on centuries-old music that preceded today's major and minor scales; these include the Dorian, Phrygian, Lydian, Mixolydian, Ionian, Locrian, and Aeolian modes.

moderato   Tempo marking for a moderate pace.

modulation   A change of key within a piece of music.

molto   Modifier for tempo markings; means "very."

motet   Short, unaccompanied vocal work for two or more voices.

motif (or **motive**)   A brief melodic or rhythmic idea.

neighboring tone   A tone one diatonic step above or below the main tone.

notation   The art of writing musical notes on paper.

note   A symbol used to indicate the duration and pitch of a sound, as in whole notes, half notes, and quarter notes.

notehead   The big, oval part of a note. The stem is always attached to the notehead.

octave   Two pitches, with the same name, located 12 half steps apart.

odd time   Any non-4/4 time signature, such as 3/4, 5/4, or 9/8.

orchestra   A group of instruments organized for the performance of symphonies and other instrumental works, or to accompany an opera or other staged presentation.

orchestration   The art of scoring music for an orchestra or band. Also called arranging.

parallel motion   Two or more voices that move in identical steps, simultaneously.

passing tone   A pitch located (scale-wise) directly between two main pitches; passing tones are typically used to connect notes in a melody.

pedal point   A note sustained below changing harmonies.

pentatonic scale   A five-note scale with the intervals of whole, whole, whole and a half, whole, whole and a half; in relationship to a major scale, the scale degrees (not counting the octave) are 1-2-3-5-6.

percussion   The family of instruments that produce sound when you hit, beat, crash, shake, roll, scratch, rub, twist, or rattle them. Included in this family are various types of drums and cymbals, as well as mallet instruments (marimba, xylophone, and so forth) and timpani.

perfect pitch   The ability to hear absolute pitches in your head, without any outside assistance.

phrase   Within a piece of music, a segment that is unified by rhythms, melodies, or harmonies and that comes to some sort of closure. Typically composed in groups of 2, 4, 8, 16, or 32 measures.

pianissimo   Very soft. (Abbreviated as pp.)

pianississimo   Very, very soft. (Abbreviated as ppp.)

piano   (1) Soft. (Abbreviated as p.) (2) An 88-key keyboard instrument, also known as the pianoforte.

pitch   The highness or lowness of a tone. (In scientific terms, a specific frequency.)

polyphony   The mixing together of several simultaneous melodic lines.

polyrhythm   Two or more rhythms played simultaneously, or against each other.

polytonality   Employing more than one tonality simultaneously.

prestissimo   Tempo marking for an extremely fast tempo, faster than presto.

presto   Tempo marking for a very fast tempo.

primary chords   The most important chords in a key: I, IV, V.

rallentando   Gradually slow down. (Abbreviated as rall.)

relative keys   Keys that share the same key signature, but not the same root. For example, A minor and C Major are relative keys.

resolve   The act of moving a suspended note down to a chord tone of the chord.

rest   A symbol used to denote silence or not playing a particular note.

rhythm   The organization of sound in time; the arrangement of beats and accents in music.

rhythm section   Those instruments providing the rhythmic pulse in a larger ensemble, typically consisting of keyboards, guitars, bass, and drums.

ritardando   Gradually slow down. (Abbreviated as rit. or ritard.)

ritenuto   Hold back the tempo. (Abbreviated as riten.)

root   The fundamental note in a chord.

SATB   Shorthand for soprano, alto, tenor, and bass. (Choral scores are sometimes called SATB scores.)

scale   A sequence of related pitches, arranged in ascending or descending order.

score   (1) The written depiction of all the individual parts played of each of the instruments in an ensemble. (2) To orchestrate a composition.

semitone   The interval of a half step.

sharp   The raising of any pitch by a half step; signified by the ♯ sign.

shuffle   A rhythmic feel based on triplets or a dotted eighth note/sixteenth note pattern.

similar motion   Two or more voices that move in the same direction, but not with the same intervals.

sonata   A piece of instrumental music performed in distinct and contrasting movements.

song form   The structure of a short piece of music; usually diagramed as A-A-B-A.

soprano voice   The highest female voice.

staff   An assemblage of horizontal lines and spaces that represent different pitches (as defined by the clef used).

string orchestra   An ensemble consisting of the five primary instruments of the string section, sometimes accompanied by piano.

string quartet   A four-piece ensemble consisting of first and second violin, viola, and cello.

strings   The family of instruments that produces sound by moving a bow across a string. The string family includes the violin, viola, cello, and double bass.

subdominant   The fourth degree of the scale, or the chord built on the fourth degree (IV).

submediant   The sixth degree of a scale, or the chord built on that degree (vi).

subtonic   The seventh degree of a scale, or the chord built on that degree (vii°). (In classical theory, the subtonic is the lowered seventh, whereas the normal seventh is called the leading tone.)

supertonic   The second degree of a scale, or the chord built on that degree (ii).

suspension   A nonchord note used within a chord to create tension. The suspended note is typically the fourth of the chord, which then resolves down to the third.

symphonic orchestra   *See* orchestra.

syncopation   An accent on an unexpected beat—or the lack of an accent on an expected beat.

tempo   The rate of speed at which beats are played in a song.

tempo primo   Return to the tempo designated at the beginning of a piece.

tenor voice   The highest male voice.

theme   A recurring melodic or rhythmic pattern or idea; the main melodic phrase in a composition.

third   The interval between the first and third degree of a scale; can be either minor (three half steps) or major (two whole steps).

tie   A curved line over or under two or more notes that "ties" the two notes together into one.

timbre   Sound quality (as in, "That trumpet player has a rich timbre").

time signature   A symbol with two numbers, one on top of the other (like a fraction), that indicates the basic meter of a song. The upper number indicates how many beats are in a measure; the bottom number indicates the type of note that receives one beat.

tonality   The organization of musical notes around a tonic, or home pitch, based on a major or minor scale or mode.

tone   A sound played or sung at a specific pitch. (The term is also used sometimes to indicate timbre, or sound quality.)

tonic   The primary note in a scale or key; the first degree of a scale or a chord built on that degree (I).

transcribing   The art of writing down melodies and chords by ear, without the benefit of any other written notation.

transpose   *See* transposition.

transposing instruments   Those instruments that are not notated at their true pitch. For example, the trumpet is notated a full step higher than it sounds; when a trumpet plays what it reads as a C, it actually sounds a B♭ in concert pitch.

transposition   Translating one pitch to another.

treble clef   A clef, used by higher-pitched voices and instruments, that places middle C on the first ledger line below the staff.

triad   Three notes, each a third apart from the previous. Most chords are built on triads.

triplet   A group of three notes performed in the space of two.

tritone   An interval consisting of three whole steps. Sometimes called "the Devil's interval."

unison   (1) Two notes of the same pitch. (2) Voices or instruments all singing or playing the same pitch.

upbeat   The eighth-note "and" after the downbeat.

vivace   Tempo marking for a lively tempo.

voice   Melodic or harmonic lines.

voice leading   The motion of a melodic line as it moves from one chord to another.

voicing   The way the notes of a chord are arranged.

whole step   An interval equal to two half steps.

woodwind   The family of instruments that produces sound by vibrating a wooden reed. The woodwind family includes the clarinet, saxophone, oboe, and bassoon. Also included are the flute and the piccolo, which do not use reeds.

Music Theory Ear Training Course

Welcome to the *Music Theory Ear Training Course!* This audio course leads you step-by-step through the essential concepts of music theory, including pitches, scales, intervals, rhythms, chords, and melodies. The course itself is online, at this book's website: idiotsguides.com/musictheory. From there, you can listen to the streaming audio tracks on any computer or connected mobile device by clicking each track in turn.

To work through the *Music Theory Ear Training Course,* all you have to do is listen to the examples on the website and then test yourself with the audio exercises. Click to listen to each exercise and then write down your answer on a piece of blank staff paper. Feel free to repeat each exercise as many times as necessary. You can then check your answers against those in this appendix.

Track Listing

Track	Contents	Track	Contents
1.	Introduction	9.	Pitch Exercises 31–35
2.	Lesson One: Pitches	10.	Pitch Exercises 36–40
3.	Pitch Exercises 1–5	11.	Lesson Two: Intervals
4.	Pitch Exercises 6–10	12.	Interval Exercises 1–5
5.	Pitch Exercises 11–15	13.	Interval Exercises 6–10
6.	Pitch Exercises 16–20	14.	Interval Exercises 11–15
7.	Pitch Exercises 21–25	15.	Interval Exercises 16–20
8.	Pitch Exercises 26–30	16.	Interval Exercises 21–25

Track	Contents	Track	Contents
17.	Interval Exercises 26–30	32.	Rhythm Exercises 21–25
18.	Interval Exercises 31–35	33.	Rhythm Exercises 26–30
19.	Interval Exercises 36–40	34.	Rhythm Exercises 31–35
20.	Interval Exercises 41–45	35.	Rhythm Exercises 36–40
21.	Interval Exercises 46–50	36.	Lesson Five: Melodies
22.	Interval Exercises 51–55	37.	Melody Exercises 1–5
23.	Interval Exercises 56–60	38.	Melody Exercises 6–10
24.	Lesson Three: Scales	39.	Melody Exercises 11–15
25.	Scale Exercises 1–5	40.	Melody Exercises 16–20
26.	Scale Exercises 6–10	41.	Lesson Six: Chords
27.	Lesson Four: Rhythms	42.	Chord Exercises 1–5
28.	Rhythm Exercises 1–5	43.	Chord Exercises 6–10
29.	Rhythm Exercises 6–10	44.	Chord Exercises 11–15
30.	Rhythm Exercises 11–15	45.	Chord Exercises 16–20
31.	Rhythm Exercises 16–20	46.	Coda

Answers to Audio Exercises

Compare your answers to the audio exercises with the correct answers listed here. (Don't cheat!)

Pitch Exercises (Tracks 3 to 10)

Identify the following pitches, using the treble clef, as played on the website.

Track	Contents	Track	Contents
1.	A	5.	F♯ (or G♭, enharmonically)
2.	C	6.	B
3.	G	7.	A♭ (or G♯, enharmonically)
4.	B♭ (or A♯, enharmonically)	8.	C♯ (or D♭, enharmonically)

Track	Contents	Track	Contents
9.	D	15.	E
10.	B	16.	C
11.	E♭ (or D♯, enharmonically)	17.	C♯ (or D♭, enharmonically)
12.	B♭ (or A♯, enharmonically)	18.	F♯ (or G♭, enharmonically)
13.	F	19.	E
14.	A♭ (or G♯, enharmonically)	20.	A

Identify the following lower pitches, using the bass clef, as played on the website.

Track	Contents	Track	Contents
21.	C	31.	A
22.	B♭ (or A♯, enharmonically)	32.	C
23.	D	33.	G
24.	F	34.	B
25.	A♭ (or G♯, enharmonically)	35.	F♯ (or G♭, enharmonically)
26.	G	36.	B♭ (or A♯, enharmonically)
27.	E	37.	E
28.	C♯ (or D♭, enharmonically)	38.	E♭ (or D♯, enharmonically)
29.	E♭ (or D♯, enharmonically)	39.	A
30.	F♯ (or G♭, enharmonically)	40.	D

Interval Exercises (Tracks 12 to 23)

Identify the following ascending intervals, as played on the website.

Track	Contents	Track	Contents
1.	Perfect fifth	5.	Minor third
2.	Octave	6.	Perfect fifth
3.	Perfect fourth	7.	Major sixth
4.	Major third	8.	Major seventh

Track	Contents	Track	Contents
9.	Major second	15.	Tritone (or augmented fourth or diminished fifth, enharmonically)
10.	Minor sixth		
11.	Perfect fourth	16.	Major third
12.	Minor second	17.	Minor seventh
13.	Minor third	18.	Octave
14.	Perfect fifth	19.	Major sixth
		20.	Major seventh

Identify the following descending intervals, as played on the website.

Track	Contents	Track	Contents
21.	Major third	32.	Minor third
22.	Perfect fourth	33.	Perfect fourth
23.	Minor third	34.	Perfect fifth
24.	Octave	35.	Major third
25.	Perfect fifth	36.	Tritone (or augmented fourth or diminished fifth, enharmonically)
26.	Perfect fifth		
27.	Major sixth	37.	Minor seventh
28.	Major seventh	38.	Major sixth
29.	Major second	39.	Octave
30.	Minor sixth	40.	Major seventh
31.	Minor second		

Identify both the interval and the second note in each series, as played on the website.

Track	Contents	Track	Contents
41.	Minor third (A-C)	51.	Minor sixth (C-A♭)
42.	Perfect fifth (D-A)	52.	Minor seventh (B-A)
43.	Major seventh (G-F♯)	53.	Minor ninth (G-A♭)
44.	Minor third (B♭-D♭)	54.	Minor third (E-G)
45.	Perfect fourth (C-F)	55.	Perfect fifth (F♯-C♯)
46.	Major sixth (A♭-F)	56.	Major second (D-E)
47.	Octave (C♯-C♯)	57.	Major third (E-G♯)
48.	Tritone (G-C♯ or G-D♭, enharmonically)	58.	Major sixth (A-F♯)
49.	Major third (D-F♯)	59.	Major seventh (G-F♯)
50.	Minor second (B-C)	60.	Octave (A-A)

Scale Exercises (Tracks 25 and 26)

Identify the following scale types and the starting note of each scale, as played on the website.

Track	Contents	Track	Contents
1.	A Major	6.	E harmonic minor
2.	C Major	7.	E melodic minor (ascending)
3.	A natural minor	8.	B♭ Major
4.	F Major	9.	D natural minor
5.	E natural minor	10.	G melodic minor (ascending)

Rhythm Exercises (Tracks 28 to 35)

Transcribe the following rhythms, as played on the website.

Melody Exercises (Tracks 37 to 40)

Transcribe the following melodies, as played on the website.

Chord Exercises (Tracks 42 to 45)

Identify the chord types (major, minor, diminished, and augmented), as played on the website.

Track	Contents	Track	Contents
1.	Major	6.	Diminished
2.	Minor	7.	Major
3.	Major	8.	Augmented
4.	Major	9.	Minor
5.	Minor	10.	Diminished

Identify the following types of extended chords, as played on the website.

Track	Contents	Track	Contents
11.	Major seventh	16.	Major ninth
12.	Minor seventh	17.	Dominant seventh
13.	Dominant seventh	18.	Minor ninth
14.	Major seventh	19.	Major seventh
15.	Dominant seventh	20.	Minor seventh

Repeat the previous exercises, this time writing out the actual chord names (with the correct starting pitch) for each chord.

Track	Contents	Track	Contents
1.	C Major	11.	F Major seventh
2.	F minor	12.	G minor seventh
3.	E Major	13.	E♭ dominant seventh (E♭7)
4.	B♭ Major	14.	D Major seventh
5.	G minor	15.	A dominant seventh (A7)
6.	B diminished	16.	C Major ninth
7.	E♭ Major	17.	F dominant seventh (F7)
8.	E♭ augmented	18.	D minor ninth
9.	D minor	19.	E♭ Major seventh
10.	G diminished	20.	F♯ minor seventh

Answers to Chapter Exercises

Here are the answers to those chapter exercises that weren't open-ended in nature. (The open-ended exercises—"Write a melody to this chord progression," and the like—don't have a single correct solution so they're not included here.) If you haven't completed the exercises yet, don't cheat—go back and do the exercises before you peek at the answers!

Chapter 1

Exercise 1-1

F   B   A   E   F   D   C   G   G   C

Exercise 1-2

C   A   A   G   D   G   C   B   F   E

Exercise 1-3

A   C   G   F   B   G   D   E   D   B

Exercise 1-4

E   F   D   G   C   A   B   G   A   C

Exercise 1-5

Bass   Treble   Alto   Tenor   Treble (octave above)

Exercise 1-6

G   B   A   D   C   B   D   C   E   F

Exercise 1-7

C   D   B   A   G   F   E   C   D   B

Exercise 1-8

C F G B D E F A G B

Chapter 2

Exercise 2-1

Exercise 2-2

Exercise 2-3

Exercise 2-4

| Down three half steps (minor 3rd) | Up one half step (minor 2nd) | Up one whole step (major 2nd) | Up two whole steps (major 3rd) | Down seven half steps (perfect 5th) | Down two whole steps (major 3rd) | Up one whole step (major 2nd) | Up seven half steps (perfect 5th) | Down one whole step (major 2nd) |

Exercise 2-5

Major   third   Minor   third   Perfect   fifth   Major   third   Major   second

Exercise 2-6

Perfect   fifth   Major   third   Perfect   fourth   Minor   third   Major   second

Exercise 2-7

Exercise 2-8

Chapter 3

Exercise 3-1

A Major, D Major, B-flat Major, E-flat Major

Exercise 3-2

D minor, G minor, E minor, F minor

Exercise 3-3

A Major   Bb Major   G Major

D Major   F Major   Eb Major

Exercise 3-4

A minor   G minor   C minor

B minor   F# minor   E minor

Exercise 3-5

D minor   B minor   G minor

Exercise 3-6

Lydian   Aeolian   Dorian

Chapter 4

Exercise 4-1

G Major, A Major, F Major, E-flat Major, E Major, B-flat Major, A-flat Major, D-flat Major, D Major, B Major

Exercise 4-2

A minor, C minor, E minor, D minor, G minor, E-flat minor, B minor, C-sharp minor, F-sharp minor, F minor

Exercise 4-3

F Major   D Major   Eb Major   G Major   Bb Major

Exercise 4-4

C minor   D minor   E minor   C# minor   F minor

Exercise 4-5

Eb   C   Ab   G   D   Eb   Bb   F   Bb   F

Exercise 4-6

Exercise 4-7

Exercise 4-8

C   F   Bb   Eb   Ab   Db

Chapter 5

Exercise 5-1

Whole note, quarter note, sixteenth note, eighth note, half note, sixteenth notes, eighth notes, half rest, quarter rest, sixteenth rest, eighth rest, whole rest

Exercise 5-2

One two three four   One two and three and four   One e and two and ah Three e and ah four

Exercise 5-3

Exercise 5-4

Exercise 5-5

Exercise 5-6

Exercise 5-7

Exercise 5-8

Chapter 6

Exercise 6-1

3/4   7/8   2/2   5/4   9/8

Exercise 6-2

Exercise 6-3

Exercise 6-4

Exercise 6-5

Exercise 6-6

Exercise 6-7

Chapter 9

Exercise 9-1

G Major, E♭ Major, D Major, B♭ Major, B Major, A♭ Major, F Major, D Major, C Major, G♭ Major

Exercise 9-2

D minor, G minor, C minor, A♭ minor, B♭ minor, E minor, D♭ minor, A minor, E♭ minor, B minor

Exercise 9-3

Exercise 9-4

Exercise 9-5

Dm7, G7, FM7, B♭M7, CM9, Cm7 (or Cm7/E♭), Gm7, B11, C♯m7, A♭7

Exercise 9-6

A7   Ebmin7   C6   DMaj7   Bbm9   F11   G7   Gmmaj7   EMaj7   Fmin7

Exercise 9-7

F   Bbaug   Gmin   E

Exercise 9-8

Gsus4   G   Dsus4   D   Fsus4   F   F#sus4   F#   Bbsus4   Bb

Chapter 10

Exercise 10-1

F   C   Gmin   Dmin   Bb   Amin   C7   Edim   BbMaj7   Gmin7

I   V   ii   vi   IV   iii   V7   vii°   IVM7   iim7

Exercise 10-2

Emin   G   F#min   Bmin   C#dim   D   A7   F#min7   DMaj7   A

ii   IV   iii   vi   vii°   I   V7   iiim7   IM7   V

Exercise 10-3

Bb   Cmin   Fmin   Gmin   Ab   Eb   Ddim   Cmin7   Bb7   Absus4

V   vi   ii   iii   IV   I   vii°   vim7   V7   IVsus

Exercise 10-4

ii   V   V   I   vi   IV   IV   V   iii   vi

Exercise 10-5

E   A   D   A   E   D   A   E   E   Bmin

perfect   plagal   interrupted   imperfect   interrupted

Exercise 10-6

F   Dm   B♭   C   F   Dm   B♭   C

Chapter 12

Exercise 12-5

Exercise 12-6

Chapter 14

Exercise 14-1

Exercise 14-2

Exercise 14-3

Exercise 14-4

Chapter 15

Exercise 15-1

One possible solution is as follows:

Chapter 16

Exercise 16-1

Exercise 16-2

Chapter 17

Exercise 17-1

Exercise 17-2

Exercise 17-3

Exercise 17-4

Exercise 17-5

Exercise 17-7

Tan-ger-ine el-e-phants high in the sky   croc-o-dile tears in my beer - - -

Chapter 20

Exercise 20-1

Trumpet

Exercise 20-2

Alto Sax

Exercise 20-3

Fr. Horn

Exercise 20-4

Index

Numbers

I chord, 139-140
I-ii-IV chord progression, 146
I-ii-IV-V chord progression, 146
I-IV chord progression, 144
I-IV-V chord progression, 145
I-IV-V-IV chord progression,
  145-146
I-V chord progression, 144
I-V-vi-IV chord progression, 146
I-vi-ii-V chord progression, 146
I-vi-ii-V7-ii chord progression,
  147
I-vi-IV-V chord progression, 147
ii-V-I chord progression, 148
IV-I-IV-V chord progression, 147
2/2 time, 84
4/4 time, 82
5/4 time, 85
6/8 time, 85
7/4 time, 86

A

a cappella, 275
A Major
  major keys, 56
  scales, 35
A minor
  harmonic minor scales, 41
  melodic minor scales, 43
  minor keys, 57
  natural minor scales, 39
a tempo, 93
above staff notes, 12
accelerando, 92
accent marks, 95-97
accidentals, 20-21, 60-61
accompaniment
  arpeggiated, 184-185
  bass, 185-186
  block chord, 181-182
  chord sheets, 179
  forms, 181
  lead sheets, 178-179
  melodies, 179-180
  rhythmic, 182-184
  tips, 186
  without music, 180-181
active listening, ear training,
  165-173
  chords, 173
  intervals, 168-171
  keys, 172
  melodies, 172
  rhythms, 171-172
  tonal memory, 167-168
adagietto tempo, 91
adagio tempo, 91
Adler, Samuel, *Study of
  Orchestration, The*, 298
Aeolian mode, 48-49
A-flat Major
  major keys, 56
  major scales, 35
A-flat minor
  harmonic minor scales, 41
  melodic minor scales, 43
  minor keys, 58
  natural minor scales, 39
allegretto tempo, 91
allegro tempo, 91
alphabet tone names, 9-10
altered bass chords, 217
altered chords, 126-127
alto clef, 15
altos, voice characteristics, 266
andante tempo, 91
andantino tempo, 91
arias, 242
arpeggiated accompaniment,
  116, 184-185
arrangements
  instrumental
    big bands, 279-280
    brass, 269
    chamber orchestra
      ensemble, 277
    choosing instruments,
      274-275
    concert bands, 278
    good and bad keys, 273-274
    guitars, 268
    keyboards, 269-270
    marching bands, 278-279
    percussion, 270
    rock bands, 280
    string orchestra ensembles,
      278

string quartets, 278
strings, 267-268
symphonic orchestras, 276-277
transpositions, 270-273
woodwinds, 269
vocal
choir ensembles, 275-276
ranges, 266-267
voice characteristics, 266
Arranging and Composing, David Baker, 298
Arranging Concepts Complete, Dick Grove, 298
ascending melodic minor scale, 43
A-sharp minor
harmonic minor scales, 41
melodic minor scales, 43
minor keys, 57
natural minor scales, 39
augmented chords, 120-121
augmented intervals, 25-26
augmented seventh chord, 124

B

B Major
major keys, 56
scales, 35
B minor
harmonic minor scales, 41
melodic minor scales, 43
minor keys, 57
natural minor scales, 39
Bach, Johann Sebastian, *Minuet in G,* 108
Baker, David, *Arranging and Composing,* 298
ballets, 241
bands, instrumental arrangements
big bands, 279-280
concert bands, 278

marching bands, 278-279
rock bands, 280
baritones, voice characteristics, 266
Baroque classical music, 240
bass
accompaniment, 185-186
altered bass chords, 217
voice characteristics, 266
walking bass line, 185
bass clefs, 14
beats
counting notes, 72
measures, 68
note values, 68
dotted notes, 73-74
eighth notes, 71
half notes, 69-70
quarter notes, 70
rests, 73
sixteenth notes, 71-72
whole notes, 69
tempo
beats per minute, 90
changes, 92-93
fast, 91
fermata, 93
Italian musical terms, 91-92
moderate, 91
slow, 91
ties, 74-75
time signatures
2/2, 84
4/4, 82
5/4, 85
6/8, 85
7/4, 86
changes, 84-85
eighth-note, 82
grouping beats, 85-86
half-note, 83-84
meters, 80
quarter-note, 80-82
triplets, 75

beats per minute. *See* bpm
bebop-style jazz, 244
below staff notes, 12-13
B-flat Major
major keys, 56
scales, 35
B-flat minor
harmonic minor scales, 41
melodic minor scales, 43
minor keys, 57
natural minor scales, 39
big-band swing music, 244
big bands
instrumental arrangements, 279-280
scores, 290-291
blank staff, 11
block chord accompaniment, 181-182
blues chord progressions, 149
blues music
blues progression, 243
scales, 243
bpm (beats per minute), 90
brass instruments, arrangements, 269
bridges, songs, 159

C

C Major
major keys, 55
scales, 34
C minor
harmonic minor scales, 40
melodic minor scales, 42
minor keys, 57
natural minor scales, 38
cadences
imperfect, 143
interrupted, 143-144
perfect, 142-143
plagal, 143

Canon in D, Johann Pachelbel, 109-110, 151-152
canons, 241
C-flat Major
  major keys, 56
  scales, 35
challenges
  counterpoints, 212-213
  harmonies, 212-213
chamber choirs, 275
chamber music, 242
chamber orchestra ensembles, 277
changes
  chords, 130
  dynamics
    crescendos, 95
    decrescendo, 95
  tempo, 92-93
  time signatures, 84-85
choir ensembles
  chamber, 275
  large, 276
  madrigal, 275
  quartets, 275
  swing, 276
  trios, 275
choral scores, 289-290
chord leading, compositions, 251
chord progressions
  altered bass chords, 217
  blues, 149, 243
  cadences
    imperfect, 143
    interrupted, 143-144
    perfect, 142-143
    plagal, 143
  chord substitutions
    diatonic, 218-219
    dominant seventh, 220-221
    functional, 221-222
    major, 219-220
    minor, 220
  chromatic circle of fifths, 148-149

circle of fifths, 148
compound chords, 218
creating, 139
extensions, 216-217
home chords, 139-140
I chords, 145-148
leading references, 140-142
melodies, 149
  perfect fit, 150-152
  writing tips, 152-154
scale-based, 136-138
turnarounds, 222-224
chord sheets, 179, 286
chords
  altered, 126-127
  arpeggiated, 116, 232
  block chord accompaniment, 181-182
  changes, 130
  comping, 131
  compositions, 250
    chord leading, 251
    harmonic rhythm, 251-252
    melody-based, 252-254
  ear training, 173
  extensions
    eleventh, 126
    ninth, 125
    seventh, 121-124
    sixth, 124-125
  fitting to melodies, compositions, 260-263
  forms, 116
  inversions,
    first, 129
    root, 129
    second, 129
  inverted, 130
  power, 128-129
  roots, 116
  suspended, 127-128
  symbols, 130
  triad, 116

types
  augmented, 120-121
  diminished, 119-120
  major, 117-118
  minor, 118-119
  voicing, 129, 204-206
  written music, 130-132
chorus, songs, 158
chromatic circle of fifths, 148-149
  chord progression, 148-149
  key signatures, 58-59
chromatic notes, 60
chromatic scales, 32
church modes, 44
circle of fifths
  chord progression, 148-149
  key signatures, 58-59
classical music
  arias, 242
  ballets, 241
  canons, 241
  chamber music, 242
  concertos, 241
  eras
    Baroque, 240
    Classical, 240
    Medieval, 240
    Renaissance, 240
    Romantic, 240
    Twentieth Century, 240
  forms, 241
  grand motet, 241
  Gregorian chants, 241
  madrigals, 241
  Mass, 241
  motet, 241
  operas, 242
  operettas, 242
  oratorios, 242
  plainsongs, 241
  sonatas, 241
  suites, 242
  symphonic poems, 242
  symphonies, 242

clefs
bass, 14
grand, 15
specialty
alto clef, 15
percussion clef, 16
tenor clef, 15-16
treble, 13-14
click tracks, 90
coda, 98
common time, 82-84
comping, 131
composing melodies, 111-114
compositions, 248
chords, 250
chord leading, 251
harmonic rhythm, 251-252
melody-based, 252-254
harmonic, 249
holistic, 249
layering approach, 249
melodic, 249
melodies
endings, 255
fitting chords to, 260-263
harmonic tensions, 259-260
home pitch, 254-255
hooks, 256
lyrics, 260
motion, 257-258
pentatonic scales, 255-256
ranges, 258-259
skip-wise, 258
step-wise, 258
variations, 256-257
overview, 248
writing your own music, 249-250
compound chords, 218
compound intervals, 26-27
computer notation programs, 296
concert bands, 278, 292

concert key, 191
good and bad keys, 273-274
transpositions, 272-273
concertos, 241
contrary motion, counterpoints, 211
cool jazz, 244
Copland, Aaron, *What to Listen for in Music,* 298
counterpoint, 208
contrary motion, 211
creating, 209-212
mistakes to avoid
big leaps, 212
dissonant intervals, 213
extended parallel movement, 212
versus harmony, 202-203
counting notes, 72
country music
alt country, 245
Americana, 245
bluegrass, 245
contemporary country, 245
country rock, 245
countrypolitan, 245
forms, 245
honky tonk, 245
Western swing, 245
crescendos, 95
C-sharp Major
major keys, 55
scales, 34
C-sharp minor
harmonic minor scales, 40
melodic minor scales, 42
minor keys, 57
natural minor scales, 38
cut time, 84
cycles per second, 6

D

D Major
major keys, 55
scales, 34
D minor
harmonic minor scales, 40
melodic minor scales, 42
minor keys, 57
natural minor scales, 38
dal capo. *See* D.C.
dal segno. *See* D.S.
D.C. (dal capo), 98
D.C. al Coda, 98
D.C. al Fine, 98
deceptive cadence, 144
decrescendo, 95
degree-wise transpositions, 193-194
degrees, scales, 22-23
descending melodic minor scale, 43
D-flat Major
major keys, 55
scales, 34
diatonic chord substitutions, 218-219
diatonic notes, 33
diminished chords, 119-120
diminished intervals, 25-26
dissonant intervals, 213
dominant, 22-23
dominant seventh chords, 122, 220-221
doppio movimento, 93
Dorian mode, 45-46
dotted notes, 73-74
D.S. (dal segno), 98
D.S. al Coda, 98
D.S. al Fine, 98
D-sharp minor
harmonic minor scales, 40
melodic minor scales, 42

minor keys, 57
natural minor scales, 38
Dvořák, Antonín, *New World Symphony*, a.k.a. *Symphony #9 in E minor ("From the New World")*, 107
dynamics
accent marks, 95-97
changes
crescendos, 95
decrescendo, 95
marcatos, 95
markings, 94

E

E Major
major keys, 56
scale, 34
E minor
harmonic minor scales, 40
melodic minor scales, 43
minor keys, 58
natural minor scales, 38
ear training
listening, 165-166
chords, 173
intervals, 168-171
keys, 172
melodies, 172
rhythms, 171-172
tonal memory, 167-168
transcribing music, 164-165, 173-174
E-flat Major
major keys, 56
scales, 34
E-flat minor
harmonic minor scales, 40
melodic minor scales, 42
minor keys, 58
natural minor scales, 38

eight-measure phrase rule, 159-160
eighth-note time signatures, 82
eighth notes, 71
eleventh chords, 126
endings
chord progressions, 142-144
melody compositions, 255
songs, 159
enharmonic notes, 21
ensembles
instrumental
big bands, 279-280
chamber orchestras, 277
concert bands, 278
marching bands, 278-279
rock bands, 280
string orchestras, 278
string quartets, 278
symphonic orchestras, 276-277
vocal
choir, 275-276
trios, 275
eras, classical music
Baroque, 240
Classical, 240
Medieval, 240
Renaissance, 240
Romantic, 240
Twentieth Century, 240
extensions
chord progressions, 216-217
chords
eleventh, 126
ninth, 125
seventh, 121-124
sixth, 124-125

F

F Major
major keys, 56
scales, 35
F minor
harmonic minor scales, 40
melodic minor scales, 43
minor keys, 58
natural minor scales, 38
fast tempos, 91
fermata, 93
first inversion, 129
flags, 71
flats, 20-21
folk music, 245
forms
accompaniment, 181
chords, 116
forte, 94
fortissimo, 94
fortississimo, 94
forzando, 96
free jazz, 244
frequency, tones, 6-7
F-sharp Major
major keys, 56
scales, 35
F-sharp minor
harmonic minor scales, 41
melodic minor scales, 43
minor keys, 58
natural minor scales, 38
functional chord substitutions, 221-222
fusion, 244

G

G Major
major keys, 56
scales, 35

G minor
    harmonic minor scales, 41
    melodic minor scales, 43
    minor keys, 58
    natural minor scales, 38
genres, music
    blues, 243
    classical
        arias, 242
        ballets, 241
        Baroque era, 240
        canons, 241
        chamber music, 242
        Classical era, 240
        concertos, 241
        grand motet, 241
        Gregorian chants, 241
        madrigals, 241
        Mass, 241
        Medieval era, 240
        motet, 241
        operas, 242
        operettas, 242
        oratorios, 242
        plainsong, 241
        Renaissance era, 240
        Romantic era, 240
        sonatas, 241
        suites, 242
        symphonic poems, 242
        symphonies, 242
        Twentieth Century era, 240
    country music
        alt country, 245
        Americana, 245
        bluegrass, 245
        contemporary country, 245
        country rock, 245
        countrypolitan, 245
        honky tonk, 245
        Western swing, 245
    folk, 245
    Great American Songbook,
        245
    jazz
        bebop, 244
        cool jazz, 244
        free jazz, 244
        fusion, 244
        hot jazz, 244
        modal jazz, 244
        New Orleans jazz, 244
        smooth jazz, 244
        soul jazz, 244
        swing, 244
    rap and hip hop, 245
    R&B (rhythm and blues), 245
    rock music
        British Invasion, 245
        disco, 245
        folk rock, 245
        forms, 245-246
        grunge, 245
        heavy metal, 245
        New Wave, 245
        progressive rock, 245
        psychedelic rock, 245
        punk rock, 245
        surf music, 245
G-flat Major
    major keys, 56
    scales, 35
glissandos, notation guidelines,
    232
Gorow, Ron, 298
grace notes, notation guidelines,
    230
grand clefs, 15
grand motets, 241
grave tempo, 91
Great American Songbook music,
    245
Gregorian chants, 44, 241
grouping beats, time signatures,
    85-86
Grove, Dick, *Arranging Concepts
    Complete*, 298

G-sharp minor
    harmonic minor scales, 41
    melodic minor scales, 43
    minor keys, 58
    natural minor scales, 38
guitars, instrumental
    arrangements, 268

H

half-diminished seventh chord,
    124
half-note time signatures, 83-84
half notes, 69-70
half steps, 8, 21
    intervals, 27-28
    semitones, 21
harmonic compositions, 249
harmonic minor scales
    intervals, 39-40
    notes, 40-41
harmonic rhythms, 251-252
harmonic tensions, 259-260
harmonies
    inversions, 204-206
    mistakes to avoid
        big leaps, 212
        dissonant intervals, 213
        extended parallel
            movement, 212
    swapping notes, 206
    versus counterpoint, 202-203
    voice leading, 206-208
    voicing, 204-206
hearing development, 166
    chords, 173
    intervals, 168-171
    keys, 172
    melodies, 172
    rhythms, 171-172
    tonal memory, 167-168
hip hop music, 245

holistic compositions, 249
home chords, 139-140
home pitch, 254-255
hooks, melody compositions, 256
hot jazz, 244

I

imperfect cadences, 143
indefinite pitch clef, 16
instrumental arrangements
   big bands, 279-280
   brass, 269
   chamber orchestra ensembles, 277
   choosing instruments, 274-275
   concert bands, 278
   good and bad keys, 273-274
   guitars, 268
   keyboards, 269-270
   marching bands, 278-279
   percussion, 270
   rock bands, 280
   string orchestra ensembles, 278
   string quartets, 278
   strings, 267-268
   symphonic orchestras, 276-277
   transpositions, 270-273
   woodwinds, 269
interrupted cadences, 143-144
interval-based transpositions, 194-195
intervals
   Aeolian mode, 48
   augmented, 25-26
   compound, 26-27
   diminished, 25-26
   dissonant, 213
   Dorian mode, 45-46
   ear training, 168-171
   flats and sharps, 20-21

   half steps, 21-22, 27-28
   harmonic minor scales, 39-41
   Ionian mode, 45
   Locrian mode, 49, 54
   Lydian mode, 47
   major, 23-24
   major scales, 33-36
   melodic minor scales, 42
   minor, 23-24
   Mixolydian mode, 48
   Mod-12 system, 28
   natural minor scales, 37
   perfect, 24-25
   Phrygian mode, 46
   scale degrees, 22-23
introductions, songs, 158
inversions, harmony, 204-206
inverted chords, 129-130
   first, 129
   root, 129
   second, 129
Ionian mode, 45
Italian musical terms, 91-92

J

jazz music
   bebop, 244
   cool jazz, 244
   free jazz, 244
   fusion, 244
   hot jazz, 244
   modal jazz, 244
   New Orleans jazz, 244
   scores, 290-291
   smooth jazz, 244
   soul jazz, 244
   swing, 244
   turnarounds, 222-224

K

keyboards
   instrumental arrangements, 269-270
   naming tones, 10
keys
   concert, 191
      good and bad keys, 273-274
      transpositions, 272-273
   ear training, 172
   major, 55-56
   minor, 57-58
   modulating, 61-62
   sharps and flats, 20-21
   signatures
      accidentals, 60-61
      circle of fifths, 58-59
      determining, 54-55
      using, 54
   transpositions
      common reasons, 190-191
      degree-wise, 193-194
      interval-based, 194-195
      octave, 190
      software-based, 195-196
      step-wise, 191-192

L

large choirs, 276
larghetto tempo, 91
largo tempo, 91
layering approach, compositions, 249
lead sheets, 178-179, 285-286
leading chord references, 140-142
leading notes, 22, 36
leaps, avoiding, 212
ledger lines, 13

lento tempo, 91
listening, ear training, 165-173
    chords, 173
    intervals, 168-171
    keys, 172
    melodies, 172
    rhythms, 171-172
    tonal memory, 167-168
Locrian mode, 49
long melodic phrases, 111
Lydian mode, 47
lyrics
    melody compositions, 260
    notation guidelines, 233-234

M

madrigals, 241, 275
major chords, 117
    notations, 118
    substitutions, 219-220
major intervals, 23-24
major keys, 55-56
major scales
    intervals, 33-36
    modes, 44
        Aeolian, 48-49
        Dorian, 45-46
        Ionian, 45
        Locrian, 49
        Lydian, 47
        Mixolydian, 47-48
        Phrygian, 46-47
    notes, 34-35
major seventh chord, 122-123
Mancini, Henry, 298
marcatos, 95
marching bands, 278-279
marks
    staccatos, 230
    tenutos, 229
"Mary Had a Little Lamb," chord
  progression, 152

Mass music form, 241
measure repeat sign, 99
measures, beats, 68
mediant, 22
Medieval classical music, 240
melodic compositions, 249
melodic minor scales, 41
    intervals, 42
    notes, 42-44
melodies
    accompaniment, 179-180
    chord-based compositions,
      252-254
    chord progressions, 149
        perfect fit, 150-152
        writing tips, 152-154
    composing, 111-114
    compositions
        endings, 255
        fitting chords to, 260-263
        harmonic tensions, 259-260
        home pitch, 254-255
        hooks, 256
        lyrics, 260
        motion, 257-258
        pentatonic scales, 255-256
        ranges, 258-259
        skip-wise, 258
        step-wise, 258
        variations, 256-257
    counterpoint, 202-203, 208
        contrary motion, 211
        creation, 209-212
        mistakes to avoid, 212-213
    ear training, 172
    harmonies, 202-203
        mistakes to avoid, 212-213
        swapping notes, 206
        voice leading, 206-208
        voicing and inversions,
          204-206
    long melodic phrases, 111
    motifs, 110
    short melodic phrases, 110-111

techniques, 106
    Canon in D, Johann
      Pachelbel, 109-110
    "Michael, Row the Boat
      Ashore," 108-109
    Minuet in G, Johann
      Sebastian Bach, 108
    New World Symphony, a.k.a.
      *Symphony #9 in E minor
      ("From the New World"),*
      Antonín Dvořák, 107
    tones and rhythms, 106
meter signatures
    2/2, 84
    4/4, 82
    5/4, 85
    6/8, 85
    7/4, 86
    changes, 84-85
    eighth-note, 82
    grouping beats, 85-86
    half-note, 83-84
    meters, 80
    quarter-note, 80-82
meters, 80
metronomes, 90
mezzo forte, 94
mezzo piano, 94
"Michael, Row the Boat Ashore,"
  108-109
minor chords
    notations, 118-119
    substitutions, 220
minor intervals, 23-24
minor keys, 57-58
minor major seventh chord, 124
minor scales, 33
    harmonic
        intervals, 39-40
        notes, 40-41
    melodic, 41
        intervals, 42
        notes, 42-44

natural, 36
  intervals, 37
  notes, 38-39
minor seventh chord, 123
Minuet in G, Johann Sebastian
  Bach, 108, 150-151
Mixolydian mode, 47-48
Mod-12 system, 28
modal jazz, 244
moderate tempo, 91
moderato tempo, 91
modes, 44
  Aeolian, 48-49
  Dorian, 45-46
  Ionian, 45
  Locrian, 49
  Lydian, 47
  Mixolydian, 47-48
  Phrygian, 46-47
modulating, 61-62
motets, 241
motifs, 110, 256
motion, melody compositions,
  257-258
music
  accompaniment
    arpeggiated, 184-185
    bass, 185-186
    block chord, 181-182
    chord sheets, 179
    forms, 181
    lead sheets, 178-179
    melodies, 179-180
    rhythmic, 182-184
    tips, 186
    without music, 180-181
  arrangements
    choir ensembles, 275-276
    good and bad keys, 274
    instrumental, 267-275
    instrumental ensembles,
      276-280
    vocal, 266-267

compositions, 248
  chords, 250-254
  harmonic, 249
  holistic, 249
  layering approach, 249
  melodic, 249
  melodies, 254-263
  overview, 248
  writing your own music,
    249-250
forms
  blues, 243
  classical, 240-242
  country, 245
  folk, 245
  Great American Songbook,
    245
  jazz, 244
  rap and hip hop, 245
  R&B (rhythm and blues),
    245
  rock, 245-246
transcribing, 174
  active listening, 165-166
  ear training, 164-165
  hearing development,
    166-173
written music
  big bands, 290-291
  choral scores, 289-290
  computer notation
    programs, 296
  concert bands, 292
  notation guidelines,
    228-234, 284-288
  SATB (soprano, alto, tenor,
    and bass) choral score,
    289-290
  symphonic orchestras,
    294-295

N

names, tones
  alphabet, 9-10
  piano keyboards, 10
  staff, 11-13
Nashville Number System,
  notation guidelines, 287-288
natural minor scales, 36
  intervals, 37
  notes, 38-39
natural notes, 20-21
neighboring tones, 113
New Orleans jazz, 244
New World Symphony, a.k.a.
  *Symphony #9 in E minor ("From the
  New World"),* Antonín Dvořák,
  107, 151
ninth chords, 125
notations
  augmented chords, 120-121
  computer notation programs,
    296
  diminished chords, 119-120
  major chords, 118
  minor chords, 118-119
  written music guidelines
    chord sheets, 286
    glissandos, 232
    grace notes, 230
    lead sheets, 285-286
    lyrics, 233-234
    Nashville Number System,
      287-288
    overview, 284-285
    phrases, 229
    roles, 232
    slurs, 228
    staccato marks, 230
    swing music, 232-233
    tenuto marks, 229
    ties, 228

trills, 231
turns, 231
note repeat notations, 99-100
noteheads, 70
notes
   accidentals, 20, 60-61
   chord progressions, 136-138
   chromatic, 60
   counting, 72
   enharmonic, 21
   flags, 71
   leading, 22, 36
   measures, 68
   naturals, 21
   notation guidelines
      glissandos, 232
      grace notes, 230
      phrases, 229
      roles, 232
      slurs, 228
      staccatos, 230
      swing music, 232-233
      tenutos, 229
      ties, 228
      trills, 231
      turns, 231
   pickup notes, 109
   roots, 23
   scale degrees, 22-23
   scales
      chromatic, 32
      diatonic, 33
      major, 33-36
      minor, 33, 36-44
      modes, 44-49
   sharps and flats, 20-21
   staff
      above, 12
      below, 12-13
      blank, 11
      clefs, 13-16
      treble clef, 11-12
   swapping, harmony, 206
   ties, 74-75

time signatures
   2/2, 84
   4/4, 82
   5/4, 85
   6/8, 85
   7/4, 86
   eighth-note, 82
   half-note, 83-84
   quarter-note, 80-82
transpositions
   common reasons, 190-191
   degree-wise, 193-194
   interval-based, 194-195
   octave, 190
   software-based, 195-196
   step-wise, 191-192
triplets, 75
values, 68
   dotted notes, 73-74
   eighth notes, 71
   half notes, 69-70
   quarter notes, 70
   rests, 73
   sixteenth notes, 71-72
   whole notes, 69
numbers, tones, 7-8

O

octave clefs, 16
octaves, 23, 190
operas, 242
operettas, 242
oratorios, 242
orchestras, scores, 294-295

P

Pachelbel, Johann, *Canon in D*,
   109-110
parallel fifths, 128

parallel movement, voices, 212
parts, songs
   bridge, 159
   chorus, 158
   ending, 159
   introduction, 158
   verse, 158
passing tones, 112
pentatonic scales, 255-256
percussion, instrumental
   arrangements, 270
percussion clefs, 16
perfect cadences, 142-143
perfect intervals, 24-25
perfect pitch, 6
Perricone, Jack, 298
phrases
   eight-measure phrase rule,
      159-160
   notation guidelines, 229
Phrygian mode, 46-47
pianissimo, 94
pianississimo, 94
piano keyboards
   black keys, 20-21
   naming tones, 10
   white keys, 10
pickup notes, 109
pitch, 4-5
   clefs
      bass, 14
      grand, 15
      specialty, 15-16
      treble, 13-14
   concert, 191
   ear training, 167-168
   frequency, 6-7
   half steps, 8
   home pitch, 254-255
   intervals
      augmented, 25-26
      compound, 26-27
      diminished, 25-26
      flats and sharps, 20-21

half steps, 21-22, 27-28
  major, 23-24
  minor, 23-24
  Mod-12 system, 28
  perfect, 24-25
  scale degrees, 22-23
names, alphabet, 9-10
numbers, 7-8
perfect, 6
scales, 7
scientific, 10
staff, 11
standard, 7
tonal memory, 167-168
tuning fork, 6
plagal cadences, 143
plainsongs, 241
poems, symphonic, 242
pop music, 246
power chords, 128-129
prestissimo tempo, 91
presto tempo, 91

Q

quarter-note time signatures,
  80-82
quarter notes, 70
quartets, 275

R

rallentando, 93
ranges
  melody compositions, 258-259
  vocal, 266-267
rap music, 245
R&B (rhythm and blues), 245
Renaissance classical music, 240

repeat marks, 97-101
  measure repeat sign, 99
  note repeat, 99-100
  rests, 100-101
rests, 73, 100-101
rhythm
  counting notes, 72
  measures, 68
  note values, 68
    dotted notes, 73-74
    eighth notes, 71
    half notes, 69-70
    quarter notes, 70
    rests, 73
    sixteenth notes, 71-72
    whole notes, 69
  ties, 74-75
  triplets, 75
rhythm and blues. *See* R&B
rhythmic accompaniment,
  182-184
rhythmic memory, 171
rhythms
  ear training, 171-172
  harmonic, 251-252
  melodies, 106
  triplets, 75
ritardando, 92
ritenuto, 93
rock bands, instrumental arrangements, 280
rock music
  British Invasion, 245
  disco, 245
  folk rock, 245
  forms, 245-246
  grunge, 245
  heavy metal, 245
  New Wave, 245
  progressive rock, 245
  psychedelic rock, 245
  punk rock, 245
  surf music, 245

romantic classical music, 240
roots, 23
  chords, 116
  inversions, 129

S

SATB (soprano, alto, tenor, and
  bass) choral score, 289-290
scales
  blues, 243
  C Major, Solfeggio method, 9
  chord progressions, 136-138
  chromatic, 32
  diatonic, 33
  keys
    concert, 191, 272-274
    ear training, 172
    major, 55-56
    minor, 57-58
    modulating, 61-62
    sharps and flats, 20-21
    signatures, 54-55, 58-61
    transpositions, 190-196
  major
    intervals, 33-36
    notes, 34-35
  minor, 33
    harmonic, 39-41
    melodic, 41-44
    natural, 36-39
  modes, 44
    Aeolian, 48-49
    Dorian, 45-46
    Ionian, 45
    Locrian, 49
    Lydian, 47
    Mixolydian, 47-48
    Phrygian, 46-47
  numbers, 22-23
  pentatonic, 255-256

scientific pitch, 10
scores, 284
  big bands, 290-291
  choral scores, 289-290
  computer notation programs, 296
  concert bands, 292
  SATB (soprano, alto, tenor, and bass) choral score, 289-290
  symphonic orchestras, 294-295
second inversion, 129
segno, 98
semitones, 21
seventh chords, 121
  augmented, 124
  dominant, 122
  half-diminished, 124
  major, 122-123
  minor, 123
  minor major, 124
sforzando, 96
sharps, 20-21
short melodic phrases, 110-111
sight reading, 283
signature keys
  accidentals, 60-61
  circle of fifths, 58-59
  determining, 54-55
  using, 54
sixteenth notes, 71-72
sixth chords, 124-125
skip-wise motion, 258
slash chords, 217
slow tempos, 91
slurs, 74, 228
smooth jazz, 244
software-based transpositions, 195-196
Solfeggio method, 8-9
sonatas, 241
songs
  compositions, 248
    chords, 250-254
    harmonic, 249

holistic, 249
  layering approach, 249
  melodic, 249
  melodies, 254-263
  overview, 248
  writing your own music, 249-250
degree-wise, 193-194
eight-measure phrase rule, 159-160
interval-based, 194-195
parts
  bridge, 159
  chorus, 158
  ending, 159
  introduction, 158
  verse, 158
software-based, 195-196
step-wise, 191-192
songwriting, 248
soprano, alto, tenor, and bass (SATB) choral score. *See* SATB
sopranos, voice characteristics, 266
soul jazz, 244
specialty clefs
  alto clef, 15
  octave clef, 16
  percussion clef, 16
  tenor clef, 15-16
staccatos, notation guidelines, 230
staffs
  above, 12
  below, 12-13
  blank, 11
  clefs
    bass, 14
    grand, 15
    specialty, 15-16
    treble, 11-14
standard pitch, 7
step-wise motion, 258
step-wise transpositions, 191-192
string orchestra ensembles, 278

string quartets, 278
strings, instrumental arrangements, 267-268
Study of Orchestration, The, Samuel Adler, 298
subdominant, 22
submediant, 22
substitutions, chords
  diatonic, 218-219
  dominant seventh, 220-221
  functional, 221-222
  major, 219-220
  minor, 220
suites, 242
supertonic, 22
suspended chords, 127-128
swing choirs, 276
swing jazz, 244
swing music, notation guidelines, 232-233
symbols, chords, 130
symphonic orchestras
  ensembles, 276-277
  scores, 294-295
symphonic poems, 242
symphonies, 242
Symphony #9 in E minor ("From the New World"), a.k.a. *New World Symphony,* Antonín Dvořák, 107-108

T-U

tablature, 131
tempo
  beats per minute, 90
  changes, 92-93
  fast, 91
  fermata, 93
  Italian musical terms, 91-92
  moderate, 91
  slow, 91
tempo primo, 93

tenor clefs, 15-16
tenors, voice characteristics, 266
tensions, harmonic, 259-260
tenutos, notation guidelines, 229
ties, 74-75, 228
time signatures
  2/2, 84
  4/4, 82
  5/4, 85
  6/8, 85
  7/4, 86
  changes, 84-85
  eighth-note, 82
  grouping beats, 85-86
  half-note, 83-84
  meters, 80
  quarter-note, 80-82
Tin Pan Alley, 245
tonal memory, 167-168
tones
  melodies, 106
  names
    alphabet, 9-10
    piano keyboards, 10
    staff, 11-13
  neighboring, 113
  passing, 112
  pitch, 4-5
  values
    frequency, 6-7
    numbers, 7-8
    Solfeggio method, 8-9
  whole steps, 21
tonic, 23
transcribing music, 174
  active listening, 165-166
  ear training, 164-165
  hearing development, 166
    chords, 173
    intervals, 168-171
    keys, 172
    melodies, 172
    rhythms, 171-172
    tonal memory, 167-168

transpositions
  common reasons, 190-191
  concert keys, 272-273
  degree-wise, 193-194
  instrumental arrangements, 270-273
  interval-based, 194-195
  octaves, 190
  software-based, 195-196
  step-wise, 191-192
treble clefs, 11-14
triads, chords, 116
trills, notation guidelines, 231
trios, 275
triplets, 75
tuning fork, 6
turnarounds, 147
  chord progressions, 222-224
  common, 223
turns, notation guidelines, 231
Twentieth Century classical music, 240

unison, 23

V

values
  notes, 68
    dotted notes, 73-74
    eighth notes, 71
    half notes, 69-70
    quarter notes, 70
    rests, 73
    sixteenth notes, 71-72
    whole notes, 69
  tones
    frequency, 6-7
    numbers, 7-8
    Solfeggio method, 8-9
variations, melody compositions, 256-257

verses, songs, 158
vivace tempo, 91
vocal arrangements
  choir ensembles
    chamber, 275
    large, 276
    madrigal, 275
    quartets, 275
    swing, 276
  ranges, 266-267
  voice characteristics
    altos, 266
    baritones, 266
    bass, 266
    sopranos, 266
    tenors, 266
voice leading, harmony, 206-208
voices
  altos, 266
  baritones, 266
  bass, 266
  parallel movement, 212
  sopranos, 266
  tenors, 266
voicing
  chords, 129
  harmony, 204-206

W-X-Y-Z

walking bass line, 185
Webb, Jimmy, 298
What to Listen for in Music, Aaron Copland, 298
whole notes, 69
whole steps, 21
woodwinds, instrumental arrangements, 269
written music
  big bands, 290-291
  choral scores, 289-290
  chords, 130-132

chords to melodies, 152-153

compositions, 248

    chords, 250-254

    harmonic, 249

    holistic, 249

    layering approach, 249

    melodic, 249

    melodies, 254-263

    overview, 248

    writing your own music, 249-250

computer notation programs, 296

concert bands, 292

melodies to chords, 153-154

notation guidelines

    chord sheets, 286

    glissandos, 232

    grace notes, 230

    lead sheets, 285-286

    lyrics, 233-234

    Nashville Number System, 287-288

    overview, 284-285

    phrases, 229

    roles, 232

    slurs, 228

    staccato marks, 230

    swing music, 232-233

    tenuto marks, 229

    ties, 228

    trills, 231

    turns, 231

SATB (soprano, alto, tenor, and bass) choral score, 289-290

symphonic orchestras, 294-295

transcribing, 174

    active listening, 165-166

    ear training, 164-165

    hearing development, 166-173